KV-483-127

WITHDRAWN
FROM
UNIVERSITY OF PLYMOUTH
LIBRARY SERVICES

This book is to be returned on
or before the date stamped below

22. MAY 1998 CANCELLED	- 4 MAY 2000
CANCELLED	- 1 JUN 2000
12 MAR 1999	- 7 JUN 2000
6 a 9 may	- 8 MAR 2001
-7. JUN. 1999 CANCELLED	26 APR 2001
	15 JUN 2001

UNIVERSITY OF PLYMOUTH

PLYMOUTH LIBRARY

Tel: (0752) 232323
This book is subject to recall if required by another reader
Books may be renewed by phone
CHARGES WILL BE MADE FOR OVERDUE BOOKS

STUDIES IN ETHNOMETHODOLOGY AND CONVERSATION ANALYSIS
No. 1

GEORGE PSATHAS
EDITOR

INTERACTION COMPETENCE

1990

International Institute for Ethnomethodology and Conversation Analysis & University Press of America
Washington, D.C.

Copyright 1990 by the
International Institute for Ethnomethodology and
Conversation Analysis

University Press of America®, Inc.
4720 Boston Way
Lanham, Maryland 20706

3 Henrietta Street
London WC2E 8LU England

All rights reserved
Printed in the United States of America
British Cataloging in Publication Information Available

Co-published by arrangement with the
International Institute for Ethnomethodology and
Conversation Analysis

Library of Congress Cataloging-in-Publication Data

Interaction competence / edited by George Psathas.
p. cm.
Studies in Ethnomethodology and Conversation Analysis No. 1
1. Conversation. 2. Oral communication.
3. Social interaction. I. Psathas, George.
P95.45.I55 1989 302.3'46—dc20 89–27546 CIP

ISBN 0–8191–7635–4 (alk. paper)

UNIVERSITY OF PLYMOUTH
LIBRARY SERVICES
Item No. 900 165159-9
Class No. 302.346 INT
Contl No. 0819176354

The paper used in this publication meets the minimum requirements of American National Standard for Information Sciences—Permanence of Paper for Printed Library Materials, ANSI Z39.48–1984.

Studies in Ethnomethodology and Conversation Analysis
is co-published by
The International Institute for Ethnomethodology and Conversation Analysis
and
University Press of America, Inc.

Editorial Board

George Psathas, *Chairman* • Boston University

Jorg R. Bergmann • Universitat Konstanz

Egon Bittner • Brandeis University

Graham Button • Polytechnic South West, Plymouth

Jeff Coulter • Boston University

Michael Lynch • Boston University

James Heap • Ontario Institute for Studies in Education

D.R. Watson • Manchester University

DEDICATION

FOR IRMA, CHRISTINE, DAVID AND ANTHONY

Table of Contents

Contributors

Graham Button, Department of Social and Political Studies,
Plymouth Polytechnic, Plymouth, Devon, England

Jeff Coulter, Department of Sociology,
Boston University, Boston, MA

Judy Arlene Davidson, P.O. Box 155, Buena Park, CA

Richard Frankel, School of Medicine,
Wayne State University, Detroit, MI

Gail Jefferson, Department of Sociology
University of York, York, England

George Psathas, Department of Sociology,
Boston University, Boston, MA

*Harvey Sacks, School of Social Sciences,
University of California at Irvine, Irvine, CA

Emanuel A. Schegloff, Department of Sociology,
University of California, Los Angeles, CA

D. R. Watson, Department of Sociology,
Manchester University, Manchester, England

*Deceased

Introduction: Methodological Issues and Recent Developments in the Study of Naturally Occurring Interaction

George Psathas

In this introduction I will try to delineate some of the major features of the methodological perspective brought to bear on the study of naturally occurring interaction from within the ethnomethodological paradigm.

The studies included in this volume represent instantiations of this methodological perspective though each study does not necessarily incorporate all the features to be discussed.

I will also briefly consider the relevance of this work for the study of member competencies and some of the directions evolving in recent work in what may be considered more "applied" problem areas in which particular, structured, interactional systems are studied.

Methodological Issues

Among the several questions which researchers in the ethnomethodological-conversation-interaction-analytic tradition have been asked, the one concerning "How is this kind of research actually done?" remains persistently unanswered. Discussions by ethnomethodologists and conversation analysts of methodological issues and perspectives are noticeably lacking. Schenkein's (1978) introduction is an exception but his discussion is too brief to be of practical value. He refers to the methodological perspective as an "analytic mentality" which seeks to describe the "systematic structural form (the 'organization') of the various phenomena" of interaction. The studies included in his volume thus represent

> studies of turn taking, identity negotiations, compliment responses, story cluster, the recommencement of a meeting, action sequence negotiations, conversational environments for equivocality, amplitude shifts, story beginnings and endings, and dirty jokes . . . (p. 5)

and what they are characterized as having in common is a commitment to

> building non-intuitive descriptions of the organization of conversational interaction as the technical accomplishment of member conversationalists. (p. 5)

More specifically, as Schenkein (1978; p. 6) points out, these studies share what he refers to as the "analytic mentality" of:

1) utilizing a corpus of data consisting of naturally occurring interactions
2) developing analyses grounded in the details of actual occurrences
3) viewing the study of conversation as "an essentially interactional activity"
4) focusing on "the sequential emergence of turn-by-turn talk"
5) using a "standardized transcription notation system which captures the details of conversational production"
6) sharing a commitment to a "non-intuitive" (i.e., a data-based rather than constructed, recalled or imagined) description of the interactional phenomena
7) presenting findings which describe the "organization and artfulness of natural conversation"
8) attempting to develop conceptual schemas to connect the particularities of contexts studied with the abstract culture.

Speier (1973) presents one of the best discussions yet published of the methodological perspective of such studies primarily focusing on the earliest work (prior to 1972) in conversation analysis. His discussion of the necessary suppositions for the naturalistic study of social organization is more theoretical than methodological but nevertheless provides some important groundings for the methodology we wish to describe.

One supposition is that interaction is organized or orderly. Any study of naturally occurring interaction must then use as a method for study (Speier, 1973; p. 24) 1) the selection of a "piece or segment of human interaction" and 2) develop an analysis of that piece or segment that "accounts for the manner in which it took place . . . i.e. an empirically valid structural description of it."[1]

He calls this the "method of instances." Interactional events are treated as instantial cases and their workings (organization, orderliness) are to be accounted for in such a way as to show a clear tie between the concrete instance and the abstract conceptualization and conclusions that may emerge in the analysis and description.

Furthermore, Speier (1973; p. 45-46) delineates what he refers to as the "invariant features of interactional events" as:

> main activities with practical orientations (within which mutual involvements are built up into situations and occasions), local settings, a cultural apparatus of labels or calling terms for selective identifications of interactants, temporal orientations and conversational structuring and sequencing rules. (In addition, he includes) spatial orientations . . . the proximate elements of interaction, such things as physical spacing and distancing and bodily positioning, (and the) domain of actions that fall into the classification of nonverbal communicative behaviors, e.g. gestures, facial organization, body movements, etc.

His preference, at the time of writing, was to develop formal interactional descriptions of talk, primarily because "talk (was) the most amenable data for precise and intensive analysis" and such features as spacing, body movement, facial work, gestures, etc. . . . (are) more difficult (to study) because of the problems involved in using words to represent communicative actions of this sort."[2]

The main problem I shall address is that of explicating how the work of conversation-interaction analysts is done by working through particular examples or instances of such work. Some of the theoretical and methodological assumptions on which this work is based will also be revealed in this process.

The first stages of such research can be characterized as "unmotivated looking."[3] No particular, pre-selected topics or phenomena are being searched for.

Data are obtained from any available source and setting. The prerequisites are simply that the interaction is "naturally occurring." By this is meant that the interaction would have occurred regardless of whether the researcher had come upon the scene and requested or obtained a recording of it. This meaning of "naturally occurring" would therefore include materials recorded for other purposes, e.g. interaction on TV interviews, video monitors of traffic, video or audio tapes of classroom instruction, recorded police calls, courtrooms, etc. All such materials may not lend themselves to certain types of analyses because of selection or editing procedures used by those who operated recording equipment or the noticeable on-camera performances of the participants—but no such recordings are ruled out in advance.

The interaction must be recordable using audio and/or visual recording technologies such as videotape, audiotape, film, or still photography. Such recordings may be obtained either with or without the awareness of those being recorded. The latter instances include recordings in which a recorder is simply introduced into a setting and left running. In most cases, particularly in institutional and other "sensitive" settings, permissions in writing from all those participating may be obtained as is conventionally the case in grant or contract sponsored research. Issues of protection of the rights to privacy of persons so recorded are accorded in the usual ways such as alteration of names, omission or re-naming of time and place details, modification of photographs so as not to identify persons, etc. In the majority of instances when persons are made aware of the nature of the research and how research results are reported, no serious objections are raised. If, however, such objections are made, researchers readily comply with persons' requests and cease their data collection. As can be seen from various studies, the types of interactions studied are so ordinary and so frequent that the researcher is not troubled by such refusals.

It should also be obvious from the studies reported here and elsewhere that the types of interactional phenomena being described and analyzed are not being analyzed in terms of their connection to the particularities of persons. There is thus no effort or need to identify persons. The phenomena being studied are not studied in relation to "who" the persons are but rather in terms of the organizational or structural features of the interactional phenomena themselves.

The interactional phenomena being studied in audio tape recordings are primarily utterances and their correlates (e.g., silence, turns, overlap, amplitude, timing, etc.) and, from videotape or sound film recordings, these and other non-verbal and non-auditory interactional phenomena (e.g., gaze movement, hand, head, and body movements, etc.). The use of recording technologies is now regarded as an absolute necessity for work in this area because the work of description and analysis can only begin after a recording is made. This is for two main reasons: 1) pre-selection of topics or phenomena is not part of the research strategy, and 2) the phenomena are so intricate and complex and have such restricted temporal and spatial features that no observational system relying on the ordinary senses operating in "real time" is capable of capturing them in all their constitutive details. In fact, as will be discussed later, it is not the deficiency of observational systems and the use of the senses which is the main issue as much as it is the opportunities provided by repeated listenings/viewings of interaction which enable the discovery and the detailed analyses of complex interactional phenomena.

Thus, the phenomena discovered are the emergent result of repeated listenings/viewings. The reproduction of a transcript or text provides for the possibility of other researchers noticing, collecting, and studying the same or related phenomena. A move from the logic of discovery to that of verification is made possible through such data collections.

It is these characteristics which differentiate conversation-interaction analysis from other approaches to the study of interaction in the social sciences.

What are interactional phenomena?

Any effort to explicate what those matters are which are to be included as topics of study is presumptuous, to say the least. The effort is further complicated by the fact that only as research continues and as recording technologies advance will the possibilities of what can be studied (discovered) become clearer. The phenomena are the "stuff," the minutiae, the details of everyday activities as these actually occur in the world of everyday life. Their number and variety is virtually limitless, and inexhaustible insofar as human situations in which interaction occurs are innumerable.

We will not undertake to define the phenomena of interaction since, from the epistemological position on which such work is based, no stipulative definition would be sensible. Interactional phenomena are discoverable matters. However, programmatically speaking, interaction refers to the orderly and patterned actions occurring whenever two or more persons come into one anothers' auditory or visual range in the context of everyday life situations.

The matters which we examine include utterances and activities. Activities include such matters as the movements of embodied persons, movements that are noticeable to us as viewers, and which we can claim are also noticeable to the participants. The movements which we would consider are noticeable-visible as "gross" movements.

For example, a hand is moved. It stops. Is this a movement? Yes.

An eye blinks. Is this a movement? Yes. A nose is wrinkled up. Is this a movement? Yes.

Movements are first described by us using gross characterizations similar to those we believe a co-participant would make.

For example, "He moved his hand to the pad and began writing." "He lifted his pen off the paper." "He raised his hand." "She nodded." "He moved his eyes to his hands raised in front of him."

As we proceed, we will try to develop a finer and more detailed description of such movements but we will refine our description and make every effort to use only those terms which members might or could use.

For example, "He moved his left hand from the side of the pad on to the top of the pad placing his wrist on the pad; his fingers, holding a pen, between the first three fingers, placed the tip of the pen on the pad and proceeded to move the pen on the surface of the pad, pausing in these movements, occasionally lifting the pen off the surface of the pad."

"He raised his head from a position where it was directed, face down, eyelids lowered, and gaze directed to the pad, to a position where the entire head was raised, the face directed toward the patient, the eyelids lifted and the eyes were directed to the patient."

We will rule out any finer, detailed description which is not discriminable or oriented to by members at the time in which the interaction is naturally occurring. An example of such a detailed description which adds elements ordinarily not available is: "He lifted his left hand five inches starting with a flexing of the left wrist upward, held it there for thirty seconds, and then dropped it." Although it is possible for a member to make such measurements or to estimate such measurements from a viewing of the videotape, our interest is in the study of members' perspectives in terms of those matters which are actually discriminable and oriented to by members *during the on-going course of the interaction itself.* Precise measurements are not available; rough estimates or verbal characterizations of, for example, distance, time or spatial relations, are.

But most importantly, closely ordered sequences of actions and utterances display orientations by members to the micro details of interaction. We can, therefore, include movements which co-occur as persons are co-present. For example, as one person speaks and moves, the other may speak and move at the same time or subsequently.

We assume that what is available to the speaker is his/her own utterance as it is heard and his/her bodily movements as they occur (although as a lived bodily experience and not from an outsider's perspective).

We further assume that the hearer has available the speaker's utterance as a heard or listened-to set of organized sounds and the speaker's body as it is available for viewing/monitoring from the hearer's position.

We do *not* assume that the hearer has available any such matters as:

–the speaker's intentions, purposes, or motives

–the speaker's ideas, or thoughts or cognitions or understandings

–the speaker's feelings, emotion or moods

except as, and insofar as, these matters can be "interpreted" by the hearer in the course of the speaker's actual utterance and co-occurring bodily movements.

These matters, i.e., intentions, thoughts, feelings and the like, we assume are matters that hearers "attend to" and "interpret" in the course of the interaction but that as they are "grasped" by hearers and intuitively and immediately apprehended, they are done so for all practical purposes in and of that situated occasioned production; and, further, that what is available to the hearer for such "apprehendings" is similarly available to us.

This specifically rules out the following:

–We cannot know of the hearer-speakers' past relationships, their biographies and their histories except as these are made available to and dicoverable by us in the specific instance of their current co-presence.

–We cannot know what they have or have not believed, thought, imagined, desired, hoped, wanted, understood, felt, etc. in the past.

–We cannot base our interpretation of what they are now doing on our assumptions about their characters, personalities, identities, selves, egos, ids, superegos, consciousness, unconcious, or other such psychologically based constructions.

–We cannot (nor do we need to) base our interpretation of what they are now doing on our constructive interpretations of such matters as taking the role of the other, playing a role, presenting a self, managing impressions, doing face-work, being deviant, managing the scene, defining the situation, and the like.

We specifically *set aside* all constructive analytic interpretations not because we do not accept or believe in them but because we are seeking to *discover* phenomena, not validate prior conceptualizations and interpretations *about* phenomena; and, we are *not* trying to *explain* phenomena by using such constructive analytic interpretations to say what is "really" going on, or how it is an instance of such pre-established categories as power, identity, ambition, stupidity, deviance, retardation, and the like.

Instead, if we address our attention to such constructive analytic interpretations it is because we seek to discover the features of practical reasoning which could be used to make such assertions and then probe further to describe what *that* instance is like in its actual particulars.

We specifically set aside all efforts to generalize from our discoveries to other, unexamined instances, which we commonsensically claim are "just like these," or "ones that I remember well," or "ones that I've always known," or "ones that someone told me about," or "ones in a book by an eminent scholar."

We do not use such recalled, reported or imagined instances to offer "proof" or "support" or "corroboration" of our claim that what we just said about the *actual* phenomenon *must be so*. We specifically do not engage in "arguments," "proofs," or "appeals to the literature" to support our claims. References to other literature using the same analytic perspective, although acceptable, must also include an instance of the data used in that study or, at least, in the original report there must be data available to ground any claim.

Our claim about what the phenomenon is must be based on the phenomenon itself—what any one of us can discover and "see" if we also are brought to a point where we can "see" the same phenomenon. Therefore, we are bound to the methodological position that the phenomenon must be capable of being recorded (by audio, video, film or still photography, or a combination of these). Any written, transcribed version of the phenomenon is ultimately referrable to the original recorded instance. The phenomenon, thus transformed, is available to us as analysts and to others who may read/view/hear the depictions/representations of the phenomenon which we collect and present. In fact, (anticipating a later point) we require that such representations be incorporated in our reports and/or be made available to our readers/listeners. We rely on modern technologies for collecting, recording, photographing, and reproducing the phenomena because we also hold that access to the same materials which we as analysts have had should be made available to our readers/listeners/viewers. Our claims *about* the phenomena can be assessed/evaluated/corroborated/disconfirmed/refuted/supplanted/or modified by the availability of such presentations and representations. Our belief that this is so is strongest when the representations we make available to our listener/reader/viewer are the same materials which we ourselves examined (e.g., the audio, video, still or film photograph).

We are, by virtue of this methodological position, specifically at odds with conventional field research in the social sciences.[4] Field research has traditionally been based on the observer's notes and recall about the phenomena. The researcher, as keen an observer as s/he may be, is forced to write down, either immediately or after a short while, what "actually happened." Such notes are subject to all the vagaries of attention, memory, and recall; to the observer's interests at the time; and to the amount of "understanding" and "access" available to the researcher at the time.

As notes about phenomena they are and can only remain "notes about phenomena." The phenomenon itself cannot be re-examined or reviewed under more selective conditions. We must rely exclusively on the observer for all our knowledge of the phenomena and on these notes. We find, conventionally, that these notes are never made available to us. We find, instead, that reports are carefully written, edited, and selected reports *about* phenomena. They are supplemented by quotations from persons in the field setting (as in field interviews) and by the quotations of equivalent status by the researcher, either from his/her own notes or from memory (e.g., Whyte, 1949; Whyte, 1955; Gubrium, 1975; Liebow, 1967).[5] When we are offered lengthy narratives in the form of quotations of interviews/conversations/discussions between the researcher and those being observed we are not provided with a tape recorded transcript but with a highly edited, reconstructed report of a dialog (cf. Castaneda, 1971).

We are not saying that such reports are not truthful, correct, or valuable. Nor that we cannot learn a great deal about the reported events. Nor that we distrust field researchers. Rather, our problem is that we cannot recover, in any less mediated fashion, the interactional phenomena themselves. The actual particulars, the timing, ordering, phasing, movement; the actual audio, spatial, temporal organization of the phenomena are lost to us in mediated reports. Why? Because such reports necessarily rely on the transformation of any and all interactional phenomena into words and into verbal descriptions produced at the time by observers who may not yet have "decided" what it is they are witnessing.

We have no difficulty understanding such verbal descriptions and reports but we are now quite certain, after examining recordings of how persons actually speak and move, that the details of interactional phenomena have been specifically omitted. Their omission is not the "fault" of the observer but a necessary "fault" of the reporting method, i.e., the requirement that a human observer, in a field setting, as events actually unfold, use verbal descriptors for such audio, spatio, temporal phenomena as can be observed. (I leave out for the present discussion the problem of how common sense interpretive schemes also serve to mediate such reports.)

Such phenomena, we may say, are thereby modified, transformed into "reported and described phenomena." We, as readers of such reports, are now in the position of having to rely totally and exclusively on these. If we wish to discuss or further analyze these reports we are now in the position of discussing and analyzing "reports," "accounts," "descriptions," and "analyses" although we may think that what we are doing is discussing and analyzing the interactional phenomena themselves.

What are we looking for then?

We are looking for whatever can be "found" in the sense of a discovery of a phenomenon. A phenomenon for our purposes is an interactional phenomenon. What are the characteristics of such a phenomenon?

1) It has a visual and/or auditory and/or tactual and/or kinaesthetic appearance for the participants in the actual course of their interaction.
2) It has a spatio-temporal appearance which includes:
    a) the spatio-temporal appearances of speech, utterances, silences and movements of the body
    b) the spatio-temporal relations of movements of the body of the person, i.e., the synchrony of bodily actions (movements) *within* the individual person
    c) the spatio-temporal relationships of speech, utterances, silences and movements of the bodies of the two (or more) persons, i.e., the synchrony *between* the participants
    d) a situated character, i.e., its appearance is in a setting whose features include objects, artifacts, rooms, furniture, buildings, walls, etc., as well as other persons

The social situation itself can be observed/described as it appears to the participants. But, only those aspects of the situation which are confirmably noted, oriented to, and "recognized" by the participants are those aspects of the situation with which we are concerned.[6] For example, as members may be seen or heard to notice, speak of, point to, touch or otherwise engage those aspects of the situation directly, then those aspects can be incorporated into our discoveries/descriptions/analyses of interactional phenomena.

The phenomena, further, may have the characteristics of 1) being "noticed," "reacted to," "considered," and/or "talked about" *by participants,* i.e., the phenomena are made into topics as when participants say, "What are you looking at?" "Why did you touch me?" "Let's talk about that."

2) Being unnoticed, unconsidered and not talked about but nevertheless available in and as our examination reveals that their production, in its spatio-temporal organization is "linked" to others' productions, i.e., what one speaker does or says is "linked" sequentially to what a next speaker does and says.

The phenomena have the characteristic of *inter*actional phenomena which refers to:

a) how they are organized, patterned, arranged, audio-spatio-temporally *in the course of* their production by a participant, i.e., *within* utterance or turn
b) how they are organized *between* the participants audio-spatio-temporally *in the course of* their production
c) or to *both* a and b above.

Our discovery, identification, description, and analysis of an interactional phenomenon will be oriented to in terms of:

a) its audio-spatio-temporal course
b) its constituent elements
c) its pattern, rhythm, synchrony, coordination, flow
d) its sequential properties including within as well as between persons
e) the *between*-ness of its production, i.e., the phenomenon may be of the type that involves, or includes the actions of one speaker followed by the actions of a next speaker; or the utterance of one speaker followed by a next speaker's utterance; or the movement of a hand by one person followed by the movement of an eye by the other person accompanied by the utterance of another person
f) the simultaneous synchrony of their doings and sayings, i.e., actions and utterances which occur "at the same time"

Our descriptions will try to note, in detail, how the phenomenon appears in the course of its *actual* production. Therefore all questions of what it is, how it is done, what natural units occur, what occurred first, second, third, etc., what it came to, etc., will be answered only by examining the actual produced phenomenon itself.

A first question is addressed to "what is its actual course?"

Questions as to meaning are to be answered through direct examination of "what happened before" and "what follows next" taking into account the manner in which participants themselves make sense (meaning) of what occurs.[7]

Our premise, however, is that participants do not have available to them what happens subsequently. Thus, although we, as analysts, can play or listen to or view an entire episode on tape, video, or film participants cannot. As participants interact, what is available to them from the past is what has already happened, and, from the future, only what can be expected, anticipated, or sought for. They cannot know what their actions will actually come to. Therefore, as analysts of their actions we cannot interpret what they are doing and saying in terms of what follows subsequent to their actions and utterances as though the subsequent outcome "proves" or "confirms" that that is what they "intended" to happen all along. Rather, we try to interpret what they are doing and saying in terms of what has just been done and said, since what has just been done and said *is* available to them as participants in that same way. As analysts, we will restrict ourselves to what is available to each participant. Thus, again, we specifically set aside any knowledge we may have of what the interaction came to in the future since the "future" is unavailable to the participants at the time when the interactional phenomenon occurs.

For example, in Psathas' study (this volume, page 218, lines 5-7, Interview 1, Segment 2) the movement of the interviewer's (doctor's) gaze to the pad is subsequently followed by the movement of the interviewee's (patient's) gaze to the pad. We do not interpret the interviewer's move as an *intention* to move the other's gaze although the other's gaze did subsequently move. We can describe the interviewer's gaze as moving to the pad, the interviewer's gaze as being monitorable by the other as to its movement and direction, and the other's gaze as "following," in the sequence of actions, the interviewer's gaze. The interviewer's gaze can now be retrospectively interpreted by us as "leading" or "directing" the other's gaze to the pad. But we must be clear that this retrospective interpretation is based on the actual sequence of gaze movements on the part of both parties and represents what the gaze "came to" or "accomplished" as a demonstrated matter.

However, the instance is understood as an instance of a phenomenon of the sort that we may call shifting the other's attention or "one party's gaze follows the other's." We do not claim that this way in which gaze moves in sequence is any better or worse than any other way for the achievement of gaze movement; nor that it is the only way; nor that the participant who follows is "aware" of "being led"; nor that the participant who leads is "consciously intending" to lead. We are only claiming that this is a way (method) by which gaze on the part of one participant can be (and is) coordinated with the gaze of another participant.

What the matter came to "after all" is not our concern at this point. Nor what it might mean for the (medical) interview. We specifically restrict our attention to the description and analysis of the particular interactional phenomenon. Our further examinations of the interaction may be oriented to the search for additional instances of the same phenomenon so that we can discover whether it recurs and how it recurs, i.e., whether there are variations in its recurrence which allow for the possibility that we have not noted all of its features; or that we have discovered a phenomenon which is more complex than we originally noted; or that a second "instance" reveals that the second is not an instance like the first but rather a different phenomenon in itself; or that we cannot find a second instance and that we therefore must be cautious in interpreting the "importance," or "typicality" of the instance we have discovered.

Questions of meaning are to be answered by strict reference to the actual course of the phenomenon itself; to what happens first, second, next, etc.; to what preceded it; and to what is actually done and said by the participants.

For example, is the doctor, in line 1, "asking a question"?

1. Dr. How far d'you feel you you haftuh hold yer (.2) your book before (.2) you c'n really focus
2. Pt. 'bout here

Our first characterization as to what the meaning of the utterance could be will rely on a member's competence with regard to a hearing (interpretation as to meaning). The utterance has the form of a question: it begins with "how"; it has a subject-verb inversion, "d(o) you"; it is not in the form of a statement; it is directed to another person ("you"); it implies that the speaker does not "know" what is being asked for ("how far" the other holds his book).

A further grounding of our characterization of it as a question could be based on our claim that, as members of the same community of speakers/hearers/interactants we would interpret it this way if it were directed to us, i.e., as a question. Or, we could actually ask others to interpret the utterance.

However, such claims should be modified to conform to the actual occurrence. Should the other, in his response, produce something other than an interpretation of the first speaker's utterance as a question, then we would have to consider that, *for the hearer,* the utterance was other than a question.

We note, therefore, that the hearer, in the immediate next utterance says "'bout here" and at the same time moves his hands up, in front of his body, and brings them to rest not fully extended, palms toward his face, in the position in which a book could be placed. (Lines 2-4 in Interview 1, Segment 2, page 218, this volume.)

This utterance and bodily action presented in the immediate next position following the first speaker's utterance can be interpreted as a response to the question, i.e., an answer, by virtue of its timing, content and information with regard to "how far" the book is placed "before you c'n really focus."

Again, this hearing/interpretation on our part, as analysts, also relies on our member's competence as speaker/hearers in the same language community, i.e., we are able to hear and see the response as providing information fitted to the prior speaker's utterance, now interpretable with greater certainty on our part as a question or request for information. That is, "how far" is answered by "'bout here," an answer which provides specific distance information as noticeable from the relation of the hands to the face. The positioning of the two hands resembles the two pages of a book. The hands are held palms facing the body, palms representing the "inside" of the book, and the answer follows in immediate next utterance position by the next speaker. The "you" addressed by the speaker is accepted as "me" by the hearer in producing his actions and utterance.

We are able now to note how the next speaker responds, what he says and does, and how these "responses" are fitted to the prior speaker's utterance. Our characterization of a question-answer sequence with speaker change (i.e., not a rhetorical question answered by same speaker) is a first order description based on the actual sequence. The movement of the answerer's hands to a position in front of his body, his gaze directed to his hands, as in the posture found in reading a book, is also to be considered a component part of the "answer" to the "question." The "how far" is visibly presented to the questioner by the bodily positioning. The "how far" can be assessed as to distance by noticing and "measuring" the distance in relation to the eyes. And the "'bout here" is said after the answerer's hands are actually at rest, in front of the body. We note in reviewing the videotape that the answerer has begun to move his hands to the front of his body while the doctor is saying "your: book before" and that his gaze is at his palms which are raised in position in front of his body by the time the doctor completes saying "you c'n really focus." Thus, the timing of the gesture and utterance is such that it is completed just after the interviewer has said "how far d'you feel you you haftuh hold yer (.2) your book before (.2) . . ."

We can interpret the interviewee's actions, both verbal and nonverbal, as an "answer" to the prior utterance's "question," thus, retrospectively, and presumably from the interviewee's perspective, recovering the "meaning" of the interviewer's utterance as a "question." We would, more strictly, be claiming that the interviewer's utterance is interpreted by the other as a question and that the interviewee interprets his own bodily action and utterance as an answer to that question. Our position is that a "meaning" of the utterance as "question" is interpretable from the actions and utterances which follow it and not from its syntactic and semantic components independent of the interactional context. If it were not "answered" we could interpret it, from the interviewer's perspective, as a "projected question" or as a failed "request for information." This interpretation is still operative if we shift our focus solely to what the interviewer says and does prior to the other's response. However, our interest in this discussion is on interaction so we shall want to consider what follows with regard to the other participant in the situation.

In summary, the first step in the analysis of a recorded segment of interaction consists of an open-ended process of "unmotivated looking," that is, simply attempting to become familiar with the various orders of complexity contained in the segment. No claims of exhaustiveness or conclusiveness are made with regard to the observational or interpretive possibilities contained in the segment. Instead, by providing the reader with the same raw materials used by the analyst, i.e., the audio or video record or transcription, additional possibilities are kept open for both the analyst and others. Observation and interpretation can thereby remain faithful to the original details of setting and interaction.

Once a selection has been made, greater attention can be given to describing the actions of each individual, the utterances, bodily activities, turns, etc. Once a pattern or orderly phenomenon is discovered and described it then becomes possible to consider the inter-relations of these elements as they fit together to produce patterns of action and response.

As in the example presented, the shift of gaze by the interviewer from the patient's face to the pad was followed by a change in the nature of their participation. The patient's shift of attention to the doctor's activity of writing was connected to the doctor's actions. These actions can be considered and interpreted as to their relevance for the mutual participation of the parties in the interview and for the sequences which may follow. Further, interpretations may be tentatively offered with regard to how such patterns may operate to create expectancies, obligations, rights and duties on the part of the participants specifically with regard to accomplishing the tasks of the interview (e.g., to solicit and to give information, etc.). The direction in which further work may lead cannot be specified in advance. The first stages of the analysis are to provide a detailed description and analysis of interaction, a descriptive phenomenology, which does not foreclose additional possibilities based on the review of the recorded and transcribed elements of the phenomena.

Having discovered a particular interactional phenomenon, we can begin to search through additional materials, i.e., already collected, recorded, or transcribed interactions, to find additional instances and accumulate a collection of instances. A collection of "repairs" (Schegloff, Jefferson, Sacks, 1977 and this volume), or "closings" (Button, this volume), or "openings" (Schegloff, 1979), or "compliments and responses" (Pomerantz, 1978), or "lists" (Jefferson, this volume), or "invitations," "offers," "rejections" (Davidson, this volume), or "arguments" (Coulter, this volume), or "identification and recognition in telephone openings" (Schegloff, 1979) or "question-answer sequences" (Frankel, this volume) can be accumulated from various sources. These collections can then be examined carefully to discover archetypical patterns and variations (cf. Schegloff, 1979; Button, this volume). The variations can further be examined to analyze and describe their features, to develop characterizations of types of variations, to discover sequence types, e.g., sequential patterns characteristic of types of utterances as produced between speakers in sequential utterances. Such patterns may be of two, four or multiple parts (cf. papers by Button, Davidson and Coulter, this volume).

Or, if the phenomenon originally studied is located in the initial part of a two part sequence involving speaker change, the varieties of responses by second speaker to the varieties of initial utterance types may be examined (see the papers by Button on varieties of "closings" and Davidson on modifications of "invitations, offers and rejections").

Further, as these interactional phenomena are examined more closely, the varieties of ways which speakers utilize, in first position, for dealing with possible responses by next speaker can be related to the varieties of responses which next speakers actually use. For example, Davidson examines how (1) "inviters, offerers, requestors, proposers, etc., when faced with either the possibility or the actuality of rejection may revise, modify, or add onto their invitations, offers, requests, proposals, etc. in an attempt to deal with this possible or actual rejection. Similarly (2), when rejectors are faced with the possibility or the actuality that the inviter or offerer is *not* going to go along with the rejection and may instead press for acceptance, rejectors may then in turn revise, modify, or add on to their rejections in an attempt to deal with this possibility or actuality."

Or, Button shows how movements out of closings can produce a variety of closing types and how speakers can negotiate for conversation termination or continuation. His study thus focuses on both parties in the interaction, over a sequence of utterances at the actual or possible close of a conversation, and implicates as an additional phenomenon the opening up of closings (a phenomenon originally identified and studied by Schegloff and Sacks, 1973).

In this fashion, the analyses expand and deepen our understanding. What may have begun as a first noticing, a discovery of a particular interactional phenomenon, with a detailed description and analysis of a single instance, continues, with a collection of instances, to reveal the rich complexity and diversity of the phenomenon, the varieties of its forms, and the interactional "work" that it accomplishes within particular contexts.

The further development of such work would lead in the direction of increasing formalization of the description of the structures of interaction.

Member Competencies

Notice first that we have assumed that structures, i.e., an orderly recurring pattern, an organization or "orderliness," can be found. The description and analysis of such structures remains an omnipresent requirement. Interaction research is, in this sense, not interested in ethnographic particularities, i.e., not interested in the ways of interacting as found for a particular two person group at a particular time and place or setting, e.g., Doctor S meeting with Patient Z in his office in June 1979, nor in "typical" encounters of "typical" doctors and patients, e.g., opthalmalogists meeting with first time patients.[8] Rather, the interest is in discovering the structures of interaction, the orderliness of these structures independent of cohort particulars (Garfinkel and Sacks, 1970). That is, the interest is in discovering the structures of interaction, as interactional phenomena in their own right, produced by members.[9] The particular parties in the production cannot be regarded as the sole competent producers. The interactional competencies displayed are regarded as member competencies, i.e., capable of production by anyone, any member of the common culture engaged in interaction within a similar context.

In order to support the claim that these studies have discovered such competencies, research presentations must meet at least two important conditions.

First, the researchers' way of proceeding in the reported research is included in or is recoverable from the reading of the report.

Second, the report includes all or as much of the data (in a standardized notational transcription format)[10] as the researcher actually analyzed in developing the description and analysis.[11]

Thus, any reader may examine the same materials (data) as those available to the researcher and compare his/her own interpretations with those of the researcher. Therefore, any claims by the researcher with regard to structures of interaction can be corroborated by any reader by examining the data included in the report.

The move toward formalization of analyses is exemplified in several studies, the best example being the work by Sacks, Schegloff and Jefferson (1974) on turn taking. Although the terms of such formalization may not be as abstract as those found in formal symbolic logic, the formalization is nevertheless significant in terms of its potential scope and the types of interconnections it suggests.

For example, in the study included in this volume, Schegloff, Jefferson and Sacks (1984, originally 1977) refer to the types of repair as:

Self-repair and other-repair.

- Self-repair can issue from:
  - a) self-initiation
  - b) other-initiation
- Other repair can issue from:
  - a) self-initiation
  - b) other-initiation
- Failure (to repair) can issue from:
  - a) self-initiation
  - b) other-initiation

Self-initiated repairs have their initiation in three main types of position:

a) within the same turn as their trouble source
b) in that turn's transition space
c) in third turn to the trouble-source turn

Other-initiated repairs occupy one main position:

a) in turn just subsequent to trouble-source turn,
etc.

Button, in his paper *On Varieties of Closings* in this volume, in discussing movements out of closings and varieties of closing types, bases his analysis on archetype closings which span four turns at talk (cf. Schegloff and Sacks, 1973). These are 1) offer; 2) take up of offer; 3) first terminal component; and 4) second terminal component with speaker change recurring after each turn. He then describes such additional phenomena as:

a) first turn arrangement longer than archetype closing
b) first turn arrangement abandoned closing
c) second turn solicitude longer than archetype closing
d) second turn solicitude abandoned closing
e) appreciation as archetype closing
f) appreciation extended closings
g) appreciation abandoned closings.

Thus, Button's work advances further the formal analysis of closing types and movements out of closings. Although his characterization of a "longer than" archetype is not as rigorously formal as we might prefer, nevertheless his work illustrates how the description and analysis of formal structures can be further developed in successive researches by different investigators, e.g., Schegloff and Sacks, 1973; Davidson, 1978; Button, 1980; and Button, this volume.

Another instance of formalization is in Coulter's paper on Argument Sequences wherein he presents the formal structure of argument sequences as:

Assertoric Sequences

A: Declarative Assertion
B: Counter Assertion

and

A: Simple Assertion
B: Acknowledgment

and further elaborated sequential structures such as:

A: Declarative Assertion
B: Disagreement as Pre-Counter Assertion
A: Solicit

B: Counter-Assertion

His paper continues further elaborations of the structures of argument sequences as additional data are examined.

Applied Directions

As research continues, other analysts, concerned with particular settings and particular types of activity systems[12] (e.g., the interview in contrast to "free" or "casual" conversation, Frankel and Psathas, or the police interrogation, Watson) may attempt to discover the presence and variety of these same phenomena. The noticing and discovery of similar or different phenomena in such other settings may be undertaken in order to assess the extent or range of occurrence of the original phenomenon or to study the modifications or variations of its appearance (and its "work") in such other contexts.

But, further, the focus on different activity systems may, using the same methodology, yield descriptions and analyses of these systems as particular systems in their own right. That is, the medical interview as a structured activity system with a clear differentiation of rights and responsibilities pre-allocated to the participants, may contain variations of such already discovered phenomena as question-answer adjacency pairings (Frankel), question-answer chains (Frankel), closings, story elicitation, gaze and utterance patterns (Goodwin, 1979, 1981), etc. Or, if new varieties of such phenomena are not discovered, nevertheless, the particular ways in which they are combined may be different.

Thus, the expansion of this same approach and the search for similar (or varied) instances of these same phenomena has implications both for the original study of the phenomenon in "free conversation," that is, a) it could reveal the extent to which particular structured interactional systems build upon or use as resources members' competencies in "ordinary" conversational-interactional methods, and b) it can reveal the particular characteristics of that interactional system itself.

As the move toward a more "applied" direction continues, the very ways in which the situations of "medical interview" (Frankel) or "police interrogation" (Watson) can be conceptualized will change. It becomes possible to adopt and use similar vocabularies of interactional analysis across these varied instances, e.g., regardless of "roles," persons can still be considered as speakers and hearers; regardless of the content of their utterances, turns at talk and utterance types can still be examined; and regardless of the topic used to end their encounters, such matters as closings, opening up closings, and the sequential organization of closings can still be examined.

Such conceptualizations allow us to cumulate findings across settings, discover the varieties of interactional phenomena across settings, and relate the variations found to the particular features of the settings. Presumably (and we hope) such work will lead us to develop more carefully described and analyzed features of the settings which represent the distinctive elements and configurations of interactional relevance for participants within and as members of those same settings.

A still further development is possible. The interactional phenomena which are discovered across and within the varieties of settings will enable us to state, with greater certainty, what interactional competencies are requisite to participation in those systems. As such requisites are discovered, we should be able to say what preparation, training, or prior interactional performative skills are vital for new entrants into these systems. And, if members are lacking in particular, identifiable, and describable interactional skills, we should be able to develop methods for teaching, demonstrating, or training those deficient in the requisite skills.

Thus, whether we wish to propose how members may be "taught" interactional competencies for ordinary "free conversation" or how doctors may be "trained" to become more skilled interviewers (assuming we have decided what types of interviewing are to be preferred for doctors) or how police may more "skillfully" interrogate suspects, applied research is a next phase of such work.

Applied research can be seen to have a number of components and some of the most recent studies begin to reveal directions such as the following:

First, the study of the particular interactional system as a system of interaction in order to delineate its constituent features.

Second, the comparison of the patterns of interactional phenomena found in other interaction studies, using the same perspective and methodological orientation, with the patterns found in the particular system under study.

Third, the description and analysis of the particularities of the same (and different) interactional phenomena as discovered in the particular system/setting.

Fourth, the selection of particular, typical, requisite, and mundane interactional competencies, as displayed by participants in these systems/settings, for examination and analysis with the aim of developing a method for training (teaching, demonstrating) the novice, unacquainted, or less expert participant the *hows* of such interactional productions.

Fifth, the evaluation and assessment of the extent to which such training (teaching, demonstrating) is effective, i.e., do those trained actually show change in their actual interactions in the same settings across a series of encounters with persons other than those with whom they participated in training or instructional sessions? Do trained persons display, in naturally occurring instances, the interactional patterns they have been "trained" to produce?

As this move toward application continues, we can expect to see a variety of efforts to draw on and use the findings which emerge from conversation-interactional analysis. Some of the foreseeable applications are indeed in those activity systems already studied, e.g., medical interviews (Frankel and Psathas, this volume), police calls (Meehan, 1983), police interrogation (Watson, this volume), interaction between parents and their "retarded" children (Sawzin, 1981), doctor-patient interaction (Meehan, 1981; Anderson, 1982), courtroom interaction (Atkinson and Drew, 1979); Neustein, 1982).

There is both a promise and problem in such possibilities—the promise for aiding those who lack certain interaction competencies, e.g., the impaired, disabled, deficient or less experienced, and providing assistance to them as they seek to develop interactional competencies for everyday living. In some instances, we may also find that they already possess competencies which are unnoticed or ignored by those around them. (cf. Sawzin, 1981)[13]

The promise for a humanistic science of human interaction is considerable. But the possibility also exists, as is the case in the use and application of any findings in the human sciences, for efforts to control, manipulate, and deliberately structure interaction so as to enable certain parties (and/or organizations) to advance their own ends and interests at the expense of others. We can conceive of the medical interview as being designed to preclude patient initiated inquiries, the police designing their responses to calls to mitigate blame or fault on their part, dentists designing their utterances so as to reduce patients' options to express their concerns, lawyers analyzing other lawyers' questioning procedures so as to enhance their own case presentations, etc. In short, there is the possibility for the appropriation of research studies for a variety of purposes, some of them oriented to increasing or improving the individual's power to maintain or advance his or her interests vis-a-vis more powerful economic or social institutional arrangements.

The ethical and moral considerations in application and use remain stubbornly persistent issues in the work of the human sciences. Although we do not have space here to address these, we recognize that these issues will become more pressing as the findings of conversation-interaction analysis become more widely known—and as efforts to make use of these findings for particular purposes develop.

Conclusion

As the range of studies included in this volume can demonstrate, there is a development in conversation-interaction analysis over the past several years moving from the discovery, identification, classification, description, analysis, and collection of interactional phenomena in everyday "free conversation" contexts to the study of these same and similar phenomena in particular, structured interactional systems.

The latter studies further reveal how the same theoretical and methodological perspective can yield important new insights about these systems and suggest directions for studies which can focus on the instruction or training of novice or less skilled interactants in the methods of interaction requisite for the production of the setting's interactional features.

As research continues, we expect both the formal, basic, and abstract and the more applied dimensions to continue to interrelate. Although currently the basic researches have contributed far more to our understanding of interactional phenomena, we expect that in the next several years applied research perspectives will also yield important new insights.

Member competencies in conversation-interaction and practical reasoning, in everyday settings, in the doings and sayings, the accomplishments of that everyday reality of the life-world, remain the ever present problem for study.

ACKNOWLEDGMENTS

I would like to thank Tim Anderson, Tracey Paget, and Marty Sawzin for their comments on an earlier draft of this paper and other members of the Boston Interaction Research Group, 1982–83, especially David Helm, Barry Kahn, Jim Ostrow and Kevin Pigott.

I am grateful to Gail Jefferson for bringing relevant passages from

Harvey Sacks' lectures to my attention; to Richard Frankel for his perceptive comments; and to James Heap and members of his seminar for their discussion of the issues raised by this paper. Although I have not responded to or incorporated all of their valuable suggestions, I have benefited in numerous ways.

NOTES

1. Sacks' (1966) way of stating this is that "whatever humans do can be examined to discover some way they do it, and that way would be stably describable. That is . . . there is order at all points. . . . given the possibility that there is overwhelming detailed order, it would be extremely hard not to find it, no matter how or where you looked. . . . and if one figures that that's the way things are to some extent, then it really wouldn't matter very much what it is you look at, if you look at it carefully enough."

2. Here he was specifically referring also to the necessity for film or videotape and the use of a notational system technically to refer to such phenomena. At the time Speier wrote (1973) audio tape recording was the least costly and most readily available technology. It seems clear to us now that videotape recording provided access to these latter elements and with its widespread use by interaction researchers served to finally make available for analysis more of the features of interaction.

The opportunity for repeated audio/video review, even in slow playback speeds, is one of the key technical features of such recording technologies. Movement, gesture and facial activity are subject to close detailed analysis most readily and more economically than 8 or 16mm film photography.

Sacks (1967) had earlier described his way of proceeding as follows:

> So I started working with tape recorded conversations, for the single virtue that I could replay them; that I could transcribe them somewhat and study them extendedly—however long it might take. . . . It wasn't from any large interest in language, or from some theoretical formulation of what should be studied, that I started with tape recorded conversation, but simply by virtue of that I could get my hands on it and I could study it again and again. And also, consequentially, that others could look at what I had studied and make of it what they could, if, for example, they wanted to be able to disagree with me.

3. This is, of course, a contradiction or paradox since looking *is* motivated or there would be no looking being done in the first place. It is a term which is intended to imply that the invetigator is "open" to discovering phenomena rather than searching for instances of already identified and described phenomena or for some theoretically preformulated conceptualization of what the phenomena should look like.

As Sacks stated it:

> Treating some actual conversation in an unmotivated way, i.e., giving some consideration to whatever can be found in any particular conversation you happen to have your hands on, subjecting it to investigation in any direction that can be produced off of it, can have strong payoffs. For one, recurrently what stands as a solution to some problem emerges from unmotivated examination of some piece of data, where, had you started out with a specific interest in that problem, it wouldn't have been supposed in the first instance that this piece of data would be a resource with which to consider, and come up with a solution for, that particular problem. (1970)
>
> Thus, there can be some real gains in trying to fit what you can hope to do, to anything that happens to come up. I mean that not merely in the sense of pick any data and you'll find something, but pick any data, without bringing any problems to it, and you'll find something. And how interesting what you may come up with will be, is something you cannot in the first instance say. (1967)

4. Goffman's work, as important and insightful as it is for the study of interaction, is included under this heading. The most notable exception in the corpus of his work is his paper "Radio Talk" (1981), where he selects actual recorded instances of persons speaking on the radio. These data are commercially available on LP records and in transcripts published in several books based on these records. Other scattered instances of actual recorded instances of interaction are found throughout his many papers and books but these are not reported with a standardized transcription notation nor can one obtain independent access to the same data. The other exception in his work is Gender Advertisements (1979) which presents the photographs he used as data for his analysis. However, in that work he was not explicitly concerned with the analysis of interaction.

5. Many other studies could be cited but these are selected as representative. An interesting and significant new approach to the analysis of the researcher's interaction with the respondent which provides a detailed transcription (the same as that used by conversation-interaction analysts) of the actual dialogue, is Paget's (1983) work. In contrast with conventional field work, Paget demonstrates not only what has been omitted in field research reports but how much can be gleaned from detailed attention to the actual interchanges between interviewer and interviewee.

6. Certain micro-phenomena, which may be discoverable through high speed photography or slow motion replays of the interaction may or may not be included for analysis. The critical question is whether it can be demonstrated that these micro-phenomena meet the criteria outlined here.

7. Here the issues of context, situation and activity are relevant. Obviously, the shift to various levels or frameworks for interpreting what the situation and activity is about, what persons can commonsensically be said to be doing, accomplishing, producing, creating, changing, etc., whether it be a committee meeting,

a teacher instructing a student, a boss directing an employee, a host greeting a guest, etc., i.e., whatever set of considerations the researcher may have with regard to the *meaning of actions,* is not necessarily directly addressed through conversation-interaction analysis. Discovering interactional phenomena is one matter; these can be discovered in varieties of context (e.g., the adjacency-pair phenomenon). Their relevance as structures for particular contexts or types of setting, types of action, etc., is uncertain until we begin to consider what these might be and how they might assist us in understanding the questions we are asking about social situations, organizations and institutions. That they may have relevance and may provide insight into the understanding of those questions is indeed a possibility.

There is yet another possibility, namely, that the attention to interaction structures as an approach to understanding particular activities and situations may lead us to reformulating the questions we originally were asking about these matters. That is, we may notice that our focus on interaction structures directs our attention to different ways of formulating our topic of inquiry, e.g., from "what is power" to "how do differences between participants in terms of interaction structures reveal (or allow us to describe) the assymetric relationships between them." Or, more concretely, how do teachers interact with students when they do "instruction"; how are instruction sequences organized; and how do they interact when they do "maintaining classroom order"? We believe that attention to interaction structures can and will be of value to the understanding of human action conceptualized in terms of "larger" issues of social organization, situation, conduct or action, but that relevance may also lead to changed perspectives and approaches to the questions posed.

8. Sacks (1970) proposed:

> Thus, it is not any particular conversation, as an object, that we are terribly interested in. Rather, our aim is to get into a position to transform, in what I figure is almost a literal, physical sense, our view of what happened in some particular interaction done by those particular people with the interaction being the thing we're studying, to a matter of interactions as products of a machinery, it being the machinery that we're trying to find, and for which, in order to find it, we've got to get access to its products. At this point, it is conversation which provides us such access.

9. Sacks (1964) in an earlier lecture, had stated this as the search for a grammar:

> . . . we can come to see how an activity is assembled, as with a verb and a predicate, etc., a sentence is assembled. Ideally, of course, we would have a formally describable method, as the assembling of a sentence is formally describable. The description would not only handle sentences in general, but would handle particular sentences. What we would be doing, then, is developing another grammar. And grammar, of course, is the model of routinely observable, closely ordered social activities.

10. For these studies, I am referring specifically to the transcription system developed by Gail Jefferson and reported in detail in Schenkein (1978) and Psathas (1979) and in the Appendix of this volume.

11. I have not considered here the detailed and painstaking process of listening (and/or viewing) audio-video recorded interaction in order to produce a transcript. The insights into and discoveries of interactional structures are in large measure accomplished only in and through the repeated listening/viewing of segments of interaction. Literally, hours can be spent in the examination of an interaction which lasts no more than 15 seconds. The researcher is sensitized to the material in such a way that it becomes possible to imaginatively "hear" and "see" it and recall its details for long periods of time. The production of a transcript necessarily results in the development of a close acquaintance with the particulars of the interaction. Once the transcript is produced, a reading of the transcript enables the researcher to recall the "hearing" and/or "viewing" of the original particulars. Thus, for anyone to "read a transcript" in the way in which conversation-interactional analysts are able to "read a transcript" cannot be accomplished without the experience of having oneself engaged in the painstaking process of producing a transcript from recorded materials. This is not to argue that the same recorded materials must be heard/seen by everyone who seeks to understand a report; rather, that once they have themselves engaged in the production of a transcript they will "know" how to *read* others' transcripts which employ the same transcription conventions.

12. I prefer to use "activity systems" rather than the term "speech exchange systems" in order to incorporate all of the interactional phenomena, non-verbal as well as verbal. For a discussion of this distinction see Anderson (1981).

13. Sawzin (1981), for example, in studying the interaction between a child with Downs syndrome and her mother, noted a large variety of interactional competencies on the part of the child which had been unnoticed even by those who were seeking to use behavior modification principles to improve the child's performance. The implication of such findings is that therapy can be based on the already available repertoire of interaction competencies rather than on the imposition of a structured program of training which does not first seek to discover the competencies already present.

REFERENCES

Atkinson, M. and P. Drew, *Order in Court: The Organization of Verbal Interaction in Judicial Settings.* New Jersey: Humanities Press, 1979.

Anderson, T., *Behavior in Painful Places: Aspects of Dentist-Patient Encounter,* unpublished Ph.D. dissertation, Boston University, 1981.

Button, G., Moving out of closings, in Schenkein, J., (Ed.), *Studies in the Organization of Conversation Interaction,* Vol. II. New York: Academic Press, forthcoming.

Button, G., On varieties of closings, in Psathas, G., (Ed.), *Interaction Competence.* this volume

Castaneda, C., *A Separate Reality.* New York: Simon and Shuster, 1971.

Coulter, J., Elementary properties of argument sequences, in Psathas, G., (Ed.), *Interaction Competence.* this volume

Davidson, J., An instance of negotiation in a call closing, *Sociology,* 12, No. 1, 1978, 123–133.

Davidson, J., Modifications of invitations, offers and rejections, in Psathas, G., (Ed.), *Interaction Competence.* this volume

Frankel, R., Talking in interviews: a dispreference for patient initiated questions in physician-patient encounters, in Psathas, G., (Ed.), *Interaction Competence.* this volume

Garfinkel, H., and H. Sacks, On formal structures of practical actions, in McKinney, J.C. and E.A. Tiryakian (Eds.), *Theoretical Sociology.* New York: Appleton-Century-Crofts,, 1970, 337-366.

Goffman, E., *Forms of Talk.* Philadelphia: U. of Pennsylvania, 1981.

Goffman, E., *Gender Advertisements.* New York: Harper and Row, 1979 (originally 1976).

Goodwin, C., The interactive construction of a sentence in natural conversation, in Psathas, G. (Ed.), *Everyday Language.* New York: Irvington Publishers, 1979, 97–122.

Goodwin, C., *Conversational Organization.* New York: Academic Press, 1981.

Gubrium, J., *Living and Dying in Murray Manor.* New York: St. Martin's Press, 1975.

Jefferson, G., List construction as task and resource, in Psathas, G. (Ed.), *Interaction Competence.* this volume

Liebow, E., *Tally's Corner.* Boston: Little, Brown and Co., 1967.

Meehan, J., Some conversational features of the use of medical terms by doctors and patients in interaction, in P. Atkinson and C. Heath (Eds.), *Medical Work.* London: Gower Press, 1981.

Meehan, J., *For the Record: Organizational and Interactional Practices for Producing Police Records on Juveniles,* unpublished Ph.D. dissertation, Boston University, 1983.

Neustein, A., *Courtroom Examination: An Analysis of Its Formal Properties,* unpublished Ph.D. dissertation, Boston University, 1981.

Paget, M., Experience and the construction of knowledge, *Human Studies,* 6, No. 2, 1983.

Pomerantz, A. Compliment responses: notes on the cooperation of multiple constraints, in J. Schenkein (Ed.), *Studies in the Organization of Conversational Organization.* New York: Academic Press, 1978.

Psathas, G., The organization of gaze, talk and activity in a medical interview, in Psathas, G. (Ed.), *Interaction Competence.* this volume

Sacks, H., unpublished lecture, School of Social Sciences, University of California at Irvine, Fall, 1964.

____, unpublished lecture, School of Social Sciences, University of California at Irvine, Spring, 1966.

____, unpublished lecture, School of Social Sciences, University of California at Irvine, Spring, 1967a.

____, unpublished lecture, School of Social Sciences, University of California at Irvine, Fall, 1967b.

____, unpublished lecture, School of Social Sciences, University of California at Irvine, Winter, 1970.

Sacks, H., E. A. Schegloff and G. Jefferson, A Simplest systematics for the organization of turn taking for conversation, *Language,* 50, 4, 1974, 696–735.

Sawzin, M., Deviance to difference: recognizing competencies of children with developmental disabilities through analysis of the sequential organization of their interaction, unpublished paper, Boston University Department of Sociology, 1981.

Schegloff, E., Identification and recognition in telephone conversation openings, in Psathas, G. (Ed.), *Everyday Language.* New York: Irvington Publishers, 1979.

Schegloff, E. A. and H. Sacks, Opening up closings, *Semiotica,* VIII, 1973, 289–327.

Schegloff, E. A., G. Jefferson, and H. Sacks, The preference for self correction in the organization of repair in conversation, *Language,* 53, 2, 1977, 361-382 (and this volume).

Schenkein, J., (Ed.), *Studies in the Organization of Conversational Interaction.* New York: Academic Press, 1978.

Speier, M., *How to Observe Face-to-Face Communication.* Pacific Palisades, CA: Goodyear, 1973.

Watson, D. R., Some features of the elicitation of confessions in murder interrogations, in Psathas, G. (Ed.), *Interaction Competence.* this volume

Whyte, W. F., The social structure of the restaurant, *American Journal of Sociology,* 54, January 1949, 302–310.

Whyte, W. F., *Street Corner Society.* Chicago: U. of Chicago Press, 1955 (2nd edition).

The Preference for Self-Correction in the Organization of Repair in Conversation

Emanuel A. Schegloff, Gail Jefferson, and Harvey Sacks

An "organization of repair" operates in conversation, addressed to recurrent problems in speaking, hearing, and understanding. Several features of that organization are introduced to explicate the mechanism which produces a strong empirical skewing in which self-repair predominates over other-repair, and to show the operation of a preference for self-repair in the organization of repair.

The "organization of repair" is a self-righting mechanism for the organization of language use in social interaction.

This study focuses on a significant problem in everyday interaction and shows, through careful examination of actual instances, some of the mechanisms which members use for handling the difficulties which may and do emerge in interaction.

1. **Self- and other-correction.** Among linguists and others who have at all concerned themselves with the phenomenon of "correction" (or, as we shall refer to it, "repair"; cf. below, §2.1) a distinction is commonly drawn between "self-correction" and "other-correction," i.e., correction by the speaker of that which is being corrected vs. correction by some "other."[1] Sociologists take an interest in such a distinction; its terms—"self" and "other"—have long been understood as central to the study of social organization and social interaction.[2] For our concerns in this paper, "self" and "other" are two classes of participants in interactive social organizations—in particular those which characterize the sequential organization of conversation, specifically its turn-taking system.[3]

Thought of in terms of the social organization of conversational interaction, self-correction and other-correction are not to be treated as independent types of possibilities or events, nor as structurally equivalent, equipotential, or equally "valued." Rather (and this is a central theme of our paper), self-correction and other-correction are related organizationally, with self-correction preferred to other-correction.[4]

One sort of gross, prima-facie evidence bears both on the relevance of the distinction and on the preference relationship of its components. Even casual inspection of talk in interaction finds self-correction vastly more common than other-correction. In locating a strong empirical skewing, the relevance of the distinction is afforded some initial rough support; the direction of the skewing—toward self-correction—affords one sort of evidence for the preference relationship of its components. We are, therefore, encouraged to explore the organizational mechanisms operating in any particular sequential environment—which, by their case-by-case operation, produce the observed over-all skewed distribution.[5]

In this paper, one in a series of efforts on repair organization,[6] we introduce some findings about several aspects of the organization of repair, in order to clarify the distinction between self- and other-correction, and to understand the organization that relates them in particular environments in such a manner as to produce a strong over-all skewing.

2. Correction and repair; initiation and outcome. Examination of the data of conversation requires several amplifications of the distinction between self-correction and other-correction.[7]

2.1. The term "correction" is commonly understood to refer to the replacement of an "error" or "mistake" by what is "correct." The phenomena we are addressing, however, are neither contingent upon error, nor limited to replacement.

2.11. Some occurrences, clearly in the domain with which we are concerned, do not involve the replacement of one item by another. For example, a "word search," which can occur if an item (e.g., a word) is not available to a speaker when "due," is in the domain which we address, but is not a "replacement" or a "correction":

(1) Clacia: B't, a-another one theh wentuh school with me
→ wa:s a girl na:med uh, (0.7) °Wh't th' hell wz
→ er name. °Karen. Right. Karen. [Clacia:17]

(2) Olive: → Yihknow Mary uh:::: (0.3) oh:: what was it.
→ Uh:: Tho:mpson. [NB:X:1:17]

2.12. It is a notable fact that the occurrence or distribution of repair/correction is not well-ordered by reference to the occurrence of "error." Repair/correction is sometimes found where there is no hearable error, mistake, or fault:

(3) Bernice: → Dean came up en 'e said 'I'd like—' 'Bernice?'
→ he said 'I'd like t' take you over tuh Shakey's
en buy you a beer.' [NB:IV:2:6]
(4) Ken: → Sure enough ten minutes later the bel r–
→ the doorbell rang . . . [GTS:1:2:11]
(5) L: Is his one dollar allright or should he send more
→ than that for the p– tuh cover the postage.
[Bookstore:1394]

Furthermore, hearable error does not necessarily yield the occurrence of repair/correction:

(6) Avon Lady: And for ninety-nine cents uh especially in,
→ Rapture, and the Au Coeur which is the newest
→ fragrances, uh, that is a very good value.
Customer: Uh huh, [Ladies.1:1:9:4]
(7) Bernice: → ... en I think if more parents of kids these age c'd
participate in this kind of an atmosphere, ˙hhhh it
would certainly help develop a lot of understanding. A:n' Mister Warden said that was certainly
one of the things thet he hed been considering ...
[NB:IV:2:8]

2.13. Accordingly, we will refer to "repair" rather than "correction" in order to capture the more general domain of occurrences. Self- and other-*correction*, then, are particular types in a domain more generally formulated by a distinction between self- and other-*repair*. We will refer to that which the repair addresses as the "repairable" or the "trouble source." In view of the point about repair being initiated with no apparent error, it appears that nothing is, in principle, excludable from the class "repairable."

2.2. "Self-repair" and "other-repair" (as well as the "correction" sub-types) refer to the success of a repair procedure. However, efforts at repair sometimes fail:[8]

(8) C: C'n you tell me– (1.0) D'you have any records

→ of whether you- whether you- who you sent-
→ Oh(hh) shit.
G: What'd you say?
C: I'm having the worst trouble talking. [BS:2:1:6]
(9) K: Didju know that guy up there et- oh. What th' hell is'z name usetuh work up't (Steeldinner) garage did their body work.for'em.
(1.5)
K: Uh:::ah, (0.5) Oh:: he meh- uh, (0.5) His wife ran off with Jim McCa:nn.
(3.2)
K: → Y'know 'oo I'm talking about,
M: → No:,
(0.5)
K: → °Oh:: shit.
(0.5)
K: He had. This guy had, a beautiful thirty-two O:lds.
[Goodwin, Auto Discussion:26]
Cf. also 16 below.

Given the possibility of failure, we are led to notice that it and successful repair are *outcomes,* and thereby to notice that the *initiation* of reparative segments and their completion (whether with success or with failure) can be quite distinct.

Then we note: the one who performs/accomplishes a repair is not necessarily the one who initiated the repair operation. In fact, both self-repair and other-repair (and failure as well) can be, and sometimes are, arrived at from either of the (for conversation) exclusive types of repair initiation: *self*-initiation of repair (i.e., by speaker of the trouble source) and *other*-initiation of repair (i.e., by any party other than speaker of the trouble source). Examples follow.

2.21. Self-repair can issue from self-initiation.

(10) N: She was givin me a:ll the people that
→ were go:ne this yea:r I mean this
→ quarter y' // know
J: Yeah [NJ:4]
(11) Vic: En- it nevuh happen. Now I could of
wen' up there en told the parents
→ myself but then the ma- the husbin
liable tuh come t'd'doh ... [US:4]

2.22. Self-repair can issue from other-initiation:

(12) Ken: Is Al here today?
Dan: Yeah.
(2.0)
Roger: → He is? hh eh heh
Dan: → Well he was. [GTS:5:3]

2.23. Other-repair can issue from self-initiation:

(13) B: → He had dis uh Mistuh W- whatever k- I can't
think of his first name, Watts on, the one thet wrote
// that piece,
A: → Dan Watts. [BC:Green:88]

2.24. Other-repair can issue from other-initiation;

(14) B: Where didju play ba:sk//etbaw.
A: (The) gy:m.
B: In the gy:m?
A: Yea:h. Like grou(h)p therapy. Yuh know=
B: = [Oh:::.
A: [half the group thet we had la:s' term wz there en we
jus' playing arou:nd.
B: → Uh- fooling around.
A: Eh- yeah ... [TG:3]
(Cf. also 64–69 below.)

2.25. Failure can issue from self-initiation:

(15) Mike: I never heard it eetheh.
(0.7)
Mike: → Awl I her- All I- Awl I ree- all you- all //
I ree-
Vic: → You knew duh broa//:d. [Frankel:US:26]
(Cf. also 8–9 above and 21 below.)

2.26. Failure can issue from other-initiation:

(16) Roger: It's kinduva- // kinduv weird.
Dan: heh

(2.0)
Roger: Wadda you think.
(2.0)
Ken: → Hm?
Roger: → Ferget it. [GTS:5:42]

2.27. Whereas we earlier proposed a typological amplification by shifting from a distinction between self- and other-correction to self- and other-repair, we now propose a sequence-organizational amplification with a distinction between repair-*initiation* and repair-*outcome.* This distinction is motivated by the fact that repair is a sequential phenomenon involving repair-"segments" in the course of ongoing talk—segments which have an organization of their own, including, as segment parts, "initiation" and "outcome." We have focused attention on one of these, initiation. Now we ask: Is the initial distinction between self and other (earlier applied to outcomes) relevant and viable when applied to *initiation?* If it is, it promises to be part of the organization we aim to describe, because "self" and "other" are always features of particular sequential environments, and potentially provide the focus for a mechanism that operates case by case.

3. Repair initiation by self and other. The evidence is compelling for the relevance of distinguishing, among reparative/corrective efforts, between those which are initiated by the speaker of the trouble source and those which are initiated by any other party. Three sorts of evidence may be mentioned.

3.1. Self- and other-initiations have regular, and clearly different, *placements* relative to the trouble source whose repair they initiate.[9]

3.11. Self-initiated repairs have their initiations placed in three main types of positions. First, they may be placed within the same turn as their trouble source:[10]

(17) Deb: Kin you wait til we get home? We'll be home in five minutes.
Anne: Ev//en less th'n that.
Naomi: → But c'd we– c'd I stay u:p?
(0.2)
Naomi: once we get // ho:me,
Marty: For a few minutes,
Deb: Once you get yer nightgown o:n. [Post-party:11]

(Cf. 8, 9, 11, 13, 15, and 16 above for other instances;[11] also cf. data citations in Sacks et. al. 1974, e.g., #21, p. 717).

Second, they may be placed in that turn's transition space:[12]

(18) L: An' 'en bud all of the doors 'n things were taped up=
L: → =I mean y'know they put up y'know that kinda paper 'r stuff,
L: → the brown paper. [Super-seedy:3]
(19) J: He's stage manager.
(2.0)
J: → He's actually first assistant but- he's calling the show.
J: → They take turns =
J: → =he and the production manager take turns calling the show. [MO, Family Dinner:I:9]
(Cf. also 10 above.)

Third, they may be placed in third turn to the trouble-source turn, i.e., in the turn subsequent to that which follows the trouble-source turn:

(20) Hannah: And he's going to make his own paintings.
Bea: Mm hm,
Hannah: → And- or I mean his own frames.
Bea: Yeah, [SBL:1:1:12:11]
(21) L: I read a very interesting story today,
M: uhm, what's that.
L: → w'll not today, maybe yesterday, aw who knows when, huh, it's called Dragon Stew.
[Super-seedy:SP]
(22) Annie: Which one::s are closed, and which ones are open.
Zebrach: Most of 'em. This, this, // this, this ((pointing))
Annie: → I 'on't mean on the shelters, I mean on the roads.
Zebrach: Oh:. [CDHQ:I:52]

3.12. Repair initiations by any other party occupy one main position: the turn just subsequent to the trouble-source turn. Instances abound in the various data citations that have preceded and will follow: e.g., in 8, G's turn; in 16, Ken's turn; and in 12 and 14, which have multiple other-initiations. Cf. also Sacks et al., #22, p. 717, and the ten further citations there.

3.2. Self- and other-initiations are done with regular, and clearly different, *initiator techniques.*

3.21. Self-initiations within the same turn (which contains the trouble source) use a variety of non-lexical speech perturbations, e.g., cut-offs, sound stretches, "uh"s, etc., to signal the possibility of repair-initiation immediately following:[13]

(23) A: → W- when's yer uh, weh- you have one day y'only have one course uh? [TG:5]

(24) A: She must know somebuddy because all those other teachers they got rid of .hhhh
(0.3)
B: → Yeh I bet they got rid of all the one:: Well one I had, t! ˙hhhh in the firs' term there, fer the firs' term of English, she die::d hhuh- uhh // .hhh [TG:8]

(Cf. also 1-5, 8, 11, 13, 15-17 above, as well as the data in Jefferson 1975, and passim in our other reports.)

3.22. Other-initiations use a group of turn-constructional devices to initiate repair.[14] One type is *Huh, What?*

(25) D: Wul did'e ever get married 'r anything?
C: → Hu:h?
D: Did jee ever get married?
C: I have // no idea. [CD:SP]

(26) A: Were you uh you were in therapy with a private doctor?
B: yah
A: Have you ever tried a clinic?
B: → What?
A: Have you ever tried a clinic?
B: ((sigh)) No, I don't want to go to a clinic. [NYE:2]

(27) B: Oh, I was just gonna say come out and come over here and talk this evening, but if you're going out // you can't very well do that
C: 'Talk,' you mean get drunk don't you.
B: → What?
C: It's Saturday. [JJ:1]

(Cf. also, e.g., 16 above.)

Another type consists of the question words *who, where, when:*

(28) B: Oh Sibbie's sistuh hadda ba:by bo:way.
A: → Who?
B: Sibbie's sister.

A: Oh really?
B: Myeah,
A: (That's nice.) [TG:27]

(29) F: This is nice, did you make this?
K: No, Samu made that.
F: → Who?
K: Samu. [KC-4:3-4]

(30) B: By the way, I haveta go to Lila's.
A: → Where?
B: Lila's ta get ( ) [BM:FN]

(31) J: Tsk there's Mako:(hh)
C: → Where,
J: There, [C-J:12]

(32) S: That's all. But you know what happened that night we went to camp. Forget it. She wouldn't behave for anything.
A: → W-when?
S: When we went to camp.
A: She behaved okay.
S: She did?
A: Yeah. She could've been a lot worse.
[On the Make:21-26]

Another is partial repeat of the trouble-source turn, plus a question word:

(33) Sue: Yeah we used to live, on the highway, too. And when we first moved up there, it was terrible sleeping because all these semis were going by at night.
((short silence))
Bob: → All the what?
Sue: Semis.
Bob: Oh [BH:1A:14]

(34) A: Well who'r you workin for.
B: ˙hhh Well I'm working through the Amfat Corporation.
A: → The who?
B: Amfah Corpora//tion. T's a holding company.
A: Oh
A: Yeah [C & D:9]

(35) Bea: Was last night the first time you met Missiz Kelly?
(1.0)

Marge: → Met whom?
Bea: Missiz Kelly,
Marge: Yes. [SBL:2:1:8:5]

(36) A: ... See I could ask you what you did at your party Saturday night.
B: I didn't go to a party Saturday night.
A: I thought you had a date with your boyfriend to go to a party.
B: No I went to a shower.
A: → To a where?
B: I went to a shower. [Carterette & Jones 1974:418]

Another is partial repeat of the trouble-source turn:

(37) A: Well Monday, lemme think. Monday, Wednesday, an' Fridays I'm home by one ten.
B: → One ten?
A: Two o'clock. My class ends one ten. [TG:15–16]

(38) A: What're you guys doin at the beach.
B: Nothin
A: → Nothe:::://n
B: No::,
A: Oh, good // heavens [NB:68:1:3]

A final type is *Y'mean* plus a possible understanding of prior turn:

(39) A: Why did I turn out this way.
B: → You mean homosexual?
A: Yes. [SPC: SP]
(Cf. also 65 and 68 below.)

There are, of course, additional construction types for other-initiation.[15]

3.3. The courses or trajectories from initiation to repair solution, engendered by self- and other-initiations from their respective positions with their respective initiation techniques, are regular within each type ("self" and "other"), and are different from one another. That is: most self-initiated repairs are initiated in the turn which contains the trouble source; and, of those, the vast majority are accomplished successfully within the same turn (cf. the data cited which include self-initiated repair; e.g., 1-5, 11, 17, 23, and 24.) Those initiated in transition space and third turn also are overwhelmingly successful within the turn in which they are initiated. Most repairs initiated by any other party in next turn take multiple turns (i.e., more than the next turn in which they are initiated) to get accomplished (cf. the data cited which include other-initiated repair, e.g., 12, 25-39, and see §5.2 below.)

3.4. Within-type regularities and between-type differences such as the above afford pointed support for the relevance of a distinction between self- and other-initiation of repair.

4. Relationship between self- and other-initiation of repair. Although self-initiation and other-initiation of repair are distinct types, they are not independent types or possibilities (as we argued earlier that self- and other-*correction* were not independent). There are quite compelling grounds for seeing self- and other-initiation to be related, and for seeing their relatedness to be organized. Two such grounds will be mentioned: (a) they operate on same domains, and (b) their respective placements can be characterized not only as "distinct" (as above, §3.1), but as ordered relative to each other.

4.1. Self- and other-initiated repair deal with the same trouble types. Although there may be trouble types which have their repair initiated only by speaker of the trouble source or only by others, the types of trouble sources we have investigated, and of which we know, do have repair initiated from each of the set of positions previously mentioned, and thus by either self or other.[16] Three types of trouble sources can serve to display this point: word replacement, repairs on person-reference, and repairs on next-speaker selection. For each of these types, note that repair can be initiated from each of the positions.

4.11. Word replacement (roughly the "correction" in the distinction with which we began) is initiated at several locations, as shown in the respective examples: from within same turn as the trouble source (self) [40]; at transition space following trouble-source turn (self) [41-42]; at next turn (other) [43]; and in third turn (self) [44]:

(40) Ken: He siz uh (1.0) W'l then what 'r you so
→ ha- er wuh- unhappy about. [GTS:5:6]
(Cf. also 17 above.)

(41) Roger: We're just workin on a different
→ thing, the same thing. [GTS:5:33]

(42) B: ... -then more people will show up. Cuz
they won't feel obligated tuh sell.
→ tuh buy. [SBL:3:1:2]

(43) A: Hey the first time they stopped me from sellin
cigarettes was this morning.
(1.0)
B: → From selling cigarettes?
A: From buying cigarettes. They // said uh
C: Uh huh [GTS:3:42]
(Cf. also 12, 14, 37.)

(44) J: Is it goin to be at your house?
B: Yeah=
J: → =your apartment?=
B: =my place. [New Year's Invitation:3-4]
(Cf. also 20, 21.)

4.12. Repairs on person references are initiated from the same four positions (same turn, transition space, next turn, and third turn), as shown respectively in examples 45-47, 48, 49-50, and 51:

(45) L: ... and uhn I don't know where we're
going, I really don't think there's much
→ more they- y'know anybody here c'n do for me.
[GTS:3:6]

(46) A: → And Bill- an' Bud got do:wn.
B: ˙hhh yes. [NB:IV:8:3]

(47) K: Well y'know a diagnosis like that is:
hardly (1.0) the end of the process,
→ y'know. I- I mean th- he- they, y'know
→ the guy- the th' pathologist looks at
the tissue in the microscope, y'know,
an he comes up with a label, 'n he gives
it a label, but then, what that is really
or what to do about it or what the prognosis is,
→ ˙hh requires ah the experience of somebody
→ y'know some other type of doctor. [KC-4:14]

(48) A: ... well I was the only one other than
→ the uhm tch Snows // uh Mrs. Randolph Snow?
B: (   )
B: (uh huh) [SBL:2:2:4:16]

(49) Vic: → First of a:::ll, uh Michael, came by:,
I tell you-
(0.5)
Vic: Tch!

James: →[Who's Michael.
Vic: [Picture the story.
Mike: M//e.
Vic: Michael came by. Michael ... [US:33]

(50) Ken: B't I d'know- it seems thet- when Roger en I
→ came in I d- I d'know if it wz u:s er what. B't
we- the group seem' tuh disba:nd af//ter we got
here.]
Roger: → U:s? it wz me:.] hheh ˙hh hhih ˙hh
(Note also the same-turn person reference repair
at the end of Ken's turn "... we- the group ...")
[GTS:5:9:r]

(51) A: Yeah. Well I should've known about
→ E-Ellen's bidding, the way she did over there
just the four // of us. Y'know.
B: Yeah
B: Uh huh
A: An uh an each ti- eh boy did I hesitate,
but I thought now she knows uh the
Goren rules, // an when you say "two"
it's a cut-off, an' sh- an' uh so uh –
→ I mean Elva. I thought. So I can I
can't under- I still can't under//stand.
B: Yeah.
B: Yeah. [SBL:2:2:3:45]

4.13. Repairs of next-speaker selections are also initiated from each of these positions, as shown respectively by examples 52-53, 54, 55-56, and 57:

(52) Dot: → Yer gettin s- look how // thin he's gettin.
[Travel Agency:11]

(53) Mike: → Sh'd I jist s- eh- Jim.
Jim: [Huh?
Mike: [Sh'd I j's send it or uh:::
(0.3)
Jim: Send it. [US:49:r]
(Cf. also Schegloff 1968:1081.)

(54) Ken: Hey why didn' you show up last week.
→ Either of you two. [GTS:4:1]

(55) Loren: Uhm::, will somebody pass the paperbacks- (1.0)

An:d: the (   )
Cathy: → Is that somebody me?
Loren: Mm hmm [Bookstore:SP]

(56) Louise: D'you go tuh thereapy,
(1.4)
Dan: → Do I?
(0.3)
Louise: Mm hm? [GTS:1:2:37]
(Cf. also Sacks et al., p. 723, fn.)

(57) Sam: Would the bartender or the cook put 'n apron on 'r sum'n I– we– how're we gonna know who's who.
(1.0)
Jim: I tried tuh call you by the way.
E: Yea//::h?
Jim: I think ih wz Thursday, you weren' in.
E: Thurs//dee?
Joe: No. (1.0) She w'z // gone
Jim: → No. Sam. I taw– I talked to you on Thursday.
(1.0)
Sam: [Me?
Jim: [I tried tuh talk tuh Sam on Thursday but he wasn' // home. [Schenkein:II:25]
(Also note the next-turn speaker-selection repair initiation at Sam's second turn "Me?")

Self- and other-initiated repairs, then, deal with same sorts of repairables.

4.2. The placements of self-initiation and other-initiation are organized by reference to each other. They are positioned successively (i.e., they occupy adjacent turns); and they are ordered, alternating turn-by-turn between positions for self- and other-initiation, with positions for self-initiation preceding those for other-initiation. Since the set of positions operates for same sorts of repairables, and thus potentially for some same particular repairable,[17] the different positions invite treatment as involving a serial ordering of opportunities to repair *some same* potential repairable. These are all aspects of an ordering of the positions for self- and other-initiation relative to each other. However, such an ordering could be a by-product of an organization of those positions relative to the trouble source. What we want to show is that the positions are not only *ordered* relative to each other, but that that ordering is *organizationally designed,* i.e., is the product of an organization that relates the positions to each other—not just to the trouble source, with a relation to each other as by-product.

Such an organization is most usefully explicated in the positioning of other-initiation relative to the trouble-source turn. We noted earlier (§4.1) that other-initiations occupy one main position: next turn. This distribution is organizationally achieved. The observation about the occurrence of other-initiation in next-turn position has dual import. First, out of the multiplicity of later turns by others that follow a potential repairable, very nearly all other-initiations come in just one of them, namely next turn, *and not in later turns by other(s).* Second, other-initiations *do not come earlier.* Although trouble-source turns are often interrupted for the initiation of repair, such interruptions are overwhelmingly self-interruptions by the speaker of the trouble-source turn for the self-initiation of repair, and are rarely interruptions by other-initiation. Rather, others "withhold" repair initiations from placement while trouble-source turn is in progress,[18] e.g., in the following fragment (from Jefferson 1972).

(58) Steven: ((Three children playing water tag; Steven has been tagged, and is now "It"))
Steven: One, two, three, ((pause)) four five
→ six, ((pause)) eleven eight nine ten.
Susan: → Eleven? eight, nine, ten?
Steven: → Eleven, eight, nine, ten.
Nancy: → Eleven?
Steven: Seven, eight, nine, ten.
Susan: That's better.
((Game continues)) [GJ:FN]
(Cf. also 62–63 below.[19])

Here the other-initiator clearly has an initiation technique (not to mention a correction) available on the occurrence of the repairable, but does not employ it until the trouble-source turn has come to completion.

Indeed, other-initiations regularly are withheld a bit *past* the possible completion of trouble-source turn; not only does a withhold get them specifically positioned in next turn, but it can get "next turn" itself delayed a bit. In such cases, other-initiations occur after a slight gap, the gap evidencing a withhold beyond the completion of trouble-source turn—providing an "extra" opportunity, in an expanded transition space, for speaker of trouble source to self-initiate repair (cf.

12, 43, 49).[20] Such opportunities are taken with some regularity, yielding data in which a slight gap after turn completion is followed by transition-space self-initiation, with no other-initiation at all (as in 60 below). Such data should be appreciated as evidence on the withholding of other-initiation, even though no other-initiation occurs in them. By means of the extended withhold, their occurrence is sometimes avoided entirely (a device having evidentiary bearing on a preference, which cannot be discussed here, for self- over other-initiation of repair).

The nearly invariable withhold of other-initiation until trouble-source turn's possible completion, with the frequent withhold for a bit after that possible completion, is an organized positioning of other-initiation relative not only to trouble source but also relative to same-turn post-trouble-source position for self-initiation. It provides clear evidence that self- and other-initiation are related *to each other,* that the relatedness is *organized,* and that the organization is in *repair-specific terms.*

4.3. We declared an interest above (§1 and fn. 5), informing our work on repair, in finding and describing an organization, operative in local environments and on a case-by-case basis, which cumulatively produced the aggregate orderliness of repair phenomena. Enough elements of such an organization have been introduced in passing, in the preceding discussion, to make it useful to restate them more pointedly and elaborate them slightly, although we cannot undertake a full account of that organization here. We begin by making explicit an analytic shift that has already been tacitly employed in the preceding paragraphs.

Having found that, for the types of repair considered (and for others that we know of), repair can be initiated from any of the four positions we have referred to, we note: each of the positions at which repair *does* get initiated is a position at which repair *can* get initiated. Each provides a "repair-initiation *opportunity.*" It is central to the understanding of the withholding of "other-initiation" that it is withheld in order to allow speaker of a repairable the use of an opportunity, or set of opportunities, to initiate repair himself. It should be appreciated, then, that such an opportunity attended that speaker's turn, whether or not it was taken. Thus all the data provided in this paper on next-turn repair initiation should be understood as showing, as well, opportunities *not taken* for same turn and transition-space repair initiation. And the data presented on third-turn repair initiation display instances in which opportunities for same-turn and transition-space initiation of repair were not taken by speaker of repairable, and in which opportunities for next-turn repair initiation were not taken by "others." It should, then, finally be appreciated that in instances in which there is no third-turn repair either—in which, then, no repair is initiated at any of these positions, and thus almost invariably no repair is initiated at all—that a potential repairable (and recall §2.1, where it was noted that nothing seems to be excludable from that class) has nonetheless been attended by the full complement of repair-initiation opportunities, none of which happens to have been taken. (Thus our earlier finding that even the "ripest" of repairables, i.e., "errors," are not necessarily followed by repair.) The organization of self- and other-initiation is, then, fundamentally located in the organization of repair-initiation *opportunity positions;* this operates whether or not any repair is initiated, by self or other. The "repair space" through which a repairable passes is, then, to be understood as a "repair-initiation *opportunity* space," some of whose characteristics we here briefly repeat, leaving a more elaborate treatment for discussion elsewhere.

The "repair-initiation opportunity space" is continuous and discretely bounded, composed of initiation-opportunity positions at least some of which are discretely bounded.[21] The positions are adjacent, each being directly succeeded by a next, some being themselves composed internally of a set of "sub-positions." The space is three turns long,[22] starting from (i.e., including) the trouble-source turn. Nearly all repairables on which repair *is* initiated have the repair initiated from within this space.[23] As ought to be clear from the earlier discussion, the organization of the repair space is compatible with an organizational preference for self-initiation over other-initiation of repair (a preference distinct from the preference for self-repair)—a preference which the empirical preponderance of self- over other-initiations suggests to be indeed operative.[24] A more detailed discussion of the repair-initiation opportunity space and of the preference for self-initiation of repair is reserved for another occasion.

5. Preference for self-correction. We have added to the distinction with which we began, between self- and other-correction, a distinction between self- and other-*initiation of repair;* we have found the latter distinction to catch a set of empirical types, and have found those types and their structured opportunity positions to be organizationally related. We now return to our initial hypothesis and the gross evidence for it; i.e., as between self- and other-*correction,* we should expect a social-organizational preference for self- over other-correction, a preference exhibited empirically by the preponderance of self- over other-correction. How is this preponderance produced?

5.1. The following points were noted earlier: (i) opportunities for self-initiation come before opportunities for other-initiation (cf. §4.2); (ii) massively, for those repairables on which repair is initiated, same-turn and transition-space opportunities for self-initiation *are taken* by speakers of the trouble source (cf. §4.2); (iii) the course or trajectory of same-turn initiated repairs regularly leads to successful self-repair in same turn, i.e., before the position for other-initiation (cf. §3.3).

This combination of facts, by itself, would account for a skewed distribution of corrections toward self-correction.

5.2. Furthermore, in the case of those repairables on which repair is initiated, but not in same turn or transition space, *other-initiations overwhelmingly yield self-corrections.* In the techniques employed for other-initiation of repair, we find a further basis for the empirical preponderance of self-correction, as well as decisive evidence that this preponderance is organizationally designed—the product of a preference for self-correction, independent of the preference for self-initiation.

We noted in §3.2 above that the techniques for self- and other-initiation were different. It is now in point to elaborate one aspect of their difference.

5.21. Same-turn and transition-space self-initiations/self-repairs can, and overwhelmingly do, combine the operations of locating the repairable and doing a candidate repair. To be sure, these two operations can be separated in same-turn repair:

(59) B: → nYeeah, ˙hh This feller I have- (nn)
→ 'felluh' this ma:n (0.2) t!˙hhh He ha::(s)- uff- eh- who- who I have fer Linguistics // is really too much.
[TG:8]

Or the "not X, Y" format may be used, in which the "not X" component locates the repairable, and the "Y" component supplies a candidate repair:

(60) A: → That sto:re, has terra cotta floors. ((pause))
A: → Not terra cotta. Terrazzo. [AT:FN]
(61) Louise: Isn't it next week we're outta school?
Roger: → Yeah next week. No // not next
→ week, // the week after. [GTS:1:28]

In the vast majority of cases, however, (cf. any of the same-turn repairs we have cited), the trouble-locating is compacted into the repair-candidate itself, both being done by a single component, and being done in the same turn as the trouble source. (The repair initiator, it will be recalled, is a non-lexical perturbation in same-turn repair, and neither locates repairable nor supplies repair.) The basic format for same-turn repair is, then, self-initiation with a non-lexical initiator followed by candidate repair.[25]

5.22. The format for other-initiated repair is different. The different initiator technique mentioned earlier (§3.2) engenders a different trajectory (§3.3), which results in other-initiation yielding self-repair in a next turn. For, in other-initiation, the operations of locating the repairable and supplying a candidate repair are separated. *The techniques for other-initiation are techniques for locating the trouble source.* The turn which affords others an opportunity for initiating repair is thus used to locate the trouble source; such turns are massively occupied with nothing else. They are used, then, to provide speaker of the trouble source *another* opportunity, in the turn that follows them, to repair the trouble source. They are used this way even when "other" clearly "knows" the repair or "correction," and *could* use the turn to do it:

(62) Ken: 'E likes that waider over there,
Al: → Wait-<u>er</u>?
Ken: Waitress, sorry,
Al: 'At's bedder, [GTS:II:2:54]

(63) A: It's just about three o'clock, so she's probably free. I'll call her now.
B: → <u>What</u> time is it?
A: Three, isn't it?
B: → I thought it was earlier.
A: Oh, two. Sorry. [SPC:SP]
(Cf. also 58 above.)

Thus other-initiated repair takes a multiple of turns—at least two: in the first of these, the other-initiator locates the trouble; in the second, the speaker of the trouble source essays a repair (self-correction).[26]

5.3. In sum: *self-initiated repairs yield self-correction,* and opportunities for self-initiation come first. *Other-initiated repairs also yield self-correction;* the opportunity available to other to initiate repair is used to afford speaker of a trouble source a further opportunity to self-repair, which he takes. This combination compels the conclusion that, although there is a distinction between self-correction and other-correction, *self-correction and other-correction are not alternatives.* Rather, the organization of repair in conversation provides centrally for self-correction, which can be arrived at by the alternative routes of self-initiation and other-initiation—routes which are themselves so organized as to favor self-initiated self-repair.

6. Some observations on other-correction. The preceding discussion has provided an organizational basis for a strongly skewed distribution of correction in the direction of self-correction, a skewing which is empirically found in conversational data. In view of the substantial constraints operating to restrict the occurrence of other-correction, the small number of other-corrections which *do* occur invite special attention. Several observations may be offered.

6.1. When other-corrections are done, they are frequently modulated in form. Several forms of modulation may be mentioned.

6.11. The other-correction may be downgraded on a "confidence/uncertainty" scale, e.g., by the affiliation to the correction of uncertainty markers, or by use of various types of question format:

(64) Ben: Lissena pigeons.
(0.7)
Ellen: → [Coo-coo::: coo:::
Bill: [Quail, I think.
Ben: Oh yeh?
(1.5)
Ben: No that's not quail, that's a pigeon, [JS:II:219-20]

One particularly common modulation form is *Y'mean X?* where *X* is a possible correction or replacement word.

(65) Lori: But y'know single beds'r awfully thin tuh sleep on.
Sam: What?
Lori: Single beds. // They're–
Ellen: → Y'mean narrow?
Lori: They're awfully narrow // yeah. [JS:II:97]

6.12. Some "other-corrections" are jokes; i.e., they are done jokingly, or turn out to be jokes, and not seriously-proposed corrections:

(66) Louise: We gotta nice large table fer her an' 'er husban'
→ t'demonstrate.
(1.7)

( ): hmm:::hh
(0.8)
Louise: 'Ere was a cartoon where they had, uhm think i'was in Playboy, (0.6) where they had 'n- you know, s:ex 'n hygiene,
(0.9)
Roger: → Not demonstrate, indulge .hhheh hh//hh
[GTS:I:2:56]

(67) L: Holiday, quote unquote, huh huh
Lo: Hn hn // hn
C: A(hh)re you ki(hh)dding?
(2.0)
L: (Memorial Day's a non-work day.)
J: That's- that's right.=
Lo: =huh huh!
J: → Stay home and pine about work.
Lo: huh huh huh huh huh huh huh uh huh.
L: → Not about work, about money,
Lo: huh huh huh! [BSII:2:151]

6.2. As noted above, the *Y'mean X?* form may be used to modulate an other-correction. But it may be used, quite apart from that, to check understanding, i.e., for a check by recipient-of-a-turn of his understanding of the turn—as can forms other than *Y'mean X?* E.g.,

(68) B: ... I was thinkin this morning, I was having a little trouble in the bathroom, an' I though 'Oh, boy, I- n- I- uh- uh this business of getting up at six o'clock'n being ready t' eat, is uh- is not fer me,' // heh heh
A: Uh huh
A: Well, uh th- ((clears throat))
B: Somehow you // endure it.
A: There's 'n- There's 'n answer to that too.
(2.0)
A: hhhh a physical answer t(hh)oo hhh
B: → You mean takin laxative at night.
A: No, suppositories. [SBL:2:1:8:2]

(69) Roger: En yer the only ones thet survive (h)after the cra::sh, ihh=
( ): =( )

Ken: Four months onna deserted island he:hh hnhh
(0.4)
(Roger): Aaa:h.=
Ken: =˙hi:::hh.
(0.2)
Jim: Go//t some imagina:tion don't] yuh.hheh
Ken: Home made abo(h)rtion.]
(Dan): (//)
Roger: Wha://t?
Jim: ((clears throat))
(0.2)
Jim: Some imagination.
(0.5)
Roger: → Who:se.mi:ne?
Jim: No hi:s.
Roger: hhihh ˙hh hh ˙hh [GTS:5:13:r]

Note that, in *Y'mean* and uncertainty-marked modulations, as well as in understanding checks, other-correction (and the "checked understanding") is not asserted, but is proferred for acceptance or rejection. The format employed is that of a guess, candidate, or "try" in what we have elsewhere called a "correction invitation format."[27]

These forms supply the most accommodating environment for *unmodulated other-correction.* Of the unmodulated other-corrections which *do* occur, a very large proportion occur in the turn after an understanding check or a modulated other-correction, e.g., of the form *You mean X?* They take the form *No* plus correction (see, e.g., 64, 68, and 69 above, the turns following the arrowed turns). It should be noted that these unmodulated other-corrections, in view of their occurrence after understanding checks, etc., in typically question and correction-invitation format, are (either) invited, and /or reject a modulated other-correction in prior turn. The import of the last points is that most of the other-correction which does occur is either specially marked or specially positioned; both types exhibit an orientation to its dispreferred status.

6.3. As the data cited on them should suggest, other-initiations of repair locate problems of hearing and/or understanding as "obstacles" to the production of what would otherwise occupy the sequential position in which they are placed—an appropriate "next turn" sequentially implicated by prior turn. Other-initiations of repair undertake to have such "obstacles" removed in the service of the production of a sequentially implicated next. When the hearing/understanding of a turn is adequate to the production of a correction by "other," it is adequate to allow production of a sequentially appropriate next turn. Under that circumstance, the turn's recipient ("other") should produce the next turn, not the correction (and, overwhelmingly, that is what is done). Therein lies another basis for the empirical paucity of other-corrections: those who could do them do a sequentially appropriate next turn instead. Therein, as well, lies the basis for the modulation—in particular, the "uncertainty marking"—of other-correction: if it were confidently held, it ought not to be done; only if unsurely held ought it to displace the sequentially implicated next turn. Therein, finally, is a basis for much of the other-correction which does occur being treated by its recipient on its occurrence, as involving more than correction, i.e., disagreement.[28]

6.4. We have so far in this section offered three types of observation on the occurrence of other-correction, in view of the structural constraints operating to restrict it: (i) about the form it takes, e.g., modulation; (ii) about its local sequential environment, e.g., just after modulated other-corrections and understanding checks; and (iii) about its sequential implications upon its occurrence, e.g., its treatment as disagreement.

Such observations are possible and in point because, unlike other-initiation of repair—which, in its proper position (next turn) is unrestricted in its privilege of occurrence—other-correction is highly constrained in its occurrence. It is likely that other environments can be located in which other-correction does occur. For example, one sequence-type environment in which other-correction is used, in a manner which exploits its potential relationship to disagreement, is the story-telling sequence in conversation. There, an "as-of-some-point-non-teller" of a story starting to be told, or in progress, may use other-correction of the teller as a bid, or subsequently as a vehicle, for being a co-teller of the story—making, with the initial teller, a "team." Once noted as an environment for other-correction, the "team" relationship of two parties may be further explored in other sequential environments for the presence of other-correction. Still, the investigation of such particular and restricted environments is indicative of the generally constrained occurrence of other-correction.

6.5. We want to note one apparent exception to the highly constrained occurrence of other-correction, with the reservation that we note it not on the basis of extensive taped and transcribed conversational materials, but on the basis of passing observation, plus some inspection of a limited amount of taped and transcribed data.[29] The exception is most apparent in the domain of adult-child interaction, in particular parent-child interaction; but it may well be more generally relevant to the not-yet-competent in some domain without respect to age. There, other-correction seems to be not as infrequent, and appears to be one vehicle for socialization. If that is so, then it appears that other-correction is not so much an alternative to self-correction in general, but rather a device for dealing with those who are still learning or being taught to operate with a system which requires, for its routine operation, that they be adequate self-monitors and self-correctors as a condition of competence. It is, in that sense, only a transitional usage, whose supersession by self-correction is continuously awaited.

7. "Repair" as a phenomenon for linguistics and sociology. In the recent history of linguistics, across the various changes in theoretical position and tenor it has experienced, the phenomena of correction—or, more generally, repair—have been largely ignored,[30] in spite of their massive occurrence in the overwhelmingly most common use of language—conversation. This is not another complaint against this or that theoretical school or style of analysis; "structural linguistics" did not give repair that much more attention than transformationalists have given it. When the relevance of the general domain *has* been appreciated, it has been "error" rather than repair which has been treated as the central phenomenon of interest.[31]

However, the organization of repair is the self-righting mechanism for the organization of language use in social interaction. If language is composed of systems of rules which are integrated, then it will have sources of trouble related to the modes of their integration (at the least). And if it has intrinsic sources of trouble, then it will have a mechanism for dealing with them intrinsically. An adequate theory of the organization of natural language will need to depict how a natural language handles its intrinsic troubles. Such a theory will, then, need an account of the organization of repair.

Finally, since language is a vehicle for the living of real lives with real interests in a real world, it should be appreciated that an interest in available mechanisms for handling the troubles of rule-system integration, among others, is not only (or primarily) a theoretician's interest. Not only language integration, but also social organization, require an organization of repair. Here, at the organization of repair—though not exclusively here—linguistics and sociology meet.

ACKNOWLEDGMENTS

We wish to acknowledge the help, through discussion and/or through bringing relevant data to our attention, of Jo Ann Goldberg, Anita Pomerantz, and Alene Terasaki at the University of California, Irvine, and of Francoise Brun-Cottan, Irene Daden, and Louise Kerr at the University of California, Los Angeles. Harvey Sacks was killed in an automobile accident while this paper was undergoing final revision. This paper was originally published in *Language,* 53, 2, 1977, 361-382. Permission to publish it here has been granted by the authors and the Linguistic Society of America.

NOTES

1. Bolinger ([1953] 1965:248) writes:

> What speakers avoid doing is as important as what they do. Self-correction of speech and writing, and the correction of others in conversation ("I can't understand what you say"), in classrooms, and over editorial desks is an unending business, one that determines the outlines of our speech just as acceptances determine its mass. Correction, the border beyond which we say "no" to an expression, is to language what a seacoast is to a map. Up to now, linguistic scientists have ignored it because they could see in it nothing more than the hankerings of pedants after a standard that is arbitrary, prejudiced and personal. But it goes deeper. Its motive is intelligibility, and in spite of the occasional aberrations that have distracted investigators from the central facts, it is systematic enough to be scientifically described.

Not much has been made of the distinction–in part, perhaps, because the disciplines have used it to divide up their work, self-correction being occasionally discussed by linguists (since it regularly occurs within the sentence?), e.g., Hockett 1967 and DuBois 1974, and other-correction by psychologists, e.g., Garvey, *ms.* They have rarely both been in the attention of the same investigator, who might then address himself to the relation between them.

2. Under various guises–self/other, individual/society, ego/alter–and through various understandings of the relationship between them–opposition, complimentarity, etc.–this pair of notions goes back to the origins of American sociology (G. H. Mead, Cooley, etc.), to the classical figures of European sociology (Marx, Weber, Durkheim), and beyond the origins of sociology as an academically specialized discpline to the origins of social and political philosophy. For one account of the development of the theme that "external control," i.e.,

control by others, will not adequately account for, or guarantee, social order, cf. Parsons 1937.

3. Cf. Sacks, Schegloff and Jefferson 1974.

4. We use the term "preference" technically to refer not to motivations of the participants, but to sequence- and turn-organizational features of conversation. For example, "dispreferreds" are structurally delayed in turns and sequences, and are (or may be) preceded by other items; dispreferreds may be formed as preferreds. Cf. Pomerantz 1975.

5. As in the organization of turn-taking, the gross facts which characterize large amounts of conversational data are the product of rules, and systems of rules, which operate on particular sequential environments. For example, it is a set of rules that operate on "possible turn completions" which produces the set of gross characteristics of conversation enumerated in Sacks et al. 1974, where "possible turn completion" is an instance of a "particular sequential environment." Similarly with repair, we are interested in finding mechanisms which operate on a "case-by-case" (or environment-by-environment) basis, yielding as a by-product some observable orderliness for the aggregate. One research aim in our work on the organization of repair has been to find and characterize the "value" of "environment" in terms of which "case-by-case" operation of repair is organized.

6. Cf. Jefferson 1972, 1973, 1975; Jordan and Fuller 1975; Sacks and Schegloff 1977; Sacks et al. 1974, passim; Schegloff 1976.

7. The research reported here is based on a large corpus of audio tapes (and a smaller corpus of video tapes) of naturally occurring conversation, and transcripts of those tapes. The conversations are of various sorts, with various sorts of parties, and combinations of them. For a glossary of symbols used in the data citations, see Sacks et al. (1974:731–4). Several of the notational conventions of special relevance to this paper are: a dash (–), used to indicate a cut-off of the preceding word or sound; colons (:), used to indicate stretching of the preceding sound; and numbers in parentheses (0.8), used to indicate silence in tenths of a second. In some cases the transcripts have been simplified by the omission of some symbols. Arrows indicate the location of the phenomenon for which a segment is initially cited.

8. In view of the point made above about the relation between repair and error, "failure" needs to be distinguished from those cases in which an apparent trouble has occurred, but no effort to repair it is undertaken. "Failure" refers to cases in which a repair procedure is initiated and does not yield a successful solution. "Failure" is a complex category; although it is frequently marked by an overt withdrawal of the repair effort, it has different forms and types. Such complexity is not in point for the present discussion, which takes note only of the gross possibility of failure. In that regard it should be noted that, although the possibility of failure cannot be ignored, in the vast majority of cases repair is successful and quick.

9. Elaboration of the following account of the distribution of the initiation of repair, and of that presented below in §§4.2–4.3, will be the topic of another report.

10. We reserve for another report discussion of the sub-distribution of repair-initiations at various positions within same turn.

11. Two comments about the cross-citation of data: (1) We refer in the text

to data segment 16. That segment's arrows locate the phenomenon being discussed *there.* That segment happens also to include an instance of the phenomenon being considered *here,* but it is not arrowed. For cross-citations of data in this paper, therefore, arrows are not of decisive import. (2) We occasionally make cross-reference to other papers of ours to show data that display phenomena we are discussing which have not been selected for that purpose.

12. Cf. Sacks et al. (1974:702–6). The transition space, roughly, is the environment of a turn's possible completion, at which possible transition to a next speaker becomes relevant. Although the transition space may begin a bit before the possible completion point, and last a bit into the beginning of a next turn, for our purposes here it may be thought of as the "beat" that potentially follows the possible completion point of a turn.

In the data on transition-space repair, we have put those components of a turn that follow a posssible completion (i.e., are in or after the transition space) on new lines. Thus: what is typographically represented on several new lines is, nonetheless, further talk by a same speaker with no intervening talk by another.

13. This is not to say that any occurrence of any one of these is engaged in repair initiation. Turn-terminal words, e.g., frequently contain a sound stretch.

14. Cf. Sacks et al. (1974:702–3, 720–23, et passim).

15. The construction types for other-initiation of repair are not presented in the text in a random order. They have a natural ordering, based on their relative "strength" or "power" on such parameters as their capacity to "locate" a repairable. The natural ordering is realized empirically in several facts. For instance, there is a preference for stronger over weaker initiators, such that weaker ones get self-interrupted in mid-production to be replaced by stronger ones:

(a) B: How long y'gonna be here?
A: Uh- not too long. Uh just til uh Monday.
B: → Til- oh yih mean like a week f'm tomorrow.
A: Yah. [DA:2]

Or, if more than one other-initiated sequence is needed, the other-initiators are used in order of increasing strength:

(b) A: I have a: — cousin teaches there.
D: Where.
A: Uh:, Columbia.
D: → Columbia?
A: Uh huh.
D: → You mean Manhattan?
A: No. Uh big university. Isn't that in Columbia?
D: Oh in Columbia.
A: Yeah.
(Cf. also 65, and (d) below.) [HS:FN]

Other construction types not enumerated in the text would fit into the ordering. For example: note that the "question words" in §3.22 all locate types of referents actually referred to in prior turn. There is a separate class of other initiators—in large measure using an overlapping set of lexical items—which locate as repairables referents which were not actually components of prior turn:

(c) Ben: They gotta- a garage sale.
Ellen: → Where.
Ben: On Third Avenoo. [Schenkein:70:38]
(d) Ava: I wanted t'know if ya got a uhm whatchamacallit uhm
p(hh)ark(hh)ing place this morning.
Bee: A parking place.
Ava: Mm hm.
Bee: → Where.
Ava: Oh hh just anyplace heh heh I was just kidding ya. [TG:1]

The latter class is differently graded than the former, being "stronger." We will report more fully on this whole area in another paper.

16. Some types, however, are overwhelmingly initiated by one or the other. Thus, when "errors" of grammar are made and repaired, the repair is usually initiated by speaker of the trouble source, and rarely by others. Such other-initiation may have characteristics such as those described below in §6, which generally apply to other-*correction.*

17. It does not necessarily follow, from the fact that the set of positions operates for same *sorts* of repairables, that they all operate on some *particular* repairable, i.e., that any particular repairable can have repair initiated on it from any of the positions. It is, however, empirically the case. That is most conveniently shown by instances in which some particular repairable, having had repair initiated in one position and a candidate solution achieved, has repair reinitiated on it at another position. Thus, in fragment (d) of fn. 15, *parking place* is first the target of a same-turn word-search repair, and then of a next-turn repair; and in 44, the place being referred to is self-repaired in third turn and then other-repaired in next turn. Also, repair may be initiated simultaneously or overlappingly by self and other, and thereby in different positions:

Prisc: Okay.
Marj: Okay then seeyuh- Wednesday.=
Prisc: =Ya:h,=
Marj: =Ya//h.
Prisc: → (Tha-) No // not (Wens)]
Marj: → No Thur] sday.
(0.2)
Prisc: Euh allright // (dear), [Trio:2:II:6]

18. On "withholding," cf. Jefferson (1973:61–70).

19. Consider also the following from Charles Dickens, *Bleak House* (Everyman's edition), p. 6 (emphasis supplied):

> "In reference," proceeds the Chancellor, still on Jarndyce and Jarndyce, "to the young *girl–*"
> "Begludships pardon–*boy,*" says Mister Tangle, *prematurely.*
> "In reference," proceeds the Chancellor, with extra distinctness, "to the young girl and boy, the two young people," (Mr. Tangle crushed) ...

20. The post-gap other-initiations are important on another point as well. It might be thought that the infrequency of interruptions by "others" to initiate repair is a consequence of the turn-taking organization and of the right it gives current speaker to speak to possible completion, including repair. To be sure, the turn-taking organization is relevant, and the compatibility of the organization of repair with it is a fact of considerable importance. But as noted in Sacks et al., slight overlap of current turn's completion by next turn's start is not infrequent and has various systematic bases; but when "next turn" is occupied with other-initiation of repair, it rarely overlaps prior turn. Furthermore, the turn-taking system is organized so as to minimize not only overlap but gap as well; that the "withholding" of other-initiation has a repair-specific basis separate from, and sometimes superseding, turn-taking may be seen in the "withhold to allow self-initiation" which yields a gap after the trouble-source turn. This is only one of many evidences of the independent status of the repair organization, whose operation may supersede otherwise operative aspects of the turn-taking organization.

21. The discussion of "withholding of other-initiation" shows the discrete boundedness of "same turn." The necessary research on this matter for the other positions is still incomplete.

22. A paper on the opportunity space will justify the turn metric employed here. That turns are the relevant units is somewhat evidenced in the text above.

23. Recall the observation in §§2 and 4 that not all errors yield repair. The same holds true for the more general category of "repairable"—more general, it will be recalled, because it appears that nothing is, in principle, excludable from that class.

24. Various of the points above speak to this preference, e.g., the extended withhold of other-initiation, in which a late self-initiation regularly occurs.

25. Cf. Jefferson (1975:186).

26. These two turns, and the further turns that may be engendered if the first other-initiated repair sequence is not successful, turn out to display adjacency-pair organization, as we will discuss in detail elsewhere. On adjacency-pair organization, cf. Schegloff and Sacks (1973:295–9); Sacks et al. (1974:716–18).

There is, of course, the alternative, in the turn following the other-initiation turn, of confirming or re-asserting the original version of the trouble-source:

(a)	Crandall:		... they talk about the president as a teacher.	
	Caller:	→	At- As a <u>teach</u>er?	
	Crandall:	→	Yes.	
	Caller:		Uh hu:h,	[Crandall:2-22:20]
(b)	A:		Why don't you want to tell it to me.	
	B:		I don't know why.	
	A:	→	You don't know?	
	B:	→	No I don't. I'm sorry.	[SPC:92]

27. Cf. Sacks and Schegloff 1977.

28. "Disagreement," used here in a technical sense, names a vast and elaborate aspect of the organization of sequences in conversation, partially overlapping with the organization of preference and dispreference, occasionally mentioned in the text, and commented on in fn. 4 above. The organization of repair is intricately involved with that of agreement/disagreement and preference/dispreference. Aside from the convergence mentioned in the text between other-correction

and disagreement, e.g., other forms of other-initiated repair are systematically related to "disagreement," regularly being used and understood as "pre-disagreements." The organization of agreement/disagreement and preference/dispreference is too complex to be entered into here. Its operation in one domain is illuminated by Pomerantz.

29. Use of taped and transcribed material is of two sorts: (a) inspection of materials in our corpus where a child is present, and (b) an initial, unsystematic reading of material collected by Roger Brown, whom we thank for having made it available to us.

30. There are exceptions, of course, and we have cited some of the published work elsewhere in this paper. We should note as well the work of Labov (cf., e.g., 1970:42); his suggestion that a few "editing rules" would bring most spoken sentences into conformity with the formats described by students of syntax encouraged and reinforced our own belief that there was sufficient orderliness in this area to permit successful investigation.

31. Cf. the collection edited by Fromkin (1973); but note the occasional interest expressed in "correction" or "editing," e.g., in the papers by Fry, Hockett, and Laver.

REFERENCES

Bolinger, Dwight, L. 1953. The life and death of words. *American Scholar* 22.323-35. [Reprinted in his *Forms of English: accent, morpheme, order.* Cambridge, MA: Harvard University Press, 1965.]

Carterette, Edward C., and Margaret Hubbard Jones. 1974. *Informal speech:* alphabetic and phonemic texts with statistical analyses and tables. Berkeley and Los Angeles: University of California Press.

DuBois, John W. 1974. Syntax in mid-sentence. *Berkeley studies in syntax and semantics,* I, ed. by Charles Fillmore, George Lakoff, and Robin Lakoff, pp. III.1-25. Berkeley: Department of Linguistics and Institute of Human Learning, University of California.

Fromkin, Victoria A. (ed.) 1973. *Speech errors as linguistic evidence.* The Hague: Mouton.

Fry, D. B. 1969. The linguistic evidence of speech errors. *Brno Studies in English* 8.70–74. [Reprinted in Fromkin, pp. 157–63.]

Garvey, Catherine. 1975. Contingent queries. *Ms.* Baltimore: Johns Hopkins University, Department of Psychology.

Hockett, C. F. 1967. Where the tongue slips, there slip I. To honor Roman Jakobson, 910-36. The Hague, Mouton. [Reprinted in Fromkin, pp. 93–119.]

Jefferson, Gail. 1972. Side sequences. *Studies in social interaction,* ed. by David N. Sudnow, 294–338. New York: Free Press.

____. 1973. A case of precision timing in ordinary conversation. *Semiotica* 9.47–96.

____. 1975. Error correction as an interactional resource. *Language in Society* 3.181–99.

Jordan, B., and N. Fuller. 1975. The non-fatal nature of trouble: sense-making

and trouble managing in lingua franca talk. *Semiotica* 13.11–31.
Labov, William. 1970. The study of language in its social context. *Studium Generale* 23.30–87.
Laver, John D.M. 1969. The detection and correction of slips of the tongue. Work in Progress 3, Dept. of Phonetics and Linguistics, University of Edinburgh. [Reprinted in Fromkin, pp. 132–43.]
Parsons, Talcott. 1937. *The structure of social action.* Glencoe, IL: Free Press.
Pomerantz, Anita. 1975. Second assessments: a study of some features of agreements/disagreements. Irvine: University of California dissertation.
Sacks, H., and E. Schegloff. 1979. Two preferences in the organization of reference to persons in conversation and their interaction. In G. Psathas, (ed.) *Everyday Language,* New York: Irvington, 1979.
Sacks, H.; E. Schegloff; and G. Jefferson. 1974. A simplest systematics for the organization of turn-taking for conversation. *Language* 50.696–735.
Schegloff, E. 1968. Sequencing in conversational openings. *American Anthropologist* 70.1075–95.
____. 1976. Some questions and ambiguities in conversation. Cambridge, England: Pragmatics Microfiche.
____, and H. Sacks. 1973. Opening up closings. *Semiotica* 8.289–327.

List-Construction as a Task and Resource

Gail Jefferson

The occurrence of lists in natural conversation is examined to reveal some of the interactional relevances of such list productions.

The presence of three-part lists are first noted. Speakers and hearers orient to their three-part nature. The completed list can then constitute a turn at talk and the hearer can monitor the third component as a sign of turn completion. Lists can thereby be a conversational sequential resource.

By virtue of the three-part structure of some lists, members can orient to such matters as a "weak," "absent," or "missing" third part. Third items can be used to accomplish particular interactional work, such as topic-shifting and offense avoidance.

Further, a list can be constructed by more than one speaker. This feature may be used for a range of activities, including the achievement of interactional accord in situations of impending discord.

This report is a preliminary examination of lists occurring in natural conversation. It focuses upon the work which list-construction, as a task, allots to speakers, and some uses to which list-construction, as a resource, can be put by speakers.

1. A first observation is that many lists occur as three-part units.

*This is a revision of a paper presented at the University of Massachusetts, Amherst, September 1973.

For example:

(1) [MC:I]
Sidney: While you've been talking tuh me, I mended, two nightshirts, a pillowcase? enna pair'v pants.

(2) [GTS:IV]
Roger: <u>That</u> was a vicious school there- it was about forty percent Negro, bout twenny percent Japanese, the rest were rich Jews, heh hhh

(3) [SPC]
Desk: And, ih- in general what we try to do is help people figure out what the trouble is, what kind of help they need and get it for them.

(4) [SBL]
Maybelle: I think if you exercise it an' <u>work</u> at it'n studied it chu <u>do</u> become clairvoyant.

(5) [GTS:III]
Louise: For three hundred years she's been giving him a w- mh bout ten white shirts, an' a coupla ties an' a suit.

This three-partedness shows up in its barest form in the listlike "triple singles" by which people indicate "muchness." For example:

(6) [Labov:BG]
Alice: "Well we're k-callin ar good friend Alice again en blah blah blah"

(7) [JG]
Maggie: <u>Work</u>ing working working you know how I do,

(8) [Frankel:US:I]
Carol: Did this phone ring? I dialed twice en it n- rang'n rang'n rang

(9) [NB:II]
Emma: They go on en on en on but . . .

(10) [SBL]
Chloe: God, she just kept lookin, an' lookin, an' lookin,

(11) [M:CB]
Linny: I've been eating'n eating'n eating but I'm not really hungry.

Three-partedness also shows up in elaborated forms involving three-part units as components of larger three-part units.

So, for example, in the following fragment, a three-part description is offered, of which the first part is itself a three-part list. The three description-components are set off in brackets.

(12) [Rose:Fairmount:I]
Bitsy: Gordy is there anything fer dinner,
Gordy: Yeh. [Porkchops mashed p'tatuh'n corn] 'n [everything's cooked.] [Awl y'haftuh do is heat it up.]

In the following fragment, a three-part list of "what you get" at a sale is offered. The third item of the list is itself a three-part list, consisting of two items and a "generalized list completer." (Some workings of generalized list completers will be considered shortly.) Again, the larger list-components are set off in brackets.

(13) [MFP]
Sally: There's this big meat sale, up in Paoli.
Andrea: Oh Go:d really?
Sally: A:n' whatchu get is [a side of bee:f, fer um a lower price?]
Andrea: Mmhm
Sally: Plus ā uh [fifteen pounds of chicken uh free?] Plus [fer a dollar more you get um uh five pounds of vea:l, o:r a choice of– or ten pounds of bacon? or y'know a whole range of things.]

And in the following fragment, a three-part description of an initiation test for a cavalry officer is offered. Part one is itself built of three parts. Part two is built of three parts, the first part of which is itself a three-part list. (An interesting feature of part three will be considered shortly.)

(14) [GTS:IV]

Roger: He was given [three bottles a'champagne, three horses, and three addresses of uh patronizing women] y'know.

And his object was tuh um [ride a horse t'one address, share a bottle a'champagne with'er, make love with'er,] [take the other horse t'y'know the next one] and then [the third one.]

An' if he completed it within, a certain period I think it was three hours or something, was a full fledged cavalry officer.

Three-partedness, then, is an empirically observable, recurrent phenomenon which shows up in various forms, including the "triple-single" format, and the elaborated three-part within three-part structures.

2. A next observation is that three-partedness appears to have "programmatic relevance" for the construction of lists. That is, roughly, lists not only can and do occur in three parts, but *should* so occur.

Two recurrent phenomena indicate the programmatic relevance of three-partedness for list construction. The first is: Three-part *lists* can be built of less than three *items.* The second is: Three-partedness can be found to constitute a problem for list-makers, for which at least one methodic solution is available and deployed.

First: Less-than-three-*item* three-part *lists* are recurrently constructed by occupying a third slot with a generalized list completer. For example:

(15) [JG:II(a):3]

Heather: And they had like a concession stand like at a fair where you can buy [coke and popcorn and that type of thing.]

(16) [Carey:Bar]

Ernie: I said no I <u>know</u> his name is something <u>e</u>lse. [Teddy'r <u>Tom</u>'r somethin.]

(17) [Adato]

Sy: Take up [m:<u>Me</u>trecal er, Carnation <u>Slen</u>der er something like <u>that</u>.]

(18) [Labov:Battersea]
Rudd: Oh they come from [Jamaica en, South Africa'n, all over the place,]

(19) [GTS:III]
Dan: Y:know, the 'bility for a person to [pass for twenny one, and buy booze, an' that sort of thing,]

(20) [NB:IV:10]
Emma: Did she [do the cooking en take over'n everything,]

Second: Three-partedness as problematic for list-makers can be seen in the following sorts of materials in which people appear to directly address the programmatic relevance of three-partedness for list construction by engaging in a search for a third list item.

Sometimes a third list item is found. For example:

(21) [Lamb Interviews]
Mr. B: It's not in the same league with [adultery, and murder, and – and – thievery,] but . . .

(22) [GJ:FN]
Aaron: things like [non-complete, non-objective, non – nominalized references] . . .

(An interesting aspect of the "search and discovery" procedure for third list members will be considered shortly.)

Sometimes a projected third list item is not produced. In that case, a methodic solution to the problem of three-partedness is available and used. The search for a third *item* is terminated, and the list is closed with a generalized list completer. For example:

(23) [Adato]
Jay: Samuel jus'takes things [casually en naturally en, – all that,]

(24) [Electioneering]
Keith: We were building, [camps, and airfields, and, uh, everything like that.]

This is not to say that generalized list completers are always and only produced as solutions to the problem imposed by the programmatic relevance of three-partedness for lists. A list constructed in the first place as [2 items + generalized completer] may do a specifiable sort of work, distinctive from lists constructed in the first place as [3 items]. A comparison of Fragments (1)-(14) with Fragments (15)-(20) suggests that [3 item] lists are "relatively complete"; i.e., the items named exhaust the possible array of nameables for the purposes to which this particular listing is being put. [This sort of work is dramatically evident in the "triple singles," Fragments (6)-(11).] In contrast, the [2 item + generalized completer] lists may be "relevantly incomplete"; i.e., not only do the named items not exhaust the possible array of nameables, but a third item would not do such work; i.e., there are "many more" relevant nameables which will not, and need not, be specified.

However, a list may be initiated as a [3 item] list, in the course of which it is discovered, either that an array-exhaustive third item cannot be found (i.e., only two relevant nameables have, after all, come to mind), or that any third item will not adequately exhaust the array (i.e., there are, after all, "many more" relevant nameables). In such circumstances, the list may be "revised" to a [2 item + generalized completer] list. One or the other circumstances may hold in Fragments (23) and (24).

Three-partedness, then, is not only an empirically observable, recurrent phenomenon which occurs in drastically simple and enormously elaborate structures, but appears to be the product of an oriented-to-procedure by which lists are properly constructed.

3. From time to time it can be observed that three-partedness, as an oriented-to task, implicates and is implicated by another order of phenomenon, the "poetics" of natural talk.[1] The shape of this phenomenon, and its import for the study of talk cannot be adequately explicated here. Roughly, it includes such activities as punning and "acoustic consonance" (e.g., rhyming, alliteration, etc.). And, roughly, such types of activity might be characterized as "sensitive to" a range of matters which are not being explicitly "attended in the talk."

So, for example, in his lecture of February 19, Winter 1971, Harvey Sacks proposes that words can be selected in "historically sensitive" ways; i.e., can be selected by reference to prior or projected events. They may have sounds which are similar to surrounding sounds. So, for example, in the following fragment a speaker proposes that he is "fascinated." The acoustic consonance between that word and the prior series of [F]-initiated words ("foo faw," "forth," "fire," "forth") can have "selected" "fascinated" from among a range of alternatives.

(25.a) [Crandall]
B.C.: I have heard all this- foo faw back an' forth about,
uh couldn't fire the three shots in seven seconds an'
so forth an' so on. I am fascinated by this . . .

Or, a word may stand in a punlike relationship to surrounding words, as in the following fragment involving the contrast-class "stand"/"fall."

(25.b) [Lamb Interviews]
Mr. M: I voted for Cranston in the Fall, mainly because I
couldn't stand Rafferty.

Three-part lists turn out to be a rich locus of such "historically sensitive" selection. For example, in fragment 22 a searched-for third list item, "nominalized," starts with the [N/ah] sounds of the prior two list items and the pre-search item; i.e., "non."

(22) [GJ:FN]
Aaron: things like [non-complete, non-objective, non –
nominalized references] . . .

Recurrently, however, it is not third list *items* which stand in an observably "historically sensitive" relationship to just-prior talk (and massively, to prior list items), but generalized list-completers. Such objects belong to a class which Sacks refers to as "freely occurring" units of talk. These are units which are not constrained by, for example, specifics of reference, and which are selected from among multiple candidates.[2]

The following fragment is a dramatic instance. A generalized list completer, "and crap" (selected from among such candidates as "and stuff," "and junk," "and things," etc.) is acoustically consonant with a series of prior words, including the two just-prior list items ("committee," "cannot," "cakes an' candy" → "an crap").

(26) [SBL:3:1:7]
Nora: there's only one on the ways an' means committee, an'
I cannot serve on two because- ˙hh all these [cakes an'
candy an' crap] thet I have . . .

In the following fragment, the generalized list completer "or so forth" is acoustically consonant with the prior two list items ("friend or family" → "or so forth").

(27) [SPC]
Desk: Is there anyone close to you [friend or family or so forth] that you could uh kind of be in contact with

In the following, the generalized list completer "the whole bit" is acoustically consonant with the repeated [B/it] sounds of the prior two list items ("build it," "it," "be," "it" → "the whole bit").

(28) [GTS:IV]
Ken: . . . to [build it the way he wants it to be, design it, the whole bit.]

In the following, the generalized list completer "what have you" is acoustically consonant with the [haa/yuh] series of the prior two list items ("half," "year" → "what have you").

(29) [Adato]
Jay: It would be a pity, y'know fer this guy, to, spend, uh [a half a year, a year, what have you] in jail.

In an earlier fragment, a search for a third list item is terminated and a generalized list completer is produced. That object is initiated with a [vowel/L] particle which appears in both prior list items ("casually," "naturally" → "all that").

(23) [Adato]
Jay: Samuel jus' takes things casually en naturally en, – all that,]

And in the following fragment, the generalized list completer "and junk like this" is initiated with a [juh] particle which is accoustically consonant with the last sound of the second list item ("change" → "junk").

(30) [GTS:II]
Ken: I go in there and [I uh put all the bottles in back and I uh give people change, and junk like this.]

Finally, in the following fragment, the generalized list completer "or anything else" is acoustically consonant with a [th/ing/el] series in the prior two list items ("talking," "talking," "health" → "anything else").

(31) [GTS:IV]
Dan: My idea at least in terms of [talking about normalicy, or talking about health, or anything else,] is . . .

Punlike relationships also show up. For example, in the following fragment, a list occurs in the course of a discussion of a Thanksgiving turkey. The generalized list completer "and stuff" not only invokes an activity one does to the turkey, but is in fact one among several other items which were bought on this occasion; i.e., "stuffing" would constitute an apparently-but-non-actually array-exhausting third list item, while "and stuff" proposes the list to be "relevantly incomplete."

(32) [NB:IV:10]
Emma: I brought [th'pie en the whip cream en stuff,] en they were gonna deliver the turkey.

And it may not be incidental that in Fragment (13) the generalized list completer for a list of foodstuffs stands in a punlike relationship to the appliance with which food is cooked; i.e., "range."

(13) [MFP]
Sally: Plus fer a dollar more you get um uh [five pounds of vea:l, o:r a choice of- or ten pounds of bacon? or y'know a whole range of things.]

The presence of acoustic consonance and punlike relationships as between list completers and prior list items can be sensitive to the fact that three-part construction constitutes a task and problem for speakers, where the need to produce a third list member triggers off a search through the surrounding talk (and recurrently, specifically the relevantly surrounding talk; i.e., the two prior list items) for resources out of which to construct that requisite third member.

A related phenomenon suggests that three-partedness, per se, can be "poetically" implicated in and implicative of list-relevant talk. In two earlier fragments, "non-actual" numbers (a fanciful exaggeration and an estimate, respectively), occurring in the environment of three-part structures, happen to be "three."

(5) [GTS:III]
Louise: For three hundred years she's been giving him . . .

(14) [GTS:IV]
Roger: An' if he completed it within, a certain period I
think it was three hours or something . . .

In the following two fragments (one a continuation of an earlier fragment), this phenomenon shows up. Again, a non-actual number in the environment of a three-part list happens to be "three."

(28) [GTS:IV]
Ken: . . . to [build it the way he wants it to be, design it,
the whole bit.] And that's not– that's not any three
hour job.

(33) [SBL]
Maude: . . . about three weeks ago [we was up at Maripo:sa, an'
up in the Mother Lode country we wen' all through
those ghost towns.]

Estimates, exaggerations, etc., belong to the class which Sacks refers to as "freely occurring" units of talk. In the above instances, the fact that the estimates, etc., are freed from the constraints of specific measurement makes them available to other selectional procedures. Undoubtedly "three" is in and of itself a canonical "approximator" number. But it is at least possible that the occurrence of "three" in these instances is at least in part the product of a particular sort of selection procedure; a punlike selection which is, say, "task sensitive"; which locates the achieving of a three-part structure as a task to which these speakers are observably oriented.

In this light another earlier fragment may be reexamined as an instance of an observable orientation to three-partedness; that orientation becoming utilized in the search for and discovery of a third list item. In this case, the item seems to be the product of an intricate procedure in which acoustic consonance is operating on a punlike sensitivity to the task.

(21) [Lamb Interviews]
Mr. B.: It's not in the same league with [adultery, and murder,
and – and – thievery,] but . . .

Here, we are not looking at the occurrence of "three." "Three" is not a possible list-completer for this particular list. What does occur is a possible list-completer for this particular list which can be characterized as having been selected from among a set of available alternatives (be it types of immorality/criminality or "synonyms" for this particular case; i.e., "robbery," "theft," etc.). The item which is selected turns out to stand in exquisite acoustic consonance to the "task sensitive" word "three"; i.e., "thievery." It might be not altogether unrealistic to propose as a schema of this production, something like the following.

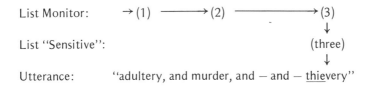

List Monitor:	→ (1) ——→	(2) ——→	(3) ↓
List "Sensitive":			(three) ↓
Utterance:	"adultery,	and murder, and – and –	thievery"

The sought-for third list item, "thievery" might more reasonably be proposed as acoustically consonant, not to the proposed "list sensitive" "three," but to the actually present pre-list word, "league." But it is at least possible that there is an intricate "poetic" phenomenon occurring here, one which is implicated in and serves as a solution to a problem imposed by the programmatic relevance of three-part list construction.[3]

So far, the programmatic relevance of three-part list construction has been examined as a task and problem for conversationalists, for the solution of which they have a variety of resources. Now, one expectable feature of such a systematic procedural program is that it provide resources. And there are observable ways in which the programmatic relevance of three-part list construction serves as a resource for the conduct of conversation.

4. *The programmatic relevance of three-part list construction can be found to serve as a sequential resource.* Three-part lists constitute turn-constructional components. Specifically, list-completion can constitute utterance completion; i.e., a point at which another can or should start talking. Crucially, forthcoming completion is projectable from the point at which a list is recognizably underway; i.e., given two items so far, a recipient can see that a third will occur, and that upon its occurrence utterance completion can have occurred whereupon it will be his turn to talk. Following are some obvious instances of a recipient monitoring a list by reference to utterance completion.

(30) [GTS:II]
Ken: I go in there and I uh [put all the bottles in back and
→ I uh give people change, and junk like this.]
[Y'know.
Roger: → [Last Saturday night I downed a litre bottle of
champagne . . .

(34) [Adato]
Matt: The good actors are all dyin out.
Tony: → They're all- they're all dyin out [yeah.
Matt: → [[Tyrone Po:wuh. Clark
Gable, Gary Cooper,]
Tony: → Now all of 'em are dyin.

(9) [NB:II]
Emma: → They go [on en on en on] [but the:hh
Nancy: → [Yeu::h.

It can be noted for each of these fragments that when overlap occurs, for both sentences [as in Fragment (34)] and lists, it is as a result of a recipient starting up at a recognizable completion point and prior speaker latching various objects to his otherwise completed utterance [Fragment (30)'s "Y'know," Fragment (34)'s "yeah," and Fragment (9)'s "But . . ."]. In principle, then, a three-part list can be used to monitor for utterance completion and turn transition.

In the following two fragments, it appears that an intended three-part list gets into trouble. What is interesting is that the trouble can be specified: In each case, the speaker has produced a recognizable *two*-part list, upon completion of which, recipient starts to talk.

(35) [SBL:2:2:3:10]
Claire: → I'm just gonna have either cheese cake, 'r a sundae,
['r–
Chloe: → [That's it.
Claire: Yeah,

(36) [SBL:2:2:4:2]
Bea: → I didn't know whether I'd be too early or too late
[or ri–
Vera: → [No::.
Vera: No, well I guess . . .

In the case of Fragment (35), the list-prefatory "either" projects a two-part list. In Fragment (36), the two list items happen to belong to a contrast-class "early"/"late," and thus constitute an array which is adequately exhaustable by those two items.

And a predictable sort of trouble occurs for the "triple singles"; i.e., "the first" is heard as "an only." Such is the case in one of the earlier fragments.

(10) [SBL:2:2:3]
Chloe: → God, she just kept lookin, [an' lookin, an' lookin,
Claire: → [Yeah, an'-
Claire: Uh huh, and she stee- starts to lead from her hand,

This fragment exhibits two features by which the recipient may be seen to be orienting to the "triple single" as a unit and as an activity. First of all, the recipient, having initially taken "the first" to be "an only," now hearing a second, understands that what is in progress is a "triple single," a three-part unit which she permits to go to its projected completion before starting to talk again.

Secondly, when the recipient does start to talk again, she produces a different token from the one with which she responded to the "first-as-only" item; i.e., she has shifted from "Yeah" to "Uh huh." Now, it is a massively recurrent phenomenon that a response which turns out to have occurred prior to completion of an ongoing utterance is "recycled" upon completion of that utterance.[4] For example:

(37) [Schenkein:II:70]
Ellen: Just on the straight. (·) [of the fabric.
Lori: → [Yeah.
Lori: → Yeah.

Roughly, the recycled response token proposes that the "early" response has turned out to have been adequate to the eventual utterance-in-toto; i.e., the additional materials were inadequate to revised response. In Fragment (10) the shift from "Yeah" to "Uh huh" is minimal (specifically, the tokens belong to a same "grade"), but it is sufficient to mark attention to and acknowledge the import of the additional materials (in this case, whatever it is that a "triple single" versus a "single" can accomplish).

Fragment (10), with its orientation to the three-partedness of the discovered "triple single," and its shifted response token which attends the import of the "listing" of a single behavioral bit, stands in sharp contrast to the following fragment, in which a recipient observably attempts to override a "listing" in progress.

(38) [NB:IV:15:2]
Guy: But it was a:ll crappy en::uh [bulged u[p 'n:::=
Len: → [Yea:h. [Yea:h.
Len: → =Ye:ah. 'hhhh[hh
Guy: [end uh::- ih wz so high I couldn't put another tile down on top of it,

Here, the response is not positioned by reference to a "first" as a possible "only," but specifically when it is clear that a list has been initiated (and that the speaker is searching for a next item); i.e., after "en::uh." And, again in contrast with Fragment (10), the next response does not await list completion but starts up by reference to the second list item. Further, the response is a repetition of the initial token; i.e., it proposes adequacy of the initial response and inadequacy of the second list item to revised response.

Whereas in Fragment (10) the recipient is acknowledging the import of the listing procedure, per se, here the recipient is treating a "first" as, say, adequately projecting and representing the two subsequent list members. In terms of sheer "substance," such treatment is not without basis. A casual review of the materials points to such a feature as "adequate representivity" of prior list member(s) vis-a-vis subsequent(s). And in the following fragment, this feature is treated as problematic for the status it allocates to an Nth list member.

(39) [NB:II:4:11]
Nancy: And uh she's very creative. She sews'n knits'n plays th- She's a very accomplished pianist.

The de-listing of a projected third list item ("'n plays th[e piano]") proposes as remediable and remedies the status which the adequate representivity of the first two items will allocate to the third. That is, it operates with and upon the fact that, as a third list member, "plays th[e piano]" will be heard as "similar" to "sews'n knits." The "free-standing" version ("She's a very accomplished pianist") specifically accounts for the preceding list-interruption as produced by reference to the "sameness" implicated by the list format. (The "informativeness" of this sort of "repair" will be considered shortly.)

The foregoing considerations indicate that the programmatic relevance of three-part list construction can serve as a basic sequential resource. Specifically, a completed list can constitute a completed turn at talk, and the projectability of third-as-final component permits a recipient to monitor for turn completion.

An inspection of materials in which a three-part list is responded-to prior to completion tends both to support the proposal of programmatic relevance [i.e., Fragment (10) exhibits recipient orientation to three-partedness] and to bring to light some possible features of list production. So, for example, Fragment (10) indicates that an intended "first list item" can be heard as a single, non-list-implicative sentence component. Such an observation raises the issue of recognizable list-initiation as a problem, for which methodic solutions may exist. Or, for example, Fragments (35) and (36) indicate that on some occasion an intended three-part list can have features which recommend it as a two-part list. Such an observation raises the issue of "list-constituency" as a problem for which, again, methodic solutions may exist. And, for example, Fragment (38) indicates that a recipient can attempt to override a recognizable list-in-progress. This final observation raised the issue of the "adequate representivity" of prior for subsequent list member(s). And this feature will be focused on in the following consideration of programmatic three-partedness as an interactional resource.

5. The programmatic relevance of three-part list construction can be found to serve as an interactional resource. For one, a projectable three-part array can be "informatively" manipulated. Secondly, third list members can be encumbered with a range of businesses.

First: The manipulation of a projectable three-part array can be informative. So, for example, one can be recognizably "trying" to fill three slots and "having difficulty," as an accomplice to a denigration. For example:

(40) [Adato]
Bob: En this wine here is nothing but [alcohol, colored wa:ter,]
— en that's it.

In this instance, a search for a third list item is terminated by an announcement of discovery that the two prior items are, after all, array-exhaustive. This fragment stands in sharp contrast to Fragment (39) in which, accomplice to a praising, a projected third list item is discovered, in the course of its production, to be inadequately represented by the prior two list items.

(39) [NB:II:4:11]

Nancy: And uh she's very creative. [She sews'n knits'n plays th-]
She's a very accomplished pianist.

In each instance, the exhibited "discovery" of adequacy or inadequacy respectively, tends to support the "case" being built. It provides that the object now under itemization is even more denegration- or praiseworthy than this speaker had intended to propose at the onset of the list; i.e., the "case" emerges from the shape of the list itself.[5]

In the following two fragments, "damning with faint praise" is achieved, in part by "having difficulty" finding items for a list of positive attributes.

(41) [Parker]
Janice: ehh hah! You make'r sound like a spiteful old witch. –
No, she's been [pretty nice en helpful'n] – I don't
know – [she's worked with me] . . .

In this case, a third list item is eventually produced, but it is observably "weak"; i.e., is more or less a recycle of the second item. In the next instance, a recipient collaborates in a coparticipant's failure to achieve a complete three-part list by turning to another matter.

(42) [SBL:1:12:25]
Marva: And she's really a lovely person. At least I like her,
I-you know what I mean, she's a [forthright,] uh, (1.0)
[hardworking,] you know,
Bea: Where's she from. Where did she train.

And in the following fragment, accomplice to a teasing, a possible two-item list is marked as possibly incomplete. The "missing" third list item is requested, and delivered a bit at a time.

(43) [GJ:ST]
John: Who all is over there.
Kitty: Oh, [Marcia and Judy] stopped by,
(pause)
John: Who else.
(pause)
Kitty: Oh, what's his name,

(pause)

Kitty: [Tom.]
John: Oh.

In the first place, an itemization of actual, such as this, is constrainable by candidates for itemization; i.e., there may in fact be no further listables. But, for one, a list-elicitor such as "Who all . . . ?" may expect a series, and there are ways to acknowledge and revise such an expectation, for example, by prefacing the "short list" with "only," "just," etc. Thus, the two-item list here may be designedly possibly incomplete; the two items possibly not exhausting the array of listables.

The possibility of a non-exhausted array not only raises the question which is asked ("Who else"), but may stand as a "clue" to why (at least) an other available candidate was not listed. One reason for non-inclusion might be that the current items are not adequately representative of (at least) that other. And possible non-represented attributes can be found; where, that they have been treated by lister as non-represented attributes can be informative (e.g., in this case, that the two current list members are female can locate that the other(s) might be male, and *that* this feature warrants such partitioning might begin to select out a or some particular male(s) from among many initial possibles).

As the interchange unfolds, it turns out, first, that the other is indeed, male, and then that male is identified. Whether or not the recipient has made an identification of that male, and whether or not that identification was correct, is not available in the fragment.[6]

In a range of ways, then, "weak," "absent," or "missing" third list members can be accomplice to a variety of interactional businesses. Third list members may also be the locus of special work; e.g., the expectable sameness provided by the adequate representivity feature exploited to design for "surprise," "punchline," etc.[7] In the following two fragments, third list members are recruited to the service of such disparate activities as topic shifting and offense-avoidance, respectively.

(44) [NB:II:2:4(r)]
((re. the Robert Kennedy Assasination that week))
Nancy: Ya:h it's been a rough week ah everbuddy is (·) you know,
(0.2)
Emma: Mm[hm
Nancy: [talkin about it'n e'rbuddy course I don't know
→ whether it's [that er jst thet wir jst (0.2) completely
bogging down et work,h] ˙hhhhhhh=

Nancy: → =e[r whata WI:H] WITH ME: WITH MY FI] NALS?hhhh
Emma: [Oh:: well ev]rybuddy's s a : d.]
Nancy: ˙uh˙u[h ˙u] hh
Emma: [OH] how'd yuh do with yer finals.

In roughest outline, a three-part list manages a three-step movement from one topic to a next; the first list item exhibiting departure from a prior, the third fully achieving arrival at the next, while at no point fully disjuncting from the prior. In slightly more detail, the first list item, "that," while it directly refers to the prior topic, tends recurrently to contrast with "it" or "this," and tends to convey "distance" in contrast to the "participatory" implicature of "it" or "this."[8] The second list item, which includes a reference to speaker's circumstances, while it might be utterly unrelated to the prior topic, *can* be heard as related, and perhaps via the adequate representivity feature *should* be heard as related (in any event, recipient exhibits sucha hearing with her "Oh:: well evrybuddy's sa:d."). The third list item arrives at an event for which speaker is focal, and while it manages to preserve a tiedness to the prior topic (again, in part via the sheer principaledness of adequate representivity), such a response as "Oh, I'm sure everyone's work suffered" would be dense to the import of "er whata WI:H WITH ME: WITH MY FINALS?" (and again, in any event, recipient exhibits a "proper" appreciation of the third list item's import with her "OH how'd yuh do with yer finals."). The third list member, with its almost purely formal tiedness to the prior topic, has brought about a circumstance in which it is not this speaker, but the recipient who markedly disjuncts from the prior topic and recognizably initiates an altogether new business.

In the following fragment, third position in a list is used to introduce a matter which might give offense to coparticipant; a gift to someone other than coparticipant (who, as speaker's sister, is a strong candidate for a gift of this sort on this occasion).

(45) [NB:IV:10:46]
Lottie: → 'n then comin home [I bought, they had tangerines ten
pounds fer a dollar, so I got [ten pounds=
Emma: [Mm:::.
Lottie: → =en I got some casaba'n then I bought uh::, uh Edna
back a box a'dates] [c'z,
Emma: [Oh at's ni[ce.
Lottie: [Yihknow=

Lottie: =[[she-
Emma: That's [nice Lottie,
Lottie: [sh'fed the ca:t, ['n
Emma: [That's beautiful.

Again, in roughest outline, by virtue of its position in the list, the gift to Edna is proposed as a "by the way," "afterthought" in the course of Lottie's buying bargains for herself.[9] In slightly more detail, the feature of adequate representivity may be exploited here to convey without actually stating (and thus potentially lying) that all the items were bought on the cheap, including the gift.

That the gift is conveyed-but-not-stated to be a cheap afterthought can both pacify a potentially offended coparticipant and avoid arming her with "information" of just the sort that a disgruntled non-gift-recipient might pass on to a gift's recipient or relevant others.

Parenthetically, by reference to earlier considerations of the three-part list as monitorable for completion, and the "adequacy" proposals of recycled responses, it can be noticed that the coparticipant starts to talk at a proper place; i.e., immediately upon completion of the three-part list, thus overlapping an "account initiation," "c'z." While the initial assessment may be called for, and may specifically properly occur with such alacrity,[10] the subsequent overlap-competitive recycle and escalation manage to recognizably disattend the explanation (which proposes not a gift, but a payment for services rendered) and propose that the "gift" was of sufficient status to constitute grounds for offense.

In a range of ways, then, a speaker can exploit the programmatic relevance of three-part list construction and the feature of adequate representivity, weakening/omitting or encumbering third list members accomplice to a range of interactional businesses. A final consideration turns to the ways in which list construction can be used by more than one speaker.

6. *A phenomenon which may be characterized as List Assimilation may be most simply stated as: A list can be constructed by more than one speaker.* The simplest form of List Assimilation is Additive Assimilation, in which a non-speaker of a list-in-progress becomes a party to that listing by adding member(s) to the list-in-progress.

So, for example, in the following fragment, a couple, each of whom tend to talk about their commonly-owned pets as "mine," are telling a third party about their latest acquisition, a kitten.

(46) [Frankel:US:I:82]
Carol: → So I got th' dawg 'n, the k-parakeet,
Vic: → (en- [en the cat.)
Carol: [en the kitten.

Simply enough, a "link term" (like "and," "or") can be used to achieve partyship to a listing.[11] With this simple device a complex order of business can be invoked and managed, roughly having to do with "entitled current speakership" for an utterance and the matter to which it refers. The current considerations will focus on negotiated speakership. The issue of "entitlement" will be tracked, but not developed.

Following is another simple instance of additive assimilation. In this case, Martha has asked Emma for some advice on how to make tacos. As it happens, it is the advice recipient who starts listing ingredients.

(47) [NB:IV:3:1(r)]
Martha: → So- d'you need, you need uh hamburger, don'tcha.
Emma: Yeahhs [en you need [some:] uh:,]
Martha: → [en- [s- s-] sh::]redded lettuce?
Emma: → Shredded lettuce, en chee::se,
Martha: Oh. Any s- particular kind?

Each next list item is prefaced by a link term (including the advice-giver's item-introductory "en you need some: uh:,). A non-linked repeat acknowledges the correctness of one of advice-recipient's candidate items and is itself followed by a link-prefaced next list item.

Another issue in which "list assimilation" seems to be recurrently implicated is that of possible "dispute" (e.g., argument or correction). That issue will be tracked in the various fragments under consideration. Following are two dramatic instances in which sheer "assimilation" and "list assimilation" respectively, show up in environments of, first, argument, and second, correction.

(48) [M.Goodwin:9-15-70-11] ((dispute about the color of a bike))
Terry: orange,
(0.4)
Pam: Gol:d.
(0.4)
Terry: → Orange.

Pam: → It's gold.
Vincent: → It's mix[ed.
Terry: [OR::ANGE::,
Pam: Gol:d

(49) [GTS:IV:23-24(r):S]
Jim: He went right down on that fie:ld'n'e w'js sittin there
talkin like a nigger en all the guys (mean) all these
→ niggers er a:ll [up there in-]
Roger: → [You mean Ne]egro: don'tcha.
(·)
Jim: Weh en [ther all-ih-uh] The [r- ther A:LL up in the sta:nds
Ken: → [An' J i : g,] [hunh

In Fragment (49) a third party to a proposed correction from "nigger" to "Negro" uses a link-term-prefaced possible co-class item, "Jig," to propose that what is occurring here is, not correction, but listing. In contrast to Fragments (46) and (47) in which next items are positioned by reference to a list in progress, here, the link-term-prefaced candidate list item performs "retroactive listing." In the following fragments (50) and (51), another sort of retroactive listing, with another sort of link term, is performed. And in each of them, both "entitled current speakership" and "possible argument or correction" appear to be relevant.

In Fragment (50) Lorna is the grandmother of the little boy they're talking about. Lorna was visiting Gwen when Lorna's family showed up and were directed by a neighbor over to Gwen's house, where they spent some time. In this subsequent conversation, a key issue seems to be whether Gwen's incidental access to the child in question entitles her to assess him. At one point, the following occurs.

(50) [Rahman:B:2(14):3]
Lorna: Mindju eez good Gwenny, 'e wz mischeevious but w-'e wz
good.
Gwen: → Oo 'e wz beautiful heahr [wuuzn't'ee.=
Lorna: [Yes.
Gwen: ='E [wz verry well be[he:ved.
Lorna: [Yes. ['E wz well behaved he:uh [too:.
Gwen: [Ye:s ther
luvly little boy:s,

Roughly: A proposal which might stand as contrastive and thereby transparent for its work vis-a-vis an entitlement dispute is, with the link term "too," proposed to be not contrastive, but additive. As it happens, the coparticipant has initiated a "no contest" response by reference to the contrastive proposal (i.e., simultaneously with the link term). Having initiated it, she does not cut off or otherwise acknowledge the work of "too"; i.e., from the standpoint of its recipient, the utterance in question remains contrastive/argumentative, and/but is not being argued with.

Similarly, in the following fragment, the link term "too" retroactively proposes "addition not contrast." In this case, one participant has found a new recipe for popcorn balls sprinkled with Jello powder, which she is telling to her recipient.

(51) [TCI(b):16:65]
Linda: You c'd almos (·) y- I don'even think you'd haftih use
the Jello, that jis kinda gives it a l[ittle bit'v] :::]=
Joan: → [gives it co] lor]
Linda: → =flavor[:
Joan: [Yea:[ah.
Linda: → [too,=
Linda: =jist a teeny bit [more fla] vor en=
Joan: [Ye:::ah.]
Linda: =˙hhhhhh But I thought oo tha' rilly sounded goo:d.

Focusing on the immediately relevant segment: The recipient produces a "collaborative utterance competion" thus at least becoming a party to, and perhaps claiming "current speakership" for, as well as possibly terminating, the utterance in progress.[12]

Teller, however, delays her own completion until recipient has reached completion, whereupon teller produces a completion component. The two completion items are different, and possibly contrastive. That teller's version has followed recipient's, and that it is not preceded by such a link term as "and" provides at least the possibility that teller's item is responsive to recipient's [cf. Fragment (47)]. And the observable difference between the two items may specifically implicate "dispute." On the other hand, that the item is produced as a syntactically coherent component of an utterance in progress can be exhibiting a "no hearing" of recipient's candidate, and thus, no argument with it.

Subsequently, both parties work to provide for the "no argument" alternative. Recipient produces an acknowledgment token which, in effect, "deletes" her own prior talk and takes up teller's. Almost simultaneously, but perhaps specifically in response to recipient's display of "no argument," teller adds the link term "too," which provides that an item which heretofore constituted either a "no hearing" of or a "dispute" with recipient's item, is now properly to be heard as neither of those, but as an "addition" to recipient's item.

In both Fragments (50) and (51), then, retroactive list assimilation is used to provide for a "no argument" situation on the occurrence of items which are otherwise possibly argumentative. In the following fragment, both retroactive and additive list assimilation are used. Here again, entitled speakership may be relevant. In this case, Jessie has announced the death of a mutual friend. The news-recipient, Goldie, had not been in contact with the friend for some time prior to her death.

(52) [D.A.2:13:S]
Jessie: I, I-I jis couldn' take thē constant repetition of
[uh::: [:::
Goldie: → [of- [of the same story. Oh don' I kno:w=
Jessie: → =or how enla:rged it was or why huhr artery wz: five
times larger or this that,=
Goldie: → =en [e v r y b o d y o] wes me a livi [n g 'n,]
Jessie: [the othuh thing,] [·hhhhh] hhhhhh k-
Jessie: Well uh- (·) uhhhh this is something that uh:: yihknow
uh evrybody owes hurh.

In terms of sheer speakership, most roughly: Something like a "single utterance" undergoes three changes of "current speakership." 1) Recipient produces a collaborative completion which terminates an utterance in progress with herself as its current speaker. 2) Teller, however, produces an item prefaced by the link term "or,"[13] thus re-opening the utterance as, now, a list in progress with herself as its current speaker. Subsequently, teller undercuts the "*co*-production" feature of this listing by producing a prototypical three-part list within her own utterance; a [2 item + generalized completer] format with the elaborated three-within-three structure considered earlier; i.e., the generalized list completer is itself a three part unit ("this that, the other thing"). That is, having deployed retroactive list assimilation to establish herself as a party to a list in progress, teller then moves to provide for sole speakership of an adequate complete list, which is specifically marked as "terminating" with herself as its speaker. 3) However, now it is the recipient who utilizes "listing" to reclaim speakership. She deploys the device of additive list assimilation, intersecting the list-terminal generalized completer with a link-term-prefaced next list item.

In terms of sheer speakership, each participant can be seen to be attempting to close off another's utterance with herself as its current speaker, each attempt countered by a re-opening (and attempted close) of that utterance with prior speaker as, again, current speaker. In terms of "entitled" speakership, it can at least be noticed that the paticipant with recent access produces current, specific, news-relevant items, while the participant with lapsed access produces generalized, proverbial items, proposing them as equally adequate for speakership on this matter.[14] It appears, then, that the speakership negotiation is, at least in part, addressed to the relevance of current, versus lapsed access.

In the following fragment, again, a candidate collaborative completion is retroactively assimilated to a list. The business here seems rather similar to that of Fragment (49) in which a third list member assimilates two "antagonistic" terms as list co-members. In that fragment it is possibly happenstance that the proposed third list member embeds the contentious term as a second, between two co-graded items [nigger, NEGRO, and jig]. But in the following fragment, a co-grade embedding is the product of visible work.

And again, "possible dispute" appears to be present and managed, and "entitlement" [of the equal-access versus categorial-privilege type seen in Fragment (50)] may be relevant. Here, initial speaker is the therapist in a group-therapy session and coparticipant is one of the patients.

(53) [GTS:I:2:34]
Dan: Well I do know last week that uh Mike was certainly very
(0.6)
Roger: → pissed [off,
Dan: → [upset, 'n pissed off, 'n angry,

The therapist intersects the patient's candidate collaborative completion with a non-link-prefaced item which, as in Fragment (51), is alternatively a possible "delayed" completion of his own utterance; in effect a "no hearing" of patient's candidate completion, or a possible response to that candidate; specifically, a grade-shifted alternative to it; i.e., a "correction" or "counter." The subsequent production of a link-term-prefaced repeat of the patient's candidate exhibits both that a "hearing" has occurred, and that "dispute" is not occurring; i.e., again, as in Fragment (51), the activity of the moment is subsequently exhibited to be neither of the initial possible alternatives, but another order of activity; i.e., a "(co)-listing."

In terms of achieved list organization, in this case, not only is a possible utterance completer retroactively assimilated to a list in progress, but the list is re-ordered. It is specifically initiated with an item of a different grade from the patient's candidate, and thereafter the patient's candidate is incorporated, as a link-term-prefaced second list item, whereupon a third list item is produced. The third list item is of the same grade as the list-initial item and thus the patient's candidate is embedded between two co-grade items [upset, 'n PISSED OFF, 'n angry]. The obviously achieved grade-ordering here is very similar to the possibly happenstance ordering of Fragment (49) [nigger, NEGRO, and jig].

Not only can the retroactive assimilation deployed in both these fragments deprive a problematic item of whatever sequential implicativeness it might have had in its original sequential position, but the particular list-ordering can further operate upon it. The ordering can combinedly exhibit the item as mis-fitted and thus possibly inappropriate, while providing a "balanced weighting" across the list, which may propose an "impartiality" on the list-maker's part. That is, a problematic item is in no way explicitly disputed, indeed it is observably being treated "impartially." Its inappropriateness is simply there to be seen. Thus, in a manner similar to the "denegration" and "damning with faint praise" of Fragments (40)-(42), in Fragments (49) and (53) "inappropriateness" is exhibited by, and emerges from, the shape of the list itself.[15]

Finally, in the following fragment, an object which, on its occurrence, constitutes the proferring of an alternative term in response to a prior speaker's two proposals, and thus might be, for example, a "candidate solution to a word-search" arrived at with the aid of two prior "clues," or a "technical specification" of two prior "lay approximations," or a "correction" of two prior "errors," is reformulated as a "third list item equivalent to two prior list items." Here, the initial speaker is a temporary employee, the coparticipants are permanent staff. Possibly at issue is, say, entitled access to technical terminology. The negotiation is conducted with exquisite economy; a free-standing item is consecutively assimilated to and partitioned from a list.

(54) [Adato:5:1:s]

Jay: I-I told Jim thet uh, I wz going to:: leave you my um,
my box of, – thet I use?
Sy: What box.
Jay: → fer the slips? 'n papers?
Jim: → Forms.
(pause)
Jay: → 'n forms?
Jim: → Forms.
(pause)
Sy: Oh thẹ, thē uh, [thē uh, index deal
Jay: [Mm-hm,

Briefly: On its occurence, the free-standing alternate term is not a member of the prior listlike series, its speaker not a party to it. The observable activity is the proferring of a correct term, possibly the doing of "correction." Prior speaker assimilates the proferred term to his own prior utterance by reproducing it, now prefaced with a link term, and preserving the intonation contour of that prior utterance. The "product" is: "Fer the slips? 'n papers? 'n forms?", a coherent, self-contained three-part list.

A slightly less economical and utterly transparent instance of this use of list-assimilation is found in the following fragment.

(55) [O'Hare:B:JP:4]

Leah: Ahn ahn ahn the mahrried men en the mahrried women ez
bahd ez [bahd ez the chill] d-
Maureen: → [Ney wuhrss]
Leah: → and- n- wo:r[se.
Maureen: → [Yeah wuhrss, cause . . .

Here, a specifically counterposed item is list-assimilated and thus reformulated as an "additional" item. In Fragment (54) by means of list-assimilation, a free-standing possible correction of a prior utterance becomes a third item on a list. The correction-proferrer becomes a contributor to a list initiated by a prior speaker; a list which, at its end, has its initiator as its current speaker; that current speaker having uttered each of its three items. In effect, the proferrer of an item has become its audience. And, as list co-members, the various items now fall under the list-constructional principle of adequate representivity. They now no longer stand in such a relationship as [word-search clues

← candidate solution] or [lay approximations ← technical specification] or [errors ← correction], but as [list item 1 + list item 2 + list item 3], the first two items observably adequate to this listing and to this list's third list item.

With his subsequent free-standing repeat, the coparticipant can be seen to be orienting to and managing this treatment of his proferred alternative item. In contrast to Fragment (55), in which, although a repetition of the term in question makes its proferrer once again its speaker, but an acknowledgment token at least formally accepts the status as list co-member of the prior "correction," and at least formally exhibits recipientship of the item this speaker had initially proferred, in Fragment (54) the free-standing repeat not only makes the initial proferrer of the term in question once again its speaker, but partitions the item off of the list to which it has been assimilated, (re)reformulating it as, not "an adequate term of reference among others," but "the uniquely proper reference term." Via such a (re)reformulation, the prior items are, again, proposed to be inadequate. [This procedure may be seen as a next-speaker's correlate of the same-speaker "de-listing" seen in Fragment (39)].

The foregoing considerations indicate that list construction can serve as a methodic resource for the conduct of interactional negotiations.[16] Specifically, a list may be partially characterized as a serial recycling of a given "turn constructional unit" (word, phrase, sentence, etc.), each unit consisting of or containing an item which is adequately representative of and adequately represented by each other unit's item. If a next speaker produces a possible "next list member," then the serial-unit-replication feature of list construction provides that what might otherwise constitute a "response to a prior completed utterance" can appropriately be seen as the "co-production of a list in progress," and the adequate-cross-item-representivity feature provides that what might otherwise constitute a "counterposed alternative to a prior utterance's item" can appropriately be seen as an "equivalent co-member with a list's prior item." Thus, a combination of list-constructional features can be exploited such that matters which might potentiate interactional discord are attendable to under the auspices of methodically exhibitable interactional accord.

Summary

Preliminary observations of lists in conversation indicate that three-partedness is a basic structural principle, the construction of a three-item list constituting a task for speakers, a task for the accomplishment of which methodic resources are available and used. Further, it appears that principled list construction serves as a methodic resource for the organization of conversational sequencing, establishing an analog to sentences and other "turn constructional units" and thus enabling the achievement of precise transition from a current speaker to a next. Finally, it appears that such list-constructional principles as serial unit-replication and adequate cross-item representivity can serve as methodic resources for the conduct of interactional negotiations. Specifically, that a potentially "counterposed response" can be reformulated as an "equivalent list co-member" provides a means by which matters implicative of discord can be managed under the auspices of accord.

NOTES

1. Over the course of his lectures, Harvey Sacks notices and develops the phenomenon of everyday "poetics." See, for example, Fall 1965, Lecture 7, p. 10; Spring 1967, Lecture 4, pp. 4 and 9; Winter 1969, Lecture 8, pp. 4–6; Spring 1970, Lecture 6, pp. 5–10; Winter 1971, February 19, pp. 1–5; Winter 1971, March 4, pp. 2–8 and 18–19; Winter 1971, March 11, pp. 3–12; Spring 1971, April 5, pp. 2–5; Spring 1971, April 9, pp. 11–12; Spring 1971, May 3, p. 13; Spring 1971, May 17, pp. 1–10; Fall 1971, Lecture 1, pp. 5–13; Fall 1971, Lecture 2, pp. 1–13; Fall 1971, Lecture 3, pp. 7–9 and 11; Fall 1971, Lecture 10, pp. 4–5; and Fall 1971, Lecture 14, pp. 11–12. See also, Sacks (1974).

2. See, for example, the lecture of March 4, Winter 1971, in which Sacks considers "expletives" as "freely occurring" units.

3. In a discussion of this domain of phenomenon, February 19, Winter 1971, Sacks proposes: "When you have an investigative aim such as mine, which is to try to discover sorts of detailed relationships that might turn out to exist, you must first permit yourself to notice a possible phenomenon. The question can then be asked, well, is there anything to it? Noticing it, you get the possibility of investigating it. Laughing it off in the first instance, or not even allowing yourself to notice it, of course it becomes impossible to find out whether there is anything to it."

4. For a consideration of recycled versus changed responses, see Jefferson (forthcoming).

5. Throughout his lectures Harvey Sacks notices and considers occurrences of interactionally informative "error." See, in particular, Fall 1976, Lecture 3, pp. 2–4, a discussion of a recognizably "unplanned rebuke." For the phenomenon in general, see, for example, Fall 1965, Lecture 7, pp. 8–9; Fall 1967, Lecture 9, p. 7; Winter 1969, Lecture 9, pp. 11–13; and Fall 1971, Lecture 2, pp. 11–12. See also, Jefferson (1974).

6. Specifically, while the "Oh" might indicate an "orientational shift" and thus propose that recipient had located someone else, it might also constitute an

"information receipt," opaque for his identification of that third list member. For some consideration of "Oh," see Heritage (1979).

7. For a consideration of third list members as "punchlines," see Sacks (1978).

8. For a brief consideration of this matter, see Jefferson, Sacks and Schegloff (in press).

9. For a consideration of the implicativeness of the ordering of report components for the hearable ordering of the events being reported, see Sacks (1972).

10. For some considerations of response-timings and their implications vis-a-vis interactional accord, see Pomerantz (1976), Jefferson, Sacks and Schegloff (in press), and Pomerantz (in press).

11. This sort of work is a version of the phenomenon, Collaborative Utterances, introduced by Harvey Sacks (see, for example, Fall 1965, Lecture 1, pp. 2–7; Fall 1967, Lecture 4, pp. 9–15, and Lecture 5, pp. 8–18; Fall 1968, Lecture 5, pp. 1–9; etc.) and currently being developed by Gene Lerner in his forthcoming doctoral dissertation.

12. A coparticipant starting up in the course of an utterance in progress may design his talk to achieve "current *co*-speakership"; i.e., to be saying the same thing at the same time, by formatting and positioning his talk in such a way as to "fit into" the utterance in progress at the point his talk starts up [see Fragments (46) and (47) for such a format- and placement-designed possibility). Such is not the case here. Recipient's talk is not designed to "fit into" the utterance in progress at the point of overlap. Thus, it may specifically, designedly be claiming "current (independent) *speaker*ship."

13. "Or" provides a contrastive linkage [see, e.g., Fragments (35) and (36)] and might, on this occasion, constitute "correction" of or "argument" with the candidate completion item. In other materials, in which such activities are clearly relevant, "or" can be seen as obviously, or interestingly equivocally, operating as a "correction" or "argument" item. So, for example, it can be noticed that teller's proposed "next" list item ("how enla:rged it was") has no local referrent (data not shown) and is thus possibly deficient, and that the subsequent "why huhr artery wz: five times larger" contains a candidate for the "missing" referrent (i.e., "it" = "artery") and thus that "correction" is relevant as between these two components and the "or" which precedes the latter component is interestingly equivocal as to whether it is proposing "replacement" or "nextness." Thus, in this list-production, there are two problematic uses of "or." That the generalized list completer is also "or"-prefaced may be designed to exhibit that the activity of the moment is not 1) dispute and not 2) self-correction, but, across the utterance and its items, "co-production of a list," with "or" as the list-local link term. That the recipient's additive assimilation is prefaced, not with "or," but with "and" may exhibit a certain sensitivity to the problematic workings of the prior "or" series.

14. For a related discussion by reference to the phenomenon of Assessments, see Pomerantz (1976).

15. In this light it may be noticed that in Fragment (49) there is close acoustic consonance between a subsequent speaker's term and the term with which it may be seen to be achieving list-exhibited "affiliation"; i.e., [nIGGer/jIG], and in Fragment (53) there is close acoustic consonance between a next speaker's term and the term with which it may be seen to be achieving list-exhibited "disaffiliation"; i.e., [PiSSed/uPSet]. That is, the "sensitivity" in these instances may

not merely be list-historical, but, specifically, interaction-historical.

16. It has been mentioned in passing that lists are recurrently implicated in negotiations vis-a-vis such an issue as "entitlement to speak on a given matter." Whether this implicature has to do with the status of a multi-party-produced list as a sub-class of "collaborative utterances," or whether there are some list-specific features which lend this organization, in particular, to such negotiations, remains to be seen. This report has not focused upon the work that list organization may be designed, in the first place, to accomplish, but rather upon the work which list-construction, as a task, allots to speakers, and some uses to which list-construction, as a resource, can be put by speakers.

REFERENCES

Heritage, J., A "news" receipt token and its placement in some sequential environments, paper presented at a Sociology of Language Group meeting, University of York, December, 1979.

Jefferson, G., Error correction as an interactional resource, *Language in Society,* 13, 1974.

____, The Abominable 'Neh?': an exploration of post response pursuit of response, in The University of Manchester Occasional Papers, forthcoming. (A revised short version to appear in *Sprache der Gegenwart,* a publication of the Institut fur Deutsche Sprache.)

Jefferson, G., H. Sacks, and E. A. Schegloff, Notes on laughter in the pursuit of intimacy, in J. Schenkein (Ed.), *Studies in the Organization of Conversational Interaction, Volume II.* New York: Academic Press, in press.

Pomerantz, A., Agreeing and disagreeing with assessments, unpublished manuscript, 1976.

Pomerantz, A., Pursuing a response, in J. Schenkein (Ed.), *Studies in the Organization of Conversational Interaction, Volume II.* New York: Academic Press, in press.

Sacks, H., On the analyzability of stories by children, in J. J. Gumperz and D. H. Hymes (Eds.), *Directions in Sociolinguistics.* New York: Holt, Rinehart and Winston, 1972.

____, On some puns with some intimations, *Annual Georgetown Roundtable in Linguistics.* Washington, D.C.: Georgetown University Press, 1974.

____, A technical analysis of a dirty joke, in J. Schenkein (Ed.), *Studies in the Organization of Conversational Interaction.* New York: Academic Press, 1978.

On Varieties of Closings

Graham Button

The examination of closing segments of telephone conversations provides us with a rich variety of closing types which are analyzed and classified in this paper.

Prior studies of closings by Schegloff and Sacks (1973), Davidson (1978) and Button (1980) are further extended in this work. These studies had described closings as having a four-part design–initial components offer and accept closings and terminal components produce and display termination.

Movement out of closings can also be made by the production of such sequence types as "arrangements," "solicitudes," "reason-for-call reiterations," and "appreciations." Some of these movements can be drastic and abandon the closing entirely. Some of the sequence types which achieve such results are "back-references," "in-conversation objects," and "topic initial elicitors." Such movements out of closings are examined in more detail in this paper.

The major findings of this work are that movements out of closings can produce a variety of closing types. Thus, the movements out of closings have an organization which can be described and analyzed. Within the varieties of closing types, Button shows that speakers can, in "delicate and systematic ways," negotiate for conversation termination or continuation.

This work expands our understanding of the termination phase of conversations and shows that the sequential organization of closings is both complex and orderly. Speakers are continually involved in close-order organization of their talk up to the very last closing components in the conversation.

I. Introduction

Before moving to the bulk of the analysis, two previous considerations of closings for conversation must be briefly introduced since they form a resource for what follows. The first documented a closing section for conversation (Schegloff and Sacks, 1973), and the second examined movements out of closings (Button, 1987).

Schegloff and Sacks describe closings as having a sectional design that spans four turns at talk. This closing design coordinates the mutual and warranted suspension of a turn's transition relevance. A first closing turn occurs within a closing implicative environment,[1] and "offers" closing. A second closing turn reciprocates or "takes up the offer," and legitimizes the production of a first terminal component which, in turn, provides for a second terminal. First and second closing turns are occupied by close components such as "okay" and "alright." They offer and accept closings in a closing implicative environment by neither continuing nor initiating topical material, and display the relevancy of termination. Both speakers provide terminal components such as "goodbye" and "bye," and preserve actual termination as mutually accomplished. This is the archetype closing.

[NB:IV:14:26]
    Emma: And, u-uh I'm w- I'm with you,
    Lottie: Yeah,
*→ Emma: Oright,
*→ Lottie: Okay [honey,
*→ Emma: [Bye, dear =
*→ Lottie: = Bye.

— end call —

[Campbell:7:12]
    Annie: And I <u>w</u>on't forget,
*→ Mac: ('Kay),
*→ Annie: <u>O</u>kay,
*→ Mac: Bah
*→ Annie: <u>Bye</u>:,

— end call —

The second analysis mentioned above examined a number of "sequence" types" that could be initiated within a closing secion. In part, these were described in terms of the trajectory of movement out of closings projected by the sequence type initial. Two categories of movement were found: minimal and drastic movements. A minimal movement out of closings takes place where a sequence type initial turn projects to next turn a sequentially relevant next activity that is not the production of a closing component, but where the sequence type is closing implicative and provides for the relevancy of reinitiating closings. Thus, in the following example Portia initiates closings, but within that turn introduces arrangement material. This is responded to in next turn by a "jokey solicitude," which receives a minimal response, following which closings are reinitiated. Portia makes a minimal movement out of closing but preserves the relevancy of closing, which is also preserved in the next two turns.

[NB:IV:4:18-19]
Portia: Yeh but chu late tuh be put down all the time,
Agnes: I know it,
Portia: Yeah,
Agnes: Wuh HAVE FUN
(0.5)
(*) → Portia: OKAY I'LL CALL YIH IN A LI'L WHILE SOON
→ EZ I HAVE MY BREAKFUSS READ THE
→ [PAPER
→ Agnes: [ehh'. hnh heh hahh HA(h)PP(h)Y
→ Breakfest ehh heh .hhh
→ Portia: Yeah,
* → Agnes: Alright honey,
* → Portia: O[kay hon,
* → Agnes: [Bye, ˙hh
* → Portia: Bye bye,
– end call –

Sequence types that regularly produce, and are typically designed for a minimal movement out of closings are "arrangements," "solicitudes," "reason-for-call reiterations" and "appreciations."

A drastic movement out of closings occurs where the sequence type initial projects to next turn a sequentially relevant next activity, but where it does not provide for the relevancy of closing reinitiation. Drastic movements out of closings abandon the closing. So, in the next fragment, Mark back-references to prior talk about "Thanksgiving." This provides for an appropriate response from Bob which would be to answer the enquiry. Neither the back-reference turn, nor the response protects the relevancy of reinitiating closings. There is a drastic movement out of closings that abandons the closing.

[Lerner:SF:II:26–27]
* → Bob: Alright [Mark.] =
° → Mark: [Wuh-]
Bob: =[[Hm?
° → Mark: [[Wudderyih doin fer Thanksgiving.
* → Bob: Oh I'm :: visiting my parents.
((continues))

Sequence types that are used, and designed in this respect, are "back-references," "in-conversation objects," and "topic initial elicitors." All sequence type initials, whether making a minimal or a drastic movement are optimally designed for particular positions within closings.

An observation was made in the investigation of movements out of closing that although the sequence types project a certain trajectory for conversation which is regularly preserved, each of the sequence types could result in a movement out of closings that does not preserve the sequence type trajectory. Thus a sequence type that regularly produces a minimal movement can, on occasions, eventuate in a drastic movement, and a sequence type that regularly produces a drastic movement can eventuate in a minimal movement. Also, although a sequence type initial may be optimally designed for a particular position within a closing in order to regularly accomplish a particular interactional task, it can be found to be used in other positions. A promise was made that these aspects of moving out of closings would be examined at a later date. This present paper is partly occupied with attempting to fulfill this promise. It will be found that together with the archetype closing and two variants on the archetype closing, various movements out of closings can produce a variety of closing types. Within these closing types, and within sequences of movements in and out of closings, speakers can, in very delicate and systematic ways, negotiate for conversation termination or conversation continuation.

II. Movements out of Closings and Varieties of Closing Types

The types of movement out of closings can be examined in terms of closing types that the movements produce.[2] Thus, typically an arrangement in first closing turn produces a longer-than-archetype closing, and a back-reference in second turn produces an abandoned closing. However, the fact that the typical sequence trajectory of a sequence type may not be preserved, and that the sequence type initial can occur in other places to that which it is regularly used, means that further varieties of closing associated with the sequence type can be produced. The sequence types can, accordingly, be re-examined in terms of the varieties of closings they can produce. In addition, other devices to the sequence types that were previously documented can be found that operate to move, or instigate a move, out of closings, and these too can produce yet further varieties of closings.

1. Arrangements in first and second turn.

a) *In first turn.* Typically arrangements are used in first closing turn and take the form of arrangement reiteration. They make a minimal movement out of closings that is preserved in next turn by a minimal response. Following this minimal response closings are reinitiated. A "first turn arrangement closing" is used by first speaker to project a longer-than-archetype closing that can operate to implicate second speaker in closing implicative material. This can be most forcibly seen in the example that follows where in next turn to the arrangement reiteration Emma minimally returns with an item that can operate both as a minimal response, and as a close component.[3] Next turn does not continue with a terminal component but with another close component. This is attentive to the fact that a movement out of closings has taken place. Typically then, an arrangement in first turn makes a minimal movement out of closings which is reciprocated in next turn by a minimal return, following which closings are reinitiated.

[NB:IV:10:56]

```
         Emma:   um [sleep good t'night swee[tie,
(*) → Lottie:       [Okeh-                   [Okay well I'll-I'll see y' in
    →            the mor[ning.
(*) → Emma:             [A:right,
 *  → Lottie:    A'right,
```

```
*  → Emma:    B'ye bye de[ar,
*  → Lottie:             [Bye bye,
                                  – end call –
```

An arrangement in first turn can, then, result in a "first turn arrangement longer-than-archetype closing."

However, although this is the typical shape of a first turn arrangement closing, an arrangement in first turn can eventuate in a drastic movement out of closings. This can result because although an arrangement reiteration may project the relevancy of closing reinitiation following a minimal return, nevertheless it is not an unequivocal close component that is bereft of topical features. Although it does not, itself, make a drastic movement out of closings that undercuts the relevancy of closings, it can provide an occasion for an accelerated and drastic movement that does undercut closing relevancy by 1) providing material that can be topically developed, 2) by touching off a further topic.

First, in the following two examples there is development of the arrangement material introduced into the first closing turn. This undercuts the relevancy of closing reinitiation and a drastic movement out of closings is made.

```
[JG:I:8:4]
           Colin:  Oh I see.
           Marge:  ˙h[hh
(*)  →     Colin:     [Oka:y well tell'm duh: (0.2) gimme a ring en let me
     →             know what he's: uh let-leave um no-note theyuh,
                                      (0.2)
     →     Marge:  Ye:s[uh huh,
     →     Colin:      [A: n' whether he wants: me tih go with im er::
     →             what 'e wants [tuh do, en then ah-] then ah'll call im=
     →     Colin:  =back.        [                    ]
     →     Marge:                 ˙hhhhhh Oh:: ah::,
                                      (.)
     →     Marge:  ˙hhh [Ye:-
 °   →     Colin:       [I s 'e still workin over there in Glenda:le?=
                                         ((continues))
```

```
[SBL:2:2:3:46]
           Cloe:   Well, it was fun Cla[ire,
           Claire:                     [Yeah. I
```

```
            Claire:  en[joyed every minute of [it
            Chloe:     [And-                  [Yeah.
(*)  →      Claire:  Okay, well then we'll see you Saturday.
     →      Chloe:   Saturday night.
     →      Claire:  Seven thirty?
     →      Chloe:   Yah.
 °   →      Claire:  You want me to bring the chairs
     →      Chloe:   Plea- No'. Yeah, I've got to get the chairs.
                                         ((continues))
```

A second way in which a drastic movement out of closings can eventuate from an arrangement in first closing turn is where the arrangement may touch off another topic. In the following example Lila begins her turn with a response to Wilbur's arrangement reiteration, but goes on to start a story about an experience she has had.

```
[Mc(Coven):53-54]
 * → Wilbur:     Okay,
   → Wilbur:     Well-well maybe we will see each other uh::: maybe
   →             not Thursday but ez soon ez you c'n get do:wn.=
   → Lila:     = [[Ye:s,
   → Wilbur:       [I'm free in the evenings,
 ° → Lila:       Yeah I'll call you-en beek- ul I'll (      ) something
 ° →             I've experienced thet I-I must tell you, I-I tried to
 ° →             get home before five o'clock since the fog . . . .
                                         ((continues))
```

An arrangement in first turn can result in a "first turn arrangement abandoned closing."

b) *In second turn.* Occasionally an arrangement may be used in second turn. In this position it can be used to curtail a movement made out of closings in first turn. In the example below Karen moves out of closings by continuing prior talk in a first closing turn. It will be seen later that a continuation of prior talk can eventuate in a drastic movement out of closings. Vicky, however, curtails this movement by minimally returning, and immediately introduces an arrangement item that can provide for the relevancy of closings. That is, in a second turn, as in a first turn, arrangements can be used to implicate next speaker in closing implicative material. In this example Karen reinitiates closings.

[Erhardt:10:4c]

Vicky: [Oh keep it.
(0.3)
(*) → Karen: ˙h Okay then ah'll give you the money [( )
→ Vicky: [Alright fi:ne.=
→ Vicky: =˙h–a:nd I:'ll u:m
(0.9)
→ Vicky: Ah'll call you timorrow when I get home fr'm work
→ about Sleepy Hollow.
(0.3)
* → Karen: Okhha:y. [Great.

Arrangements can also be used in a second turn that follows a first turn reinitiation of a closing. On these occasions it can display a continued availability for conversation without actually drastically moving out of, and itself abandoning closings. In the following example Marj (line 7) has used a topic initial elicitor[4] in third closing turn. This can be used to display availability for further conversation while providing for next speaker to introduce material for talk. Pris (line 8), however, declines to introduce further material. Marj (line 9 and 10) could then reinitiate closings but holds off doing so, and it is Pris (line 11) who reinitiates. Thus, Marj has twice shown a reluctance for closure by attempting to generate further talk and not reinitiating closings in a turn in which that is relevant, though she does not drastically move out of closings. Then, following Pris' reinitiation Marj (line 13) returns a second close component but introduces what is for this conversation an arrangement initial. Here, Marj makes a minimal movement out of closings, but in the context of previous displays of conversation availability, this arrangement introduction can also be used to continue a display of availability for conversation. Interestingly, when Pris (line 14) only minimally returns to the arrangement, Marj (line 15) again displays a reluctance for closure by continuing in-conversation and not reinitiating closings in next turn which is ripe for closing reinitiation. There is a correction of the day for meeting and a reinitiation of closings which goes to termination.

[Trio:2:6–7b]
1 Pris: Well you j's tell 'er I think ih wz stoo:pid.=
2 Marj: =eh heh heh heh he[h eh] eh eh]uh [uh,
3 Pris: [ehhh] hheh heh] [Fa:lse ala[::rm.]
4 Marj: [˙hhhh]

Marj: =O::k[y,
Pris: [O kay hon=
Marj: Nothing else happen.=
Pris: =n:Nothin.
(0.2)
Marj: Yeah.=
Pris: =Okay.
(·)
Marj: Okay then seeyuh- (·) Wednesday.=
Pris: =Ya:h,=
Marj: =ya[h.
Pris: [(Tha-) No [not (Wens)]
Marj: [No Thur] sday.
(0.2)
Pris: Euh alright [(dear)]
Marj: [O k] ay by[e bye, ehh] heh-heh-hih
Pris: [( )]
– end call –

2. *Solicitudes in first and second turn.*

a) *In first turn.* Solicitudes, like arrangements, typically occur within a first closing turn. They project that a next turn should be occupied with a proper sequential response that "heeds" the solicitude, following which closings can be reinitiated. Again, similar to arrangements, they make a minimal movement out of closings when used in a first closing turn, and are used to implicate second speaker in closings.

[JG:1:10:7.b.]

Sam: [Nice talking t'you honey
maybe I'll see yuh [Thurs[dee.
(*) → Marge: [uh: [Oh: alright love tih see you.
→ ˙hh A:n' uh tell uh:ar li'l gi:rlfriend ar o↑ther little
→ girlfrie: [nd hello an' everything like that.=
Sam: [( )
→ Sam: =I will deah.
* → Marge: O:kay.=
* → Sam: =Thank you,
* → Marge: Bey=[bye,
* → Sam: [B'bye.

– end call –

Solicitudes in a first turn can produce a longer-than-archetype closing, and this is the typical "solicitude closing." However, as for arrangements, a drastic movement can eventuate from a solicitude in first turn. This occurs when a second closing turn does not just minimally return to the solicitude in the projected manner, but in returning, introduces further material that undercuts the relevancy of reinitiating closings. In the following fragment second turn elaborates upon an initially minimal response and then latches on material that does not provide for closing reinitiation. Next turn continues on that material.

```
[TC:II:Ex.1:11]
          Char:   I:'ll remind 'er Winsdee,
          Jo:     ee Ya:: [°ah ha:°
          Char:           [(th)eh we need it Fri:dee.
          Jo:     ee Ya[h:.
          Char:        [(           )
(*) → Jo:                          [ˑhhhh Okay take care a'yerself.
    → Char:   ˑhh oh I wi:ll. I w'-I've been: u - I've had it, h (0.3)
    →         several days en I'm (·) go[nnuh be ˑhh    ]alright .hhh=
          Jo:                          [Hmm::::::::.  ]
°   → Char:   =We got ar new kid in cla:ss:::,
    → Jo:     Oh-h didjih get that bo::y, h
                                  ((continues))
```

Solicitudes in first turn can result in "first turn solicitude abandoned closings."

b) *In second turn.* Although solicitudes are typically used by first speaker in a first closing turn they can also be used, on occasions, by second speaker in second turn. Second turn is a crucial turn for second speakers to display whether or not they too are entering into closings moved into by first speaker. Typically a drastic movement out of closings is made in this turn should second speaker not enter into closings.

However, a second speaker may use a solicitude in this turn position to display that while not drastically moving out of closings, and hence displaying themselves as insensitive to closure, nevertheless they are available for conversation continuation should first speaker who has now received an in conversation response supply further material for talk. That is, they do not introduce further material or re-topicalize prior material, but in as much as they are an in-conversation response following a first closing turn, they can be used to indicate to first speaker an availability for continued conversation.

This display can be oriented to by next speaker who introduces material that drastically moves out of closings. This escalates a movement out of closing made by the solicitude, but it is in response to the displayed availability for further conversation. In the following example, Bob returns to Mark's solicitude and then introduces material that does not provide for the relevancy of reinitiating closings. Bob displays an orientation to the fact that it is Mark who may desire further conversation although it is Bob who actually makes the drastic movement. This is done by Mark making provision for Bob to talk about his plans.

[Lerner:SF:II:24]

Mark: . . . end:dah, hh ˙hh ul be talkin to yuh Friday .h
(0.2)
* → Bob: Oka:y.=
→ Mark: =Have a happy Thanksgivee:n a:nd uh (·) mm- ˙khhh
→ may all yer dreams c'm true.=
→ Bob: =W'l thank you:. thank you.
(·)
Mark: [[Ah-
° → Bob: [[Wtr' yih doin t'morruh [night anythin [:g
→ Mark: [˙hhhhhhhhhhh [Oh:::. uh
We-e:ll uh
((continues))

First speaker may, however, be unresponsive to second speaker's display of availability, and only minimally return to the solicitude in second turn. Second speaker not having drastically moved out of closings may then reinitiate closings should that availability not be taken up. The result is a solicitude in second turn that produces a longer-than-archetype closing where the solicitude's potentiality for a drastic movement is curtailed by next speaker's minimal response.

[NB:IV:14:26]

Emma: ˙hh w'l listen honey I'm g'nnuh have another cup a'
co:ffee, e[n I'll be talkin with you throughout the day.
Lottie: [Yeh I am too.
* → Lottie: Okay honey,
→ Emma: And, u-uh I'm w-I'm with you,

→ Lottie: Yeah,
* → Emma: Oright,
* → Lottie: Okay [honey,
* → Emma: [By dear=
* → Lottie: = Bye.

— end call —

Solicitudes in second turn can result in a "second turn solicitude abandoned closing" or a "second turn solicitude longer-than-archetype closing" where the latter is the result of a potential "second turn solicitude abandoned closing" having been curtailed.

3. Appreciations in first and second turn.

Appreciations are found to distribute quite evenly across first and second closing turns. This results from the fact that the initiation of closings is done independently of persons from whom appreciation may be due. Appreciations in closings produce the greatest variety of closing types associated with a particular sequence type. First, appreciations can operate as though they were closing components. Their occurrence in either a first or second turn regularly preserves the four turn closing found for the archetype closing.

[NB:IV:7:6:b]

Marian: [En you call me et nine t'morrow mor[ning.
* → Emma: [Alright
→ darling, I appreciate it.
→ Marian: Okay,
→ Emma: Bye bye
→ Marian: Buh- bye

— end call —

[JG:1:10:7.C]

Sam: = I will deah.
* → Marge: O:kay.=
* → Sam: =Thankyou,
* → Marge: Bye: [bye,
* → Sam: [B'bye.

— end call —

Second, appreciations can be reciprocated but, again, without occasioning the relevancy of reinitiating closings, and the closing continues. Here appreciations operate as an optional sequential insert and result in a type of closing extension. The closing reaches termination and there is no reinitiation of closings. This contrasts with the operation of arrangements and solicitudes in first turn where closing reinitiation is relevant.

[MC:II:6:9]

Alfred: ahh ha- ha- ha ˙hh Well, we'll see what happens.
* → Lila: Okay,
→ Alfred: Thank you very much [Missiz Asch,
→ Lila: [Thanks for calling,
* → Alfred: G' [bye,
* → Lila: [Bye bye,

– end call –

While appreciations can produce these varieties of closings it can be found that appreciations eventuate in a drastic movement out of closings. This is the product of appreciations possessing topical and topicalizable features, unlike archetype closing components. A drastic movement can eventuate if the appreciation is used as a way of introducing some further material for the conversation.

In the next extract, the segment of talk that is initiated by an appreciation goes drastic when some "problem" is revealed. Ginny has rung to inform Milly about a meeting, and offers to take her to it. But it transpires that Milly does not want to go, and Milly initiates that segment of talk with an appreciation.

[SBL:3:5:8-9]

Milly: She tol' me he was wonderful.
Ginny: Yeah.
* → Milly: Okay honey,
* → Ginny: O[::kay.
→ Milly: [Thanks fer calling me, [and uh-
Ginny: [A:lright,
→ Milly: [[I really-
Ginny: [[Well the we'll - we'll keep it y-y-you think [about it and uh-
Milly: [Yeh,
→ Milly: Well maybe [I c'n w-
Ginny: [You want me to stop by?
→ Milly: Well, you better not maybe um be cuz . . .

((continues)

Appreciations, then, can result in the following varieties of closings: "appreciation as archetype closings," "appreciation extended closings," and "appreciation abandoned closings."

4. *Back-references in first and second turns.*

a) *In second turn.* Back-references are massively used in second closing turn and drastically move out of closings. They are the prototypical way in which second speaker declines to enter into closings. A back-reference second turn retopicalizes prior talk, and typically the form that the re-topicalization takes projects to next turn a sequential developmental function. In this typical projection neither the back-reference turn, nor next turn, provides for the relevance of reinitiating closings. A drastic movement out of closings takes place producing a "second turn back-reference abandoned closing."

[Kr:D+R:14:b:1]
Robin: Hm
(2.0)
* → Robin: Awright °David°
° → David: So what did the baby say.
→ Robin: Oh: he ass:f'you. He slep' with me two nights this
→ wee:k he ass fih you in the morning . . .
((continues))

Although a back-reference in second turn may be designed to drastically move out of closings, next turns may not follow the projected trajectory, but attempt to curtail the drastic movement. In the next fragment Pam has rung Vicky to see if Vicky will help her out at work. Vicky back-references to this (lines 4, 5 and 7) following Pam's closing initiation and appreciation. But Pam does not even minimally respond to the back-reference, she specifically attempts to reinitiate closings (line 9) and curtail the potentiality for drastically moving out of closings occasioned by the back-reference. However, Vicky is unresponsive to the curtailing and continues on her back-reference (lines 10, 12, 13). Again, Pam does not develop this but attempts another closing (line 15) and this is followed by Vicky producing a question intoned close component which in turn is followed by an appreciation. Following this appreciation Vicky again back-references and this time Pam responds.

[Ernhardt:8:3]

1 Pam: I wz js calling you en finding out.
2 (·)
* → 3 Pam: ˙hnn okay. [Well thank you anyway [cuti]cle [( )
° → 4 Vicky: [°Oh:° [Yeah.] [I:-
° → 5 Vicky: I- have a: class Thursday.
6 (0.9)
° → 7 Vicky: a:nd
8 (0.9)
→ 9 Pam: O [ka::]y.
→ 10 Vicky: [yih know,]
11 (·)
→ 12 Vicky: every Thursday 'hh thou:gh starting December
→ 13 seventeenth I won't ˙hh
14 (0.3)
→ 15 Pam: ↑Oka:y,
→ 16 Vicky: Ok[a:y?
→ 17 Pam: [We:ll, then thanks anyway.
→ 18 Vicky: Yeh I'm sorry [Pam,]
→ 19 Pam: [Ohw'l] it's not yer problem.=
→ 20 Vicky: =Yeah it woulda been better if . . . .
((continues))

In the following example Mark (line 3) back-references to prior talk following Pete's closing initial. Pete curtails the drastic movement out of closings by minimally responding (line 4) and reinitiating closings (line 6). However, Mark (line 7) again back-references, and this is again curtailed by Pete (line 9) who again minimally responds and reinitiates closings.

[JG:I:6:2:2]

1 Mark: Yeah
° → 2 Pete: Okay: Uh-Mar[k
° → 3 Mark: [But j u c'n see my poi:nt,
→ 4 Pete: Yeah
5 (0.3)
* → 6 Pete: Okay Mark [I'll see yih]
° → 7 Mark: [( ) we had] so much stuff we just had tih
° → 8 clear out.=
* → 9 Pete: =Yeah. Okay Mar[k.

So, although back-references in second turn typically make a drastic movement out of closings that is followed in next turn, next turn may curtail that moment. For the examples above it can be noted that further back-references may occur following curtailing turns that reinitiate closings, and a "tussle" can develop between one speaker continuing conversation and the other attempting to close.

Curtailing turns have also been observed to operate with respect to a solicitude that could go drastic. For this instance no tussle was observed, and following a curtailing turn, closing was oriented to. This can be accounted for in terms of the typical movement out of closings made by such items. Solicitudes typically make a minimal movement out of closings and only go drastic on some particular occasions. These occasions involve the cooperation of next speaker who provides material for talk to. On occasions where they could go drastic but are curtailed, curtailing may be deferred to inasmuch as these movements going drastic do require next speaker to provide material that drastically moves out of closings. If that is not forthcoming, then, inasmuch as next speaker has curtailed, and in so doing displayed an orientation to closing, and since prior speaker has not actually drastically moved but merely provided for that, closings may be re-entered.

In the case of back-references, however, they are designed to make a drastic movement out of closings themselves, and if next speaker attempts to curtail that movement, prior speaker can continue on the back-reference and preserve the typical trajectory of movement made by a back-reference even though this has not been oriented to by the curtailing speaker.

b) *In first turn.* Although back-references are overwhelmingly used in second turn as the prototypical way for second speaker to decline to enter into closings, they can also take place in a first closing turn. Similar to back-references in second turn, prior talk is retopicalized and makes a drastic movement out of closings that does not provide for the relevancy of reinitiating closings.

[JG:I:8:2:3]

	Colin:	He has the telephone number a' my apartment (eh) it's six two ei:ght,
	Marge:	Six two: ei:ght,
	Colin:	°Seven seven° Oh: three:
		(0.8)
(*) °→	Marge:	˙hhhhhhh Alri:ght, ˙h An:d uh I don't know:w uhm:n
°→		whether he has uh: ˙hhh uh: (1) – (0.2) a ladyfriend on

°→ the side er not but he seems to go out'n stay quite late
°→ from: some ('v the-) his different thin[gs so::,
Colin: [°( )°
→ Marge: Well 'e nevuh speaks of 'em so I: I don't think j-I don't
→ think y'have anyth- fea(h)r there,
((continues))

[JG:Reel 6:10:12]
Marge: ˙hhh So then I won't put it on 'ntil later.
(0.5)
(*) °→ Marge: ˙hh Okay then I guess that's about a:ll. = I u'm
(0.5)
°→ Marge: I would certainly love to know where I could find
°→ some more of this goddamn polish. = It is absolu -
°→ fantastic as far as polish itself is concerned. But these
°→ colors. = I'd sure like to get some lighter ones.
→ Maggie: Well then wh-h-y don't y I don't see why you don't
→ call over to : uhh Save On just to see.
((continues)

Back-references made in first turn by first speakers may operate to display that although they acknowledge, through the production of a first close component, that they are in a sequentially appropriate environment for closing initiation, nevertheless they desire continued conversation. This can be elaborated upon. First speakers may find themselves in a sequential environment that is ripe for closing initiation. This can be transparently seen in example [JG:I:8:2-3] presented above, where Marge finds herself in a turn position following a last arrangement item. Arrangements are heavily closing implicative and Marge may be placed in a position where closing initiation is relevant. It is, however, possible for speakers to extract themselves from this relevancy by the introduction of further newsworthy items. That is, although in a closing implicative environment, closing initiation may be deferred by the introduction of further material for "this" conversation.

In the example below Hyla and Nancy have been talking about a nightgown that Hyla is returning to a shop. They both sequentially display to one another that the topic is exhausted but although closings could be entered into, they also indicate a reluctance for closing initiation which is eventually deferred by the introduction of new material for the conversation.

[HG:17]

Hyla: =Plus it's a size sma:[ll
Nancy: [Oh:,
(·)
Hyla: En I don't think it[I fit] mhhhhihhhh
Nancy: [No] don't think, ˙hh=
Hyla: =.k ˙huhhh hhh=
Nancy: =˙hehhh=
Hyla: = hh So:,
(·)
Hyla: ginna see wh't I c'n ::[get for it.=
Nancy: [°( )
Nancy: =°Mmhmm
(·)
Hyla: ˙tch! A:u::ha, what e:lse. ˙hhh D'you know w't
I did t'day I . . .

However, speakers may display that they do not have further newsworthy items to introduce. They can acknowledge that closings are sequentially appropriate by producing a first close component, but by back-referencing to prior material, display that although no new material is being introduced that would defer closings, continued conversation is, nevertheless, desired and provided for. They can then initiate closing and immediately drastically move out of closing by back-referencing to prior material. Thus back-references in a first turn may be done under particular circumstances where first speakers display that they do not have further newsworthy items but desire conversation continuation.

Although back-references in a first turn can, similar to back-references in second turn, operate to drastically move out of closings, they may, as again for second turn, be curtailed by next turn's response. In the example that follows, Emma (lines 2 and 5) initiates closings, introduces an arrangement item, and then back-references to prior talk. Lottie (line 6) does not develop the re-topicalized material but immediately reinitiates closings and so curtails the drastic movement made by the first turn back-reference. Overlapped with this curtailing turn Emma (line 7) has displayed some continuation of her back-reference, but this is cut off and closing is deferred to. Interestingly, Lottie (line 9) introduces a further close component which may be oriented to, and marks that "out of closing" talk has occurred, though termination is desired and results.

[NB:II:3:12]

```
         1  Lottie:  Yeah.
* →      2  Emma:    ˙hhhh Okay honey, well I'll talk with you [next week,
         3  Lottie:                                            [Uh-h-
         4  Lottie:  [[   Uh-h-
° →      5  Emma:    [[Maybe I'll stay down, I'll see.
* →      6  Lottie:  O[kay honey,
  →      7  Emma:     [Eh-
* →      8  Emma:    Alri[ght,
* →      9  Lottie:      [Right.
* →     10  Emma:    B[ye,
* →     11  Lottie:   [Bye bye.
                              — end call —
```

Back-references in first and second closing turns can produce the following closing-types: "second turn back-reference abandoned closing," "second turn back-reference longer-than-archetype closing," which is the result of a curtailed "second turn back-reference abandoned closing," "first turn back-reference abandoned closing," and "first turn back-reference longer-than-archetype closing," which is the result of a curtailed "first turn back-reference abandoned closing."

5. Continuation of prior talk in first and second turns.

a) *In first turn.* A turn begun as first closing turn can have its shape changed by the inclusion of material that continues, as opposed to reintroduces, prior talk.

[JG:III:22:4.C]

```
           Tess:    Tell Maggie I'll tell Ronnie bout this an you'll get a
                    good s:(n) good supply.
(*)  →     Marge:   Well okay [an if its rill good the next time go go up=
           Tess:              [Al-h-right
     →     Tess:    =[[Ah:(fi')
           Marge:    [[you ken bring some more
```

[Erhardt:10:4.C]

```
           Vicky:   Oh keep it.
                                 (0.3)
*    →     Karen:   ˙h Okay then ah'll give you the money [(      )
                                                          [
```

Next turns are found to respond to this continuation. A movement out of closing is made by the continuation which is reciprocated in next turn. However, next turn seems to be crucial for determining the degree of movement that eventuates from first turn prior talk continuations. In extract [JG:III:22:4.C] Marj continues prior talk by requesting Tess to bring something the next time she is at a particular place. It is revealed, though, that Tess does not go there that often and in displaying this problem the movement out of closing goes drastic, and the closing is abandoned.

[JG:III:22:4.C]
(*) → Marge: Well okay [an if it's ril good the next time you go up=
* → Tess: [Al-h-right.
Tess: = [[Ah:(fi')
→ Marge: [[you ken bring us some more
° → Tess: or the next time he comes down. We don't go up there
° → that often . . .
((continues)

In example [Erhardt:10:4:C], however, next turn curtails the movement out of closings and produces a minimal response and a closing implicative arrangement item which in next turn receives a close component.

[Erhardt:10:4:C]
(*) → Karen: ˙h Okay then ah'll give you the money [( )
→ Vicky: [Alright fi:ne.=
Vicky: =˙h- a:nd I'll u:m (0.9) ah'll call you tihmorrow when
I get home fr'm work about Sleepy Hollow.
(0.3)
* → Karen: Okhha:y [Great.

The continuation of prior talk in first closing turn can produce a "first turn continuation of prior talk abandoned closing" and a "first turn continuation of prior talk longer-than-archetype closing" which for the example examined is the result of curtailed "first turn continuation of prior talk abandoned closing."

b) *In second turn.* Second speaker can also continue prior talk in second turn.

[MC:II:1:3]
Lila: . . . I'll tell yuh about it when yuh get here.

* → Jan: Yah. Okay honey
→ Lila: En I'll straighten up ez best I can.

[JG:I:8:5]
Marge: Jayee ef [ef, ee ar: e ss,
Colin: [Yeah.
Marge: °Uh huh,°
* → Colin: O[kay [thank you ( )
→ Marge: [·hh [u-well that's oka:y ·hh uh:m:n u-he.
→ will uh just uh ring you I: ho:pe that he will
→ ring y[ou? And]

[JG:1:24:12]
Marge: So anyway ummm well take care of yourself honey=
Laura: =Oh I will anuh give me a buz:z again if you hear anything
Marge: Well I I just uh the next time I see him I'm gonna uhh I'm gonna say that you umm had called again
* → Laura: Okay
→ Marge: an: dun wondered what in the world was the matter that
→ you couldn't uh phone her back and uh (0.5) you know

The continuation of prior talk in second turn may not project a particular sequentially relevant response, and accordingly can preserve the relevancy of closings. Next turn may, then, minimally respond and a minimal movement out of closings is made, closings being reinitiated. In extract [MC:II:1:3] Jan minimally responds and within the turn produces an appreciation. Lila reinitiates closings and termination results. A "second turn continuation of prior talk longer-than-archetype closing" is produced.

[MC:II:1:3]
* → Jan: Yah. Okay honey
→ Lila: En I'll straighten up ez best I can.
→ Jan: Yah fine. Tha[nks a lot Lila,
* → Lila: [Aw-Aright dear
Lila: Yer welcome.
Jan: Ya. Bye::,
– end call –

The continuing turn may, however, introduce material that can be developed, and a drastic movement can eventuate. In fragment [JG:I:8:5] Marge continues the prior talk with further arrangement material. This is completed by Colin, but although this completion is closing implicative Marge continues in-conversation by developing further material that does not provide for the relevancy of closing. Here a "second turn continuation of prior talk abandoned closing" is the result.

[JG:I:8:5]
* → Colin: O[kay [thank you (
→ Marge: [ˈhh [u–well that's oka:y, ˈhh uh:m:n u–he will uh
→ just uh:ring you I: ho:pe thet he will ring y[ou? An:d]=
→ Colin: [An' then]
→ Marge: = [[uh:] ˈhhhh
→ Colin: [[then i]f then if iz fay:v'ble oh: ah'll call im back.
(·)
° → Marge: eYes, ˈhh Ah:: well. I tell you I certainly wish you (·)
° → would go along with im.
((continues)

Although the movement out of closings projected by the continuation of prior talk has been seen to be minimal for the above examples and goes drastic if there is development, continuation of prior talk in second turn can also drastically move out of closings when the relevancy of closing reinitiation is not preserved. In the example [JG:I: 24:12] Marge queries why Laura has not made a return call to a friend. This does not just provide for a minimal response, but projects that some explanation is in order and drastically moves out of closings. However, Laura curtails that movement by not producing an account, and following Marge's comment Laura reinitiates closing. Interestingly, Marge still continues prior talk following the reinitiation, and again this continuation is a drastic movement out of closings which eventuates in the abandonment of closings.

[JG:I:24:12]
* → Laura: Okay.
° → Marge: an:duh wondered what in the world was the matter that
° → you couldn't uh phone her back and uh (0.5) you know
→ Laura: Umhum
Marge: See what he says
* → Laura: Okay

```
° → Marge:   I mean I'll do it if you want me to
    Laura:   I don't care
    Marge:   ˙Well I mean if-if you would prefer . . .
                                        ((continues))
```

6. *Question intoned first and second close components.*

a) *Question intoned first close components.* Closings can be initiated by a question intoned close component.

```
[TC1(b):9:6:6-7]
      Walt:     Okay well (0.4) you do w't [ever you wanna do,
      Gayle:                               [hhhhh
                                  (·)
* → Walt:       O↑Kay?

[TC1(b)13:3]
      Jerry:    Well I c'n leave right now if yih want,=
      Linda:    = No:: h[hh
      Jerry:            [hhh-hh
      Linda:    hh:::::::hh so:,
                                  (0.3)
* → Linda:      Okay?

[F:TC:I:I:22]
      Shirley:  ˙p˙t En that's all that's new,
                                  (0.6)
* → Shirley:    ˙t˙hhhhhhh Oka:y?  hhhn

[Rahman:II:6]
      Ida:      Well I'll give her a ri:ng,
                                  (·)
      Jenny:    Ye[s,
      Ida:        ['n-
                                  (0.2)
      Ida:      ((off phone)) Pa:rdon Dez?
                                  (1.0)
* → Ida:        Aa:-Right. Okay then?
```

A question intoned first close component can operate in a closing section in the same manner as a close component, and produce a "first turn question intoned as archetype closing."

[TC1(b):9:6-7]
* → Walt: O↑Kay?
* → Gayle: ˙hh Okay, h[h
* → Walt: [Okeh -Bye bye.
* → Gayle: Bye::.h
— end call —

However, question intoned first close components would seem to be designed to provide for some response other than a second close component, and regularly next turns are occupied with a minimal response to the question intonation of first close component.

[TC1(b):13:3]
* → Linda: Okay:
(0.3)
→ Jerry: Yah.

[F:TC:I:1:22]
* → Shirley: ˙t˙ hhhhhh Oka:y? hhhh
→ Geri: Ye:ah, hh

[Rahman:II:6]
* → Ida: A:Right. Okay then?
→ Jerry: Yes, mm ˙hh Yeh=

Inasmuch as a question intoned first close component is designed to receive an in-conversation response it equivocably initiates closings. That is, while it can initiate closings it also provides for an in-conversation response, and in this respect can be oriented to by next speaker as slightly edging out of the very closing it initiates. However, if just a minimal in-conversation response is returned then since neither first or second speaker has actually introduced items that can be talked to, closing can be re-entered. Re-entry takes the form of closing reinitiation which displays an orientation to a slight movement out of closings having taken place.

[TC1(b)13:3]
(*) → Linda: Okay?
(0.3)
→ Jerry: Yah.

* → Linda: O:kay h[oney
* → Jerry: [Okay.
* → Linda: Bye b[ye

However, next turn to the question intoned first close component can drastically move out of closings by latching on topical material to a minimal response.

[Rahman:II:6]
(*) → Ida: Aa:–Right. Okay then?
° → Jenny: Yes, mm ˙hh Yeh –hh She was saying that Jane had
° → applie:d for the jo:b.
((continues))

So, although a question intoned first close component can be used to initiate closings it does so in an equivocable manner that invites an in-conversation response. Next speakers may then minimally return, or take an opportunity to drastically move out of closings by latching on topical material to a minimal response to the question intoned prior close component. A question intoned first close component may thus result in a "first turn question intoned longer-than-archetype closing" and a "first turn question intoned abandoned closing."

b) *Question intoned second close component.* These can operate in similar ways to question intoned first close components since they too are designed to receive an in-conversation response, and thus slightly edge out of closings. These responses are usually minimal.

[F:TC:I:1:22.b]
Shirley: :hhhhhhhh[Good w'l have coffee.
Geri: [°°( )°°
(0.3)
→ Geri: °Oka:y,°
(*) → Shirley: Alright?
Geri: Mm–h [m:?

[Erhardt:10:4]
Vicky: a ˙h– a:nd I: 'll u:m (0.9) Ah'll call you tihmorrow
when I get home fr'm work about Sleepy Hollow.
(0.3)

```
     → Karen:    Okhha:y. [Great.
(*)  → Vicky:              [Okay?
       Karen:    Great.
```

Following an in-conversation response next speaker may continue out of closings and the closing is abandoned, resulting in a "question intoned second close component abandoned closing."

```
[F:TC:I:1:22.b]
 *   → Geri:      °Oka:y°
(*)  → Shirley:   Alright?
     → Geri:      mm-h [m:?
 °   → Shirley:        [D'yih talk tih Dayna this week?
     → Geri:      ˙hhh Yeh . . .
                                 ((continues))
```

Closings may, however, be reinitiated and a "question intoned second close component longer-than-archetype closing" results.

```
[Erhardt:10:4]
 *   → Karen:    Okhha:y. [Great.
(*)  → Vicky:             [Okay?
     → Karen:    Great,
                              (·)
 *   → Vicky:    [[Alright
 *   → Karen:    [[Okay
 *   → Karen:    Thanks kid,
                             (0.2)
 *   → Vicky:    Bah[bye.
 *   → Karen:       [Bye, hh
                               – end call –
```

7. *First turn response to prior utterance.*

It was seen earlier that turns begun with close components could continue prior talk. It can also be found that first closing turns begun with a close component can also include material that responds to prior turn, but without continuing prior talk. This is one of three occasions in closings where the introduction into a closing turn of other than a close component does not systematically, and regularly, result in a movement out of closings. The other occasions are where an appreciation operates as though it were a closing component, and where appreciations are an optional sequence insert.

Responses to a prior utterance in a first closing turn that follow a first close component do not project to next turns some sequentially appropriate object, and, hence, although they do not operate to move out of closings, next turns can be occupied with a second close component. This can be seen for both of the following examples, though the first produces an extension turn, and the second has an optional appreciation insert. Neither occurrences, however, display themselves to be associated with the first closing turn's response to prior utterance, and both reach termination.

[JG:III:21:7.b]
Marge: Oh that's wonderful. Well ˙hh have a nice dinner an then I'll see you tomorrow
* → Nell: Oka:y you too
* → Marge: Okay [hon
* → Nell: [(Alright dar[lin)
* → Marge: [Bye bye=
* → Nell: Bye bye.
— end call —

[MC:II:3:5]
Lila: I'm gonna start right now tuh get some buddy in then get tuh that darn post office 'n get that air mail stuff off.
* → Bush: A'right, ve[ry good,
* → Lila: [Alright.
* → Bush: Thank you very kindly for [yer order.
* → Lila: [En thanks so much.
* → Bush: Surely.
* → Lila: [[Bye
* → Bush: [[Bye
— end call —

Response to prior utterance in first closing turn can be done by first speaker in order to mark an orientation to closure. The response to the prior utterance could have occupied a turn position following the utterance responded to, without having a close component in turn initial position, and hence without initiating closings. Next speaker could, then, initiate closings following the response to the prior utterance.

However, should this be the case, the speaker who would initiate the closing would not be the speaker providing the response to prior, and although the sequential environment might be primed for closing initiation the speaker providing the response to prior utterance has no guarantee that closings would actually be initiated by next speaker. Speakers may initiate closings before responding to prior utterance as a way of not only providing a response to prior that may have been appropriate, but also as a way of marking their orientation to closings. Inasmuch as a response to prior utterance does not project a sequentially relevant next activity, and is itself actually a response, first speaker can provide a response to prior without moving out of closings.

A movement out of a closing so initiated could be done by second speaker in second turn. However, since first speaker has, in the manner described, displayed a particular orientation to closings, next speaker may respond to that orientation and provide a second close component in preference to initiating a movement out of closings, and thus, response to prior utterance in a first turn systematically reach termination. A "first closing turn response to prior utterance as though archetype closing" is produced.

8. *First turn announcements of closure.*

First closing turn begun with a close component can continue with an announcement of closure. Next turns respond to this announcement.

[F:TC:1:28] [[Shiloh the dog is barking]]
Shirley: I c'n [hear it fr'm this [side,
Shiloh: [ragh! rugh [-ragh'.
(*) → Geri: [Okay w'l lemme get o:ff,
→ Shirley: Yeh go do yer work,

Announcements of closure are closing implicative, and next turns, although responding to closure announcement, can also preserve closing implicature. Closings can then be re-entered. The form that the reentry takes is the reinitiation of closings which displays an orientation to a movement out of closings having taken place. A minimal movement out of closings can then be produced by an announcement of closure which has the effect of producing a longer-than-archetype closing. First turn announcements of closure can produce a "first turn announcement of closures longer-than-archetype closing."

[F:TC:I:28][5]

(*) →	Geri:	[Okay w'l lemme get o:ff,
→	Shirley:	Yeh go do yer work,
→	Geri:	Yeh,
* →	Shirley:	˙t˙hh okay?=

However, unlike a close component, the announcement of closure is not bereft of topicalizable features, and next turns may topicalize that material in a way that does not provide for the reinitiation of closings. That is, announcements of closures can eventuate in a drastic movement out of closings and produce a "first turn announcement of closure abandoned closing."

[JG:IV:1:3]

	Ronald:	Wul it's a puhlitical cartoo:n.
* →	Maggie:	Oh. Okay sweetie
	Ronald:	[[Okay-
→	Maggie:	[[Wu' I'll letcha go. I'm in the middle of cleaning up this mess.
° →	Ronald:	˙hh whuddiyou - What's the mess. Some [thing-
	Maggie:	[Oh we-
	Maggie:	No no we change the clothes around. ((continues))

9. First turn reason-for-call reiteration.

Reason-for-call reiteration occurs in first closing turn and is used to soften and account for an initial movement into closings. Typically a minimal movement is made out of closings that preserves the relevancy of closing reinitiation, and similar to arrangements and solicitudes in first turn, a longer-than-archetype closing results.

[RN:9]

	John:	I'll see you over the weekend then.
	Steve:	Good thing.
(*) →	John:	Okay, and I'm glad I ra:ng nuw an sorted things
→		out.
→	Steve:	Yeh me too.
* →	John:	Okay then.
* →	Steve:	Oka:y,

```
*  → John:      B[ye.
*  → Steve:      [Bye.
                              – end call –
```

Reason-for-call reiteration in first closing turn can, consequently, produce a "reason-for-call longer-than-archetype closing."

However, again, as for other items introduced in first turn, reason for all in first turn can eventuate in a drastic movement out of closings. In the example below Vicky initiates closings but within the closing initial turn begins to reiterate reason-for-call. Karen minimally responds to this but her utterance is intercepted by Vicky who latches further material onto the reason for call. This not only does not reinitiate closings, but undercuts the relevancy of reinitiation. Again, the possibility is provided for by the fact that the reason-for-call introduces into closings material that can be developed in a way that archetype closing components cannot. Should this be developed, a drastic movement out of closings eventuates resulting in a "reason-for-call abandoned closing."

```
[Erhardt:10:3]
        Vicky:    °Good°
                              (0.2)
* →     Vicky:    Okay well I just ca:lled tu:h (0.4) teh:: (·) ask,=
        Karen:    = thanks [a lo:t,           ]
° →     Vicky:             [though've cour] se I knew
° →               [the an] swer would be no:
        Karen:    [really ]
        Karen:    Yehhh
                              ((continues))
```

The possibility that a reason-for-call in first turn can go drastic can be attended to by next speaker who can, in the manner described for solicitudes and back-references, produce a response that curtails the drastic potentiality of a reason-for-call. In the next extract Emma (line 7) initiates closings and reiterates reason for call. Lottie (line 2) returns a second close component which defers to Emma's continuing with reason-for-call. However, Lottie, overlapped with Emma, then minimally responds to the reiteration and immediately produces a close component which curtails the potentiality that the reason-for-call reiteration could go drastic. Termination is arrived at, and similar to curtailed solicitudes, a "reason-for-call longer-than-archetype closing" which is the product of a curtailed potential "reason-for-call abandoned closing" results.

[NB:IV:12:2]

```
             1 Emma:    Well I'll talk tih yuh later dear.
             2 Lottie:  We:ll,
             3 Emma:    [[I-
             4 Lottie:  [[Well I wz jus ge[tting dressed.
             5 Emma:                     [I know yer goin.
             6 Lottie:  Yeah.
(*) →        7 Emma:    A ARIGHT I
                        [JUS THOUGHT I'D TELL [YUH THERE WZ ONE HUH-
 *  →        8 Lottie:  [Okay.                [Yea:h, okay hun,
 *  →        9 Emma:    Bye,
 *  →       10 Lottie:  Bye.
```

10. Misplaced first close component.

A move may be made to initiate a closing in a closing implicative environment, such as arrangement completion, but the actual place at which the movement into closings is made results in the misplacement of the first close component vis-a-vis a prior turn. In the following examples closing implicative talk is in progress, but continuation of an utterance is marked by continuation components such as "o:r," "becuz," "a:nd," and "yihknow." A first close component is produced, but the components that are used to mark that an utterance is still in progress result in the close component but provide the continuation of the utterance marked as still in progress.

[NB:I:5:4-6]

```
       Guy:   An' if yuh c'n bring uh (1.4) Buster Brown along with
              yeh? Why bring im along.
       Eddy:  A'right, I'll see.
     → Guy:   o:r.
   * → Eddy:  O-kay,
     → Guy:   Stoveall or who ever we can.
```

[TC:II:15:Ex:2:1-2]

```
  → Jo:    Buh anyway it'll be okay: becuz [uh
* → Cher:                                  [Okay [(dear)
  → Jo:                                          [I saved the piece=
           =°huh huh°
```

[Erhardt:8:3.c]

Vicky: I have a: class Thursday.
(0.9)
→ Vicky: and
(0.2)
* → Pam: O[ka::]y.
→ Vicky: [Yih know,]
(·)
→ Vicky: evry Thursda– ˙hh th ou:gh starting December seventeenth . . .

[TC1(b)16:88]

Joan: ˙t˙ Ah'll letche go::, =
Linda: =Yeh=
Joan: = end ah::m ˙t˙ hhhh Uh::m ah'll talk tih Jack. Ah'll see ih I c'n::
(·)
Linda: ye[ah.]=
Joan: [yihknow]
Linda: [[Okay,
Joan: [[u t ell im Thi– u – This is plenny'v ti:me . . .

Although an initiation of a closing may be attempted, should that first closing turn be misplaced with regard to a continuing prior utterance, next speakers are unresponsive to closure and continue their prior utterance. Following this continuation, next speakers may attempt another closing initiation and this can be attended to by next turn as now legitimate through the production of a second close component.

[NB:I:5:4–6]

Eddy: O-okay,
Guy: Stoveall or whoever we can.
* → Eddy: Yeah. Alright,
(0.8)
* → Guy: Alright?

[Erhardt:8:3:C.]

Pam: O[ka::]y.
Vicky: [yihknow,]
(·)
Vicky: evry Thursday ˙hh thou:gh starting December

seventeenth I won't ˙hh
(0.3)
* → Pam: ↑Oka:y,
* → Vicky: Ok[a: y?

Speakers who have attempted initiation, but have misplaced a first close component, may preserve their displayed orientation to closings by initiating another closing as soon as they can. But the turn following a misplaced first close component that continues the prior utterance may be occupied with material that is no longer closing implicative, and next speakers may not be in a position to initiate closings.

[TC:II:15:Ex.2:1–2]
Jo: Buh anyway it'll be okay: becuz [uh
Char: [okay [(dear)
Jo: [I saved the piece=
Jo: =°huh huh°
° → Char: (Oh) good. Ih wz so nice of you tih do it e[h
Jo: [˙hhhhh
Jo: We[ll I enjoyed it.]
Char: [Joe is j's terr] ibly:uh (0.3) uh: impressed . . . .
((continues))

[TC1(b):16:88]
Linda: Ye[ah.
Joan: [Yihknow] =
Linda: [[Okay,
→ Joan: [[Utellim.] This-u this is plenny'v ti:me. thet he hhh
° → ˙hhhuhhh better (m) go through that book on jist mark
° → hhimshhe(h)lf (h) o(h)ff[tha[(n)at n] ight, ˙hhhehhhhh=
Linda: [Ye:ah,]
Joan: = The:n yih know
((continues))

So closings may be initiated by misplaced first close components. These receive a continuation of the utterance that was in progress, and depending upon how this utterance develops an attempt to initiate closings may or may not ensue.

11. In-conversation objects in second turn.

In-conversation objects are another way that second speaker in second turn can decline to enter into closings. Although they do not, as do back-references, introduce material for next turn to talk on, nevertheless, they typically receive next turns that do not provide for the relevancy of reinitiating closings. This material is produced as a response to the in-conversation object, and the drastic movement out of closings that ensues is initiated by the in-conversation object. Often, material that is introduced by next speaker actually displays itself as a response to the in-conversation object. This can be done by nominating a topic for talk on behalf of second speaker. Consequently, in-conversation objects produce a "second turn in-conversation object abandoned closing."

[TC1(b):16:89]
Linda: nNo I don't think there's we'll all git tihgether et the
same ti [ime.
Joan: [Ye:ah.
* → Joan: °O:ka[y.°
→ Linda: [°Ya:h°
° → Joan: °so: I wz g'nna° say:. Uh:m (0.2) ˙t˙hhh you wanna
° → go t' their hou:se? er: (·) come he:re?
° → en you:rs ahhuhh
Linda: ↑oh? h h I don't c[a ::re
Joan: [ah'll talk tih my mum tihday . . .
((continues))

There are two occasions when drastic movement out of closings that is typically associated with in-conversation objects is not realized. First, similar to back-references, the movement out of closings may be curtailed by next speaker's response. In the next example Linda marks that she is still "in-conversation" (line 4) following a close initial turn. However, Jerry (line 5) does not provide new material as is done in the example above. Rather, although his "Later" is responsive to the creation of a sequential environment for conversation continuation, it is not responsive to continuation and proposes that further conversation should be shelved.

[TC1(b)13:6]
1 Linda: . . . but ˙hhhhhhhh try'n :: try tih git Deeanna's about
2 seven.
→ 3 Jerry: Oka:y,

→ 4 Linda: So:: [I-
→ 5 Jerry: [Later
6 (·)
7 Linda: Okay honey.
8 Jerry: Gih bye.=
9 Linda: Bye bye.
– end call –

Second, next speaker may be unresponsive to the "in-conversation" marking by prior speaker. In the following fragment Mark (line 3) indicates that he is still in-conversation but no next turn is produced by Joanne (line 4). Although Joanne does not introduce conversational components that can operate to curtail Mark's movement, the non-production of further material can be oriented to by Mark as indicating that new material is not being presented. But it requires next speaker to introduce possible newsworthy items in order for this sort of drastic movement out of closings to be realized. Mark then produces closing implicative material and Joanne reinitiates closings.

[SF:I:13.b]
1 Mark: Ah'll probly see yih et Biff's.
* → 2 Joanne: Okay,
° → 3 Mark: ˙hhh so: uh:,
→ 4 (0.4)
5 Mark: Ah'll talk tih yuh later,
→ 6 Joanne: Okay Spark [thanks fer calling.

12. Second turn no-response.

It has just been observed that in-conversation objects may receive no-response and that this is consequential for closings. It can also be found that no-response can operate in relationship to the initiation of a movement out of closings. This can happen when a first closing turn receives no-response. Following no-response first speaker can move out of closings and display that their movement is in response to no-response in second turn.

[HG:15]
1 Nancy: Anyw::y,=

	2	Hyla:	=˙pk˙. A:nywa [:y,
	3	Nancy:	[So::;,
	4		(·)
	5	Hyla:	˙p=
	6	Nancy:	=You'll come abou:t (·) eight. Right?=
	7	Hyla:	=Yea::h,=
* →	8	Nancy:	=Okay.
→	9		(0.2)
→	10	Nancy:	Anything else to report,
	11		(0.3)
	12	Hyla:	Uh:::: :::m:::,
	13		(0.4)
	14	Hyla:	Getting my hair cut tihmorrow,
	15	Nancy:	=Oh rilly?
			((continues))

In this example (line 10) Nancy moves out of closings, and displays the movement as oriented to Hyla's no-response (line 9) to first closing turn (line 8). Nancy does this by not actually introducing further material for talk to, but proposes that if Hyla desires continuation she has the onus of introducing newsworthy material. That is, no-response in second turn can be oriented to by other speaker as indicating reluctance for closure. In this example a drastic movement out of closings eventuates through the introduction of further material that is topicalized. The introduction of this material is a response to prior turn which has made provision for new material to be introduced. This turn has, however, displayed itself to be responsive to second turn no-response. Thus the drastic movement that eventuates can be traced back to second turn no-response and it can, then, be observed that a "second turn no-response abandoned closing" results.

First speakers can display a high degree of sensitivity to second turn no-response. In the fragment below, Shirley moves out of closings following the "beat" in which Geri could produce a second close component. Again, this movement displays a sensitivity to second turn no-response. Shirley displays a search for something to say and eventually introduces an arrangement item. That is, she produces the arrangement item as something searched for, and in this manner displays it to be something that she might not have produced if there had been a response in second turn. There is, in this example, a reinitiation of closings though that closing is eventually abandoned as will be seen when this extract is re-examined in section III.

[F:TC:I:1:22-23]

	Geri:	Yeh ah'll cme over I wannih (g) (·) git s'm work do:ne 'n then ah'll c'm over'n ah'll help Joe [: y, en
* →	Shirley:	[Okay,
→		(·)
→	Shirley:	˙hhhhhhh [Good w'l have coffee,

13. Foreshortening in first and second turn.[6]

Foreshortening in first and second turn can be briefly noted. Foreshortening in first turn can take place where a first turn is used to produce a first close component and a first terminal component. Here the relevancy of second terminal production in next turn is provided for, and next turns can return with the sought second terminal, though this can be preceded by a second close component that re-establishes termination as mutually oriented to. Foreshortening in first turn can operate to both hasten termination and display the inappropriateness of moving out of closings. Once a second terminal is secured, first speaker may "soften" the abruptness of closings by producing another terminal and lengthen closings but without undercutting termination.

[JG:III:14]

	Rita:	Cuz I know you're [practically [starving.
* →	Maggie:	[˙hhAlright [G'bye.
* →	Rita:	Okay [bye.
* →	Maggie:	[Bye.

— end call —

Foreshortening can also be done in a second turn. Here second speaker not only produces a second close component but also a first terminal that offers the immediate relevance of second terminal production. Again foreshortening can be done in second turn to both hasten termination and to display the inappropriateness of moving out of closings.

[TC1(c):12:21-23]

	Linda:	Have a nice weeke:nd.=
	Joan:	=Yeh you too,
* →	Linda:	Okay,=
* →	Joan:	=Okay buh bye.=
* →	Linda:	=Buh bye.

– end call –

14. One further variant on the archetype closing.

In contrast to foreshortened closings, extended closings can be produced. Unlike the other closing types that have been examined where first and second turns have been the crucial turn for the production of a certain closing type, extended closings operate for third turn. Here first speaker may extend closings by the production of a further close component as opposed to a first terminal. Closing extensions can be used to display an availability for further conversation but without actually moving out of closings. Next turns can either respond to this availability by moving out of closings, or be unresponsive and produce a first terminal, though here, terminal production has been displaced and delayed.

[FD:I:66:R]

Jack: See y' later,
* → Terry: Okay.
* → Jack: Okay.
→ Terry: Okay, ˙hh [h
→ Jack: [See yuh coffeetime

[NB:II:4]

B: Lemme call yuh back'nna liddle while.
A: Fine.
* → B: Awright.
* → A: Okay dear,
→ B: Awright,
→ A: [[Bye bye
B: [[Bye bye 'oney.

– end call –

Next turn to a closing extension can also reciprocate an availability for conversation without moving out of closings with a returned extension turn. But inasmuch as neither that speaker nor second speaker have actually moved out of closings on prior occasions, talk can be found to be exhausted and a first terminal is produced.

[NB:II:27]

A: Well I'mm gonna call Neville's mother b'fore I do anything

else. So, ˙hhhh [I'll give yih a buzz'n,
B: [Wuh-
* → B: AWRIGHT ho[ney,
* → A: [Okay
→ B: Awright,
→ A: O [kay dear,
* → B: [Bye,
* → A: Bye bye

— end call —

III. Negotiating for Termination and Negotiating for Abandoning Closings [7]

The previous section identified a variety of closing types. Closings can also be constructed that utilize component parts from different closing types. In the following example Lily (line 3 and 4) initiates closings, but within the turn makes a closure announcement and produces a solicitude. In next turn Cora (line 5) produces a second close component and an arrangement item. Lily (line 6) uses another close component, and an appreciation which is followed by an in-conversation response (line 7). This receives a first terminal (line 8) and in second terminal results (line 9) conversation ends.

[TC1(b):7:3]
1 Lily: ˙hh Sa:m says how much he li:kes you:,
2 Cora: Yeah,=
3 Lily: =So:, O::ka:y, ˙hh well gee you go back tih bed'n take
4 good care a'yerse:lf.
5 Cora: Okay maybe nex'time hu:n,
6 Lily: O:kay tha:nk you:.
7 Lily: Uh[huh
8 Cora: [Bah: b[ye:.
9 Lily: [Bye:.

— end call —

Participants may use components from various closing types past first initiation of closing to termination, and, indeed, from first closing initiation to the abandonment of closings. Speakers use closing type components to negotiate with one another for conversation termination and for closing abandonment. Closings can now be re-examined to highlight these negotiations. Nine categories of negotiations will be examined. Some of these just involve instances of the closing types previously mentioned, while others involve combinations of closing type components, and various movements in and out of closings. These categories are not definitive of negotiations that can occur, but they capture many of the interactions that are found to regularly occur from the first initiation of closing to termination or closing abandonment.

1. Displayed mutual orientation for termination resulting in termination

Speakers can display a mutual orientation for termination and mutually terminate their conversation. This can be seen in the archetype closing, and the foreshortened closing.

[NB:IV:14:26]
Emma: And, u-uh I'm w- I'm with you,
Lottie: Yeah,
* → Emma: Oright,
* → Lottie: Okay [honey
* → Emma: [Bye dear=
* → Lottie: =Bye.
— end call —

[JG:III:14]
Rita: Cuz I know you're [practically [starving.
* → Maggie: [ˑhh Alright [G'bye.
* → Rita: Okay [bye.
* → Maggie: [Bye.
— end call —

[TC1(c):12:23]
Linda: <u>H</u>ave a nice <u>w</u>eeke:nd.=
Joan: =<u>Y</u>eh you too,
* → Linda: <u>O</u>kay,=
* → Joan: =Okay <u>b</u>uh bye. =
* → Linda: =Buh bye,
— end call —

It can also be seen for some of the longer-than-archetype closings. For example, first turn arrangements. It was seen that in extract [NB:

IV:10:56] that although moving out of closings the arrangement in first turn provides for the relevancy of closings reinitiation which was oriented to in next turn by the production of an item that was not only a return to the arrangement item but also reinitiated closings. Neither speaker moves out of the reinitiated closing. Both speakers thus display an orientation to closing through producing a longer-than-archetype closing.

```
[NB:IV:10:56]
         Emma:   Um [sleep good. t'night swee[tie,
*    →  Lottie:     [Okeh-                   [Okay well I'll -I'll see
     →           y' in the mor[ning.
(*)  →  Emma:                 [A:right.
     →  Lottie:  A'right,
     →  Emma:    B'ye bye de[ar,
     →  Lottie:             [Bye bye,
                              — end call —
```

Again, this can be seen for a first turn solicitude closing. In example [JG:1:10:7.b] the solicitude moves out of closings, but, as for the arrangement, it provides for the relevancy of reinitiating closings which is oriented to in next turn by a minimal response. Closings are reinitiated, neither speaker then moves out of closings, and termination results. Again, both speakers display a mutual orientation for termination through producing a longer-than-archetype closing,

```
[JG:1:10:7b]

         Sam:                    [Nice talking t'you honey
                 maybe I'll se yuh [Thurs [dee.
(*)  →  Marge:                     [Uh:   [Oh: alright love tih see
     →           you. ˙hh A:n' uh tell uh:ar li'l gi:rlfriend ar o↑ther
     →           little girlfrie[nd hello en' everything like that.=
     →  Sam:                    [(    )
     →  Sam:     = I will deah.
*    →  Marge:   O:kay.=
*    →  Sam:     =Thank you,
*    →  Marge:   Bye: [bye,
*    →  Sam:          [B'ye.
                              — end call —
```

2. *Mutually protracted closings resulting in termination.*

Speakers can, in contrast to mutually produced longer-than-archetype closings that result in mutual termination, negotiate a mutually protracted closing using components from different closing types that also results in termination.

```
[TC1(c):12:21-23]
 1 Linda:   ˙hhi:hh ˙hhih hn-hn, ˙hhhhhhuhhh [hn
 2 Joan:                                    [(She'd) know yer on
            it. hh[hh
 3 Linda:         [eh hn
 4 Joan:    O:ka[y,
 5 Linda:       [O:khay, [˙hhh
 6 Joan:                 [Well I'll talk t'you [la:t [er,
 7 Linda:                                      [˙hh  [Yeah.
 8 Linda:   Have a nice weeke:nd.=
 9 Joan:    =Yeh you too,
10 Linda:   Okay,=
11 Joan:    =Okay buh bye.=
12 Linda:   =Buh bye,
                              – end call –
```

Here, Joan (line 4) initiates closings which is followed by a second close component (line 5). Joan (line 6) introduces an arrangement item in third turn which could be occupied by a first terminal component. An arrangement in closings is usually placed in first turn and can operate, as for the example [NB:IV:10:56] given in part 1 of this section, to produce a longer-than-archetype closing. In producing an arrangement item in this turn position Joan can display a reluctance for termination at this place.

But, the arrangement item minimally moves out of closings and does not itself drastically move and undercut the relevancy of closings. Next turn can minimally respond (line 7). Joan may display a reluctance for termination, but in producing an arrangement item that can receive a minimal response, she preserves the relevancy of closing. This can also be preserved in next turn that minimally responds, and does not escalate a movement out of closings which can be, in next turn, reinitiated.

However, Linda (line 8) undercuts the relevancy of reinitiating closings by latching on a solicitude to her minimal response, thereby reciprocating a reluctance for termination. Again, this item does not drastically move out of closings. Joan (line 9) responds to the solicitude with a minimum receipt item and a returned solicitude just as Linda initially responded to the arrangement. Both of them have made a minimal movement out of closings that preserves the relevancy of closings and neither of them has attempted to drastically move out of closing.

In this manner Joan and Linda make a protracted minimal movement over four turns at talk, while they both display that neither of them is drastically moving out of closings. Linda (line 10) then reinitiates closings which is followed by a foreshortened second turn (line 11) resulting in a second terminal (line 12) and termination.

Thus Linda and Joan are able to protract their closing by using components from two closing types, yet display an orientation to closing. They negotiate a protracted closing while orienting to termination. Such a closing may be produced as a way of reaching termination while producing in-conversation talk.

This can also be seen in the next fragment.

[JG:III:18:23]

1 Mrs. B: [Well I knew I better check with you:
2 Rita: Yeah yeah.
3 Rita: ˙hh well okay then honey I'll be down there to do you in
4 the morning.
5 Mrs. B: Thank you dear
6 Rita: Ok[a:y, Oka:y=
7 Mrs. B: [Okay
8 Mrs. B: [[(Bye)
9 Rita: [[I'm in the middle of my dinner other[wise I would talk=
10 Mrs. B: [No
11 Mrs. B: =No that's alright hon[cuz I'm just getting my husband's.
12 Rita: [( )
13 Mrs. B: Tha[nk you
14 Rita: [Yes. O:kay. uh huh. Bye bye=
15 Mrs. B: =Bye bye

– end call –

Rita (line 3) initiates closings and in that turn minimally moves out of closings with an arrangement reiteration. Mrs. B (line 5) responds to this with an appreciation of the "service" indicated in the arrangement reiteration. Rita (line 6) unambiguously returns to closings, though she produces two close components within that turn. Mrs. B (line 7) returns a close component overlapped with Rita's previous first close component and displays an orientation to closings, and goes on to produce a first terminal (line 8).

Overlapped with this first terminal, Rita (line 9) makes an announcement of closure that accounts and apologizes for not being able to continue in conversation. In so doing, she displays a reluctance for termination at that point, while, nevertheless, preserving the relevancy of closings. Mrs. B (lines 10, 11) reciprocates the reluctance for closure at this point by similarly returning an announcement for closure that attends to Rita's account and apology, and displays that she is in the same circumstances as Rita. But she also preserves the relevancy of closings.

Both Rita and Mrs. B mutually produce items that minimally move out of closings and which display a reluctance for termination and closure at the places in which they make a movement out of closings. However, both movements are oriented to the relevancy of closings. They are able to mutually protract their closing while also orienting to the relevancy of termination. Mrs. B (line 13) then goes on to produce an appreciation which, inasmuch as it can operate as a closing component, edges back into closings. The protraction of the closing hangs over into Rita's turn (line 14) when she specifically responds to the appreciation before unequivocably reinitiating closings, and, although she offers the relevancy of a second terminal with the production of a first terminal, its production within the turn is delayed by the speech token "Uh huh." Mrs. B (line 15) provides a second terminal and the call is terminated.

Thus Rita and Mrs. B have, like Joan and Linda in the previous example, protracted their closing, though using components from different closing types. In both of the examples the initial minimal movement out of closings is used to display a reluctance for terminal production while also providing for the relevancy of closings. Recipients do not just minimally respond but also postpone the reinitiation of closings, while preserving the relevancy of closings. In both examples, then, the speakers mutually protract their closing while also preserving the relevancy of closing production, and none of them attempts to drastically move out of closings. Like Joan and Linda, Rita and Mrs. B may protract their closing while retaining the relevancy of closing.

3. *Mutual displays of availability for conversation continuation.*

In contrast to a mutually protracted closing where both speakers protract a closing by reciprocal minimal movements out of closings while retaining an orientation to the relevancy of closings, both speakers can, over the course of a number of turns that move in and out of closings, display to one another mutual availability for conversation continuation.

[F:TC:I:1:22]

1 Shirley: ˙t˙hhh B't anyway I made lotta money las'night
2 °so I'm happy about that°,
3 Geri: °M-hm°.
4 (0.2)
5 Shirley: ˙p˙t En that's all that's new,
6 (0.6)
7 Shirley: ˙t˙ hhhhhh Oka:y? hhhh
8 Geri: Ye:ah, hh
9 Shirley: ˙hh s c'm over later.
10 Geri: Yeh ah'll come over I wannih (g) (·) git s'm work
11 do:ne'n then ah'll c'm over'n ah'll help Joe [:y, en
12 Shirley: [Okay,
13 (·)
14 Shirley: ˙hhhhhhh [Good w'l have coffee.
15 Geri: [°°( )°°
16 (0.3)
17 Geri: °Oka:y°
18 Shirley: Alright?
19 Geri: Mm.h [m:?
20 Shirley: [D'yih talk tih Dayna this week?
21 Geri: ˙hhh Yeh . . . .
((continues))

Shirley (line 5) provides an opportunity for further conversation or for initiating closing. That is, her "En that's all thet's new" provides an opportunity for next speaker to furnish "anything that's new with her" or for declining to offer any further material and initiate closings. Geri (line 6) does not take her turn where she could provide further material, and Shirley (line 7) then initiates closings. However, she does so in an equivocal fashion using a question intoned first close component which although initiates closings also slightly edges out of the very closing it initiates. The equivocality is reciprocated by Geri (line 8) who specifically returns with an in-conversation response as opposed to a second close component. Shirley thus equivocally initiates closings.

She slightly edges out of the closing she has initiated, and thereby may display some continued availability for conversation while also initiating closings. Geri reciprocates this continued availability by returning an in-conversation object to the question intoned first close component in a position where she could unequivocally enter into closings with the production of a second close component. Neither of them drastically moves out of conversation by continuing conversation, but while not actually continuing conversation they both display availability for continuation.

Following Geri's in-conversation response Shirley could reinitiate closings. However, she (line 9) continues out of closings with an arrangement item. Shirley does not drastically move out of closing but preserves the relevancy of closings, but neither does she reinitiate closing. An arrangement item here may display a reluctance for closings without actually abandoning closings, but inasmuch as a reinitiation of closing could have taken place here, her preservation of a minimal movement out of closings may be used to display an availability for continuation without actually continuing.

Geri (lines 10 and 11) reciprocates this reluctance. She could have drastically moved out of closings at this point in response to Shirley's displayed availability for conversation or have displayed an orientation to termination through the production of a minimal response that could provide for closing reinitiation, or indeed have minimally responded and within the turn reinitiated closings. However, she actually responds to Shirley's arrangement item in an elaborative fashion which although not drastically moving out of closings could be used to reciprocate an availability for continued conversation.

Both speakers have now displayed an availability for conversation on two occasions but neither of them has picked this up. Shirley (line 12) can now reinitiate closings. However, following the "beat" (line 13) in which Geri could begin her next turn, and return a second close component, Shirley orients to that slight delay as a no-response, and as indicative of an availability for continued conversation. She introduces another arrangement item. But again this arrangement item does not undercut the relevancy of closing and does not drastically move out of closings itself, and can, again, be used to display an availability for conversation. This is overlapped with inaudible talk from Geri (line 15), and following a period of non-speech (line 16), Geri (line 17) reinitiates closings. Shirley, however, returns with a question intoned second close component which again slightly edges out of closings, and can be used to display yet a further availability for continued conversation.

To this point, then, both speakers have displayed over the course of a number of turns that move in and out of closings that while they are not drastically moving out of closings they are nevertheless available for further conversation. Also, up to this point, neither of them has picked up the display by actually drastically moving out of closings in response to displayed availability. It can be seen that Shirley may initiate these displays, but Geri has also reciprocated them. Then Geri (line 19) produces an in-conversation object following the question intoned second close component, which now eventuates in a drastic movement out of closings with the nomination of a new topic by Shirley (line 20). This is talked to by Geri (line 21) and closings are abandoned. Both speakers having made repeated displays of availability, it is only now that this availability results in a drastic movement out of closing that undercuts the relevancy of closings. Interestingly enough, the form that the actual movement takes requires a collaborative effort by both speakers. The in-conversation object does not introduce newsworthy material, and the response nominates a topic on behalf of the person who introduced the in-conversation object. This compares with a back-reference where the drastic movement out of closings is made by one speaker.

A mutual display of availability for conversation can be seen to be done over a number of turns that move in and out of closings, and utilize component parts of various closing types. In this example the mutual display is protracted and eventuates in the abandonment of closings. Another way in which a mutual display of availability may be made is in an extended closing.

For example [NB:II:27] it was seen that both speakers display an availability for conversation through closing extension close components, but that no move out of closing was made, conversation could be sequentially found to be exhausted and termination resulted.

[NB:II:27]

A: Well I'm gonna call Neville's mother b'fore I do
anything else. So, ˙hhhh [I'll give yih a buzz'n,
B: [wuh-
* → B: AWRIGHT ho[ney,
* → A: [Okay
→ B: Awright,
→ A: O [kay dear,
* → B: [Bye,
* → A: Bye bye.

— end call —

4. *One speaker displays availability for continued conversation other speaker immediately responds.*

Where mutual displays of availability for further conversation have been made, this can, in part, be found to be the result of next speaker to a first display not having immediately responded by drastically moving out of closings but just reciprocating a displayed orientation for further conversation. Next speaker to a display of availability can, however, respond by drastically moving out of closings and undercutting the relevancy of closings.

This can be observed in some of the closing types that were examined in Section II. For example, "second turn no-response abandoned closings" where for extract [HG:15] it was seen that there was a response to a second turn no-response that provided for the introduction of further material for talk to, and the closing abandoned. Here the drastic movement out of closings that eventuated was produced as a displayed response to the no-response.

```
[HG:15]
        Nancy:   Anyw::y,=
        Hyla:    = ˙pk˙. A:nywa [:y,
        Nancy:                  [So:::,
                                  (·)
        Hyla:    ˙p=
        Nancy:   =You'll come abou:t (·) eight. Right?=
        Hyla:    =Yea::h,=
  * →   Nancy:   =Okay.
    →                             (0.2)
    →   Nancy:   Anything else to report,
                                  (0.3)
    →   Hyla:    Uh:::::::m:::,
                                  (0.4)
    →   Hyla:    Getting my hair cut tihmorrow,
        Nancy:   =Oh rilly?
                                       ((continues))
```

A display of availability can also be made by a closing extension turn that does not move out of closing. Next turn can immediately respond. In example [FD:I:66:R] it was seen that Jack moves out of closing, following Terry's close component extension. This move is a minimal arrangement movement, and is sensitive to the prior display of availability inasmuch as it continues in conversation but could have been previously produced earlier in the closing. That is, Jack can come up with something that continues in-conversation, and this is responsive to a displayed availability for conversation, inasmuch as this item could have been produced earlier but was not.

[FD:I:66:R]

Jack: See y' later,
Terry: Okay,
Jack: Okay.
Terry: Okay, ˙hh [h
Jack: [See yuh coffee time,

It is possible, then, for one speaker to display availability for continued conversation and for next speaker to be responsive and provide for continuation.

5. One speaker displays availability for continued conversation other speaker is unresponsive.

One speaker can display an availability for continued conversation but next speaker may be unresponsive, and in contrast to both an immediate response that can eventuate in a drastic movement out of closings, and to a reciprocal display of availability, next speaker may not orient to the possibility of further conversation. This can occur over the course of a number of turns. One speaker can sustain an availability, to which other speaker is consistently unresponsive though that speaker also does not "coerce" closings.

[JG:III:15:2-3]

Maggie: Well then I'll go ahead ann annu start Ronald's food
Marge: Yeah go ahead an let him eat an then if uh sheda' he
doesn't come by or something I'll ring you back. Okay?
Maggie: H'ri (bruskly)
Marge: Okay?
Maggie: Bye ((bruskly))
Marge: Okay. Iz there anything else yo:u-happen today
of any interest?
Maggie: No (0.5) huh uh. ˙hh ((throat clogged)) sevente ((clears
throat)) seventeen dollar for Ronald's teeth.
(0.5)
Marge: ( ) =

13 Maggie: =That wuz the only thing an your bank kuh checks
14 Marge: ˙hh°h: well. Okay uh then I'll letchu (   ) oh well I
15 mean I won't call you if I'm gonna – if they're gonna
16 drop me off If they're not gonna drop me off then
17 I'll jus call up
18 (0.5)
19 Ah'ri ((very bruskly))
20 Marge: Okay?
21 Maggie: Bye ((very bruskly)
22 Marge: = But go ahead an feed hi[m (   ) imagine hez starving
23 Maggie: [Yeah
24 Maggie: Yeah bye ((bruskly))
25 Marge: Okay bye.

– end call –

In this extract Marge (line 3) initiates closings but with a question intoned first close component. This can be used to indicate some reluctance for closings by equivocably initiating closings. Maggie (line 4) is unresponsive to this and does not produce an in-conversation but a second close response component that would provide for a first terminal. Marge (line 5) does not produce the first terminal component but proceeds with a close component extension that is question intoned. In both respects she displays an availability for conversation without actually moving out of closings. Maggie (line 6) is again unresponsive, and produces a first terminal.

Following the first terminal Marge (line 7) does not provide a second terminal but again produces a close component onto which she latches a topic initial elicitor. While this can make a drastic movement out of closings it requires next speaker to nominate a topic in order for the relevancy of closings to be undercut. Maggie (line 9) is yet, again, unresponsive and declines to produce a topic initial. Following a silence in which Marge could reinitiate closings, Maggie does go on, but provides a particularly non-newsworthy item, and following a silence (line 11) and an inaudible utterance from Marge (line 12), closes down the movement out of closings (line 13) and provides for the relevancy of closing reinitiation with a reiteration of prior material.

Marge (line 14) reinitiates closings, but she again moves out with an announced closure changed to an elaborated arrangement. Here she minimally moves out of closings but inasmuch as she elaborately produces arrangement material, and inasmuch as she has now displayed availability for continued conversation previously, this may be seen as yet another display of availability without actually drastically moving out of closings. Once more Maggie (line 19) is unresponsive and reinitiates closings, and yet again Marge (line 20) displays continued availability with the use of a question intoned close component. Maggie, however (line 21) preserves her unresponsiveness with the production of a first terminal. Maggie (line 22), continues to display availability. She does not produce a second terminal but provides an announced closure. This movement, although it is not a drastic movement, is curtailed by Maggie (lines 23 and 24) who minimally responds and produces a first terminal. At this point where Maggie now displays the total relevancy of termination with the production of a first terminal without a reinitiation of closings with a close component, Marge (line 25) finally produces a second terminal though she does delay its immediate production with a close component. Conversation terminates.

Over the course of a series of turns Marge has utilized various components from various closing types in order to display an availability for further conversation without, herself, actually drastically moving out of closings. Marge has remained unresponsive to Maggie's displays and results in termination.

6. *One speaker displays availability for continued conversation other speaker eventually responds.*

As opposed to continued unresponsiveness as seen above, one speaker over the course of a number of turns can display availability for continued conversation but without actually drastically moving out of closings and abandoning closing, to which the other speaker is unresponsive but becomes responsive.

[Lerner:SF:II:24]

1 Mark: =having talk't JoAnn I did wanna git thee f:ful skinny.=
2 Bob: =hh-hhhhh ˙hh Okha(h)ky,
3 Mark: ˙t˙ hhhh so:: I::, hh thought I'd-give yih a bu:zz.
4 Bob: Okay Mark glad yih did.
5 Mark Oka:y en: dah, hh ˙hh ulble talkin to yuh Friday. h
6 (0.2)
7 Bob: Oka:y.:
8 Mark: =Have a happy Thanksgivee:n a:nd uh(·)mm-khhh may
9 all yer dreams c'm true.=
10 Bob: =W I thank you:. thank you.

(·)

12 Mark: [[Ah–
13 Bob: [[Wee' yih doin t'morruh [night. Anythin [:g,
14 Mark: [·hhhhhhhhhhhh [Oh:: : uh
15 we–e:ll

((continues)

Bob (line 2) initiates closings. Mark (line 3) minimally moves out of closings by reiterating reason-for-call. Bob (line 4) curtails this movement by reinitiating closings before minimally responding to the prior utterance. Mark (line 5) provides a second close component but again minimally moves out of closings with an arrangement item. Bob (line 7) curtails this movement by reinitiating closings. Mark (line 8) then produces a solicitude in second closing turn, of the reinitiated closing.

Thus Mark has minimally moved out of closings on three occasions and over the course of these movements, although not actually abandoning the relevancy of closings, can display an availability for continued conversation. On the other hand, Bob has not just been unresponsive up to this point but has curtailed even the minimal movements.

However, following Mark's solicitude Bob becomes responsive to Mark's display of availability and appreciates the solicitude (line 10), and overlapped with Mark (line 12), provides for the continuation of conversation (line 13) with an enquiry into Mark's plans for the next day. This is immediately taken up by Mark (line 13) and the closing abandoned. Mark has thus sustained a display of availability for continued conversation without actually abandoning the relevancy of closings, to which Bob has not just been unresponsive, but actually goes for termination, and then eventually responds.

7. *One speaker continues conversation other speaker responds.*

In contrast to the various displays of availability for continued conversation, one speaker may actually continue conversation, and this can be reciprocated in next turn. This can be seen for some of the second turn abandoned closings, for example "second turn back-reference abandoned closings." When example [Kr:D+R:14:b:1] was examined it was seen that a second turn back-reference can retopicalize prior material, drastically move out of closings, and provide for next speaker to produce a proper sequential response. Neither the back-reference turn nor the next turn provide for the relevancy of closings, and the closing was abandoned. Here, then, one speaker actually continues conversation and the next speaker reciprocates.

[Kr:D+R:14:b:1]

	Robin:	Hm
		(2.0)
* →	Robin:	Awright °David°
→	David:	So what did the baby say.
→	Robin:	Oh: he ass: f'yo. He slep' with me two nights this
→		wee:k he ass fih you in the morning. . . .
		((continues))

8. One speaker continues conversation other speaker goes for closing resulting in termination.

In the above example one speaker continues conversation and next speaker reciprocates. However, one speaker can continue conversation and the next speaker does not reciprocate but goes for closings. This can be seen for some of the curtailed second turn abandoned closings. For example, a curtailed second turn in-conversation object abandoned closing. It was seen when fragment [TC1(b)13:6] was examined that a second turn in-conversation object that could drastically move out of closings had this potentiality curtailed by next turn response that resulted in the reinitiation of closings that then went to termination.

[TC1(b):13:6]

	Linda:	. . . . but .hhhhhhhh try tih git Deeanna's about seven.
* →	Jerry:	Oka:y,
→	Linda:	So:: [I
→	Jerry:	[Later
		(·)
→	Linda:	Okay honey.
* →	Jerry:	Gih bye=.
* →	Linda:	=Bye bye.
		– end call –

One speaker can continue conversation, other speaker can go for closing and this can result in the continuing speaker deferring, and termination eventuates.

9. One speaker continues conversation other speaker goes for closing resulting in continuation.

One speaker may continue conversation with one of the second turn abandoned closing types, and next speaker may go for closings by curtailing the drastic movement out of closings. But in the reinitiated closing termination may not result as in the example above, but conversation may continue, through another second turn abandoned closing type being produced. For example [Erhardt:8:3] the reinitiated closing where a drastic movement is made is, again, not responded to, but the second reinitiated closing is abandoned, continuation being deferred to.

```
[Erhardt:8:3]
           Pam:    I wz js calling you en finding out.
                                   (·)
*   → Pam:    ˙hnn Okay Well thank you anyway [cuti  ]cle [(        ).
°   → Vicky:                 °Oh:°            [Yeah. ]    [I:-
°   → Vicky:  I- have a: class Thursday.
                                   (0.9)
°   → Vicky:  a:nd
                                   (0.2)
*   → Pam:    O[ka::     ]y
°   → Vicky:   [Yihknow, ]
                                   (·)
°   → Vicky:  every Thursday ˙hh thou:gh starting December
°             seventeenth I won't ˙hh
                                   (0.3)
*   → Pam:    ↑Oka:y,
(*) → Vicky:  Ok[a:y?
    → Pam:      [We:ll, then thanks anyway.
°   → Vicky:  Yeh I'm sorry [Pam,  ]
    → Pam:                  [Oh wl ] it's not yer problem=
    → Vicky:  =Yeh it woulda been better if . . . . .
```

IV. Conclusion

The conclusion is simple. Speakers can produce a variety of closing types within which negotiations for conversation continue or conversation termination can take place, and through the use of various closing type components, and in the course of movements in and out of closings, also negotiate for conversation continuation or abandonment.

Closings, indeed, provide a sequential environment in which a rich array of delicate interactions can take place.

ACKNOWLEDGMENTS

Some aspects of this paper were first considered in "No-Close Closings," presented at the International Conference on Practical Reasoning and Discourse Processes, St. Hughes College, Oxford. As on other occasions I am very grateful, and in debt, to Gail Jefferson. She provided a collated corpus of data without which this analysis could not have proceeded. She also revealed the operation of a number of devices in closings that had not been previously noted, and discussed some of the fragments of conversation presented. This does not mean that she is associated with any defects that might be found in this analysis.

NOTES

1. Closing implicative environments mark that no further newsworthy items are being introduced. Arrangements can operate in this way inasmuch as they provide for a "future" encounter and can then signal that no further newsworthy items are being introduced for "this" conversation. Reiterations of prior material can also operate in this way when they occupy a turn where a new topic could be initiated. Announcements of closure are another closing implicative environment. Others that have been pointed to are topic bounding techniques, aphoristic conclusions that draw a point (Schegloff and Sacks, 1973), "request-satisfaction topics," and "complaint-remedy topics" (Davidson, 1978). These sequential environments occasion the relevancy of closing initiation.

2. "Sequence types" that move out of closings previously examined were "arrangements," "solicitudes," "reason-for-calls," "appreciation," "back-references," "in-conversation objects," and "topic initial elicitors," (Button, 1987). Where these sequence types figure in what follows the typical trajectory they project, and their typical operation in closings that was previously examined will just be documented in the form of a brief resume. A detailed exposition will not be re-presented.

Movements out of closings will be examined in terms of first and second, and first or second closing turns. It is within these turns that movements out of closings mainly occur and the varieties of closing types mainly originate.

3. Items that are used to both minimally respond to prior and can also be possible close components, operate as "pivots" between the sequence type and the reinitiation of closings.

4. Topic initial elicitors are the only sequence type designed for third turn. Only two cases were found where they occurred elsewhere: in example [HG:15] as a response to no-response, and in a closing to a monotopical call where they operated to throw the conversation "open." Because they do not make a systematic appearance in first or second turn they will not be considered in detail. However, the following aspects of their operation can be noted because they are mentioned in section III.

Topic initial elicitors are used to provide for the introduction of further newsworthy items. They make enquiries in this respect, but can be found to "prefer" the initiation of new topics and the introduction of further newsworthy items. They require the collaboration of next speaker who produces the newsworthy item, but if that is not forthcoming closings can be re-entered. Inasmuch as they "prefer" newsworthy item presentation they make drastic movement out of closings unless a decline to present newsworthy items is produced in which case they eventuate in a minimal movement (Button, 1987). See Button and Casey (1984) for a detailed description of topic initial elicitor sequences.

5. Note that the reinitiation is a question intoned first close component. In this example the reinitiated closing does not go to termination.

6. Foreshortening and extending closings (mentioned in the next part of this section) received more extensive attention in the previous analysis of movements out of closings. They are briefly introduced here since many of the reinitiated closings for other closing types can be seen to take a foreshortened or extended form, and because reference is made to them in Section III.

7. Judy Davidson (1978) has previously investigated an instance of negotiation in closings.

REFERENCES

Button, G. 1987. Moving out of closings. In G. Button and J. R. G. Lee, Eds., *Talk and Social Organization,* Clevedon: Multilingual Matters, Ltd.

Button, G. and Casey, N. J., 1984. Generatin's topic. In J. M. Atkinson and J. Heritage, Eds., *Structures of Social Action: Studies in Conversation Analysis,* Cambridge University Press.

Davidson, J. 1978. An instance of negotiation in a call closing. *Sociology,* vol. 12, no. 1, pp. 123–133.

Schegloff, E. A., and Sacks, H. 1973. Opening up closings. *Semiotica,* VIII, pp. 289–327.

Modifications of Invitations, Offers and Rejections

Judy Arlene Davidson

Davidson examines invitations, offers, requests, and proposals in conversation to discover how these types of utterances are modified when those who make them are faced with either the possibility or actuality of rejection. And, similarly, when those who reject such invitations, offers, etc. are faced either with the possibility or actuality that the one who made the invitation or offer is not going to go along with the rejection, they may modify their rejection in an effort to deal with this possibility.

Interactants are shown to be sensitive to these possibilities and next turns display such sensitivities.

Modifications and revisions can be produced in various ways but the data show that both participants are able to recognize and deal with such changes in the course of their interaction. The study offers further corroboration of the close order monitoring by interactants of one another's utterances in the course of their production.

I. Introduction

The doing of an object such as an offer, invitation, request, proposal, etc., sets up that a relevant next object can be either an acceptance or a rejection:[1]

INSTANCE #1. Acceptance (SBL 5, p. 18)

Request A: We:ll, will you help me [ou:t.
Acceptance B: [I certainly wi:ll.

INSTANCE #2. Rejection (trip)

Offer A: You wan' me bring you anything.
Rejection (0.4)
B: No: no: nothing.

Now in turn, the doing of a *rejection* of an object such as an invitation or offer sets up that in the next turn there are at least two sequentially relevant possibilities: (1) that that rejection will be the end of the matter, i.e., inviter or offerer[2] will "accept" or go along with the rejection, or (2) that inviter or offerer will *not* go along with the rejection, such that there may be a series of re-offers or re-invitations. That is, as Harvey Sacks (1971) has pointed out, when an offer is rejected, the rejection may not be the end of the matter, and instead there may be a series of re-offers, where each successive offer may be different in some way from the prior offer. Instances #3 and #4 display these two post-rejection possibilities:

INSTANCE #3. Rejection not followed by re-offer or new offer (NB 45, p. 171)

Offer M: C'n I: add anything fuh you::?=
Rejection A: ˙hh Oh: honey thanks I think I:: I'll let
Sam go.=[Maybe he'll get some fi:sh.
M: [↓(eYes).
(·)
M: eYes.

INSTANCE #4. Rejection followed by series of offers (NB 52, p. 266)

Offer P: Don'tchu want me tuh come down'n getchu
t'morrow en take yih down: duh the beauty parlor
(0.3)
Rejection A: What ↓for.=I jus' did my hair it looks like pruh
uh pruhfessional.
(0.4)
Offer P: Oh I mean uh: you wanna go t'the store er anything

over et the Market [Basket er anything?]
A: [·hhhhhhhhhhhhhhhhhh] h=
A: =Well ho[ney (I-)]
P: [Or Ri] chard's?
(0.2)
Rejection A: I've bou:ght ev'rythai:ng,

This paper will examine two sorts of phenomena: (1) Inviters, offerers, requestors, proposers, etc., when faced with either the possibility or the actuality of rejection may revise, modify, or add onto their invitations, offers, requests, proposals, etc., in an attempt to deal with this possible or actual rejection. (2) Similarly, when rejectors are faced with either the possibility or the actuality that inviter or offerer is *not* going to go along with the rejection and may instead press for acceptance, rejectors may then in turn revise, modify, or add onto their rejections in an attempt to deal with this possibility or actuality.

II. Revised or Modified Invitations and Offers[3]

A. Post-invitation silence as possible pre-rejection.

Instances #5 and #6 have in common that in line 1, there is an invitation, followed by a silence in line 2, followed by inviter's producing some further object in line 3:

INSTANCE #5. (NB 43, p. 150)

1 C: Well yih c'n both sta:y.
2 (0.4)
3 C: [Got plenty a roo:m,
B: [Oh I-

INSTANCE #6. (NB 38, p. 92)

1 B: C'mon down he:re,=it's oka:y,
2 (0.2)
3 B: I got lotta stuff,=I got be:er en stuff 'n

It will be argued here that the silence in line 2 in each instance is taken by inviter as a display that the recipient of the invitation is finding the invitation troublesome or problematic in some way, and that the utterance in line 3 in each instance is an attempt to deal with this possible trouble. Pomerantz (1978), in talking about sequences in which an object such as an assertion is followed by a silence, states:

> What was taken for granted as adequate for its purposes at time of delivery can be called up for review by virtue of what it engenders. Gaps, faltering starts, hedges, etc. may accountably occasion a review of the prior assertion motivated to find a way to altering it to now-clear-and-understandable. (p. 4)

Although Pomerantz was talking about such objects as assertions, there is some evidence that her findings are also applicable to objects such as invitations and offers. Consider the following instance:

INSTANCE #7. (SBL 22, p. 203)

1 A: ˙hh Yihknow id be kinda ni::ce, (·) to:o,=˙hh uh(m):
2 (0.2) ˙hh I was thinking about goin– when we go over tuh
3 church w::why wouldn't it be nice tuh play ↑pa:rt↓ners.
4 (0.3)
5 A: Or wouldja li:ke that.

Now in contrast to the sorts of objects Pomerantz was examining, where the trouble was taken to be with the clarity or understandability of an assertion, note that in Instance #7, speaker A takes the silence in line 4 as displaying trouble not with issues of clarity or understandability, but specifically with issues of the *acceptability* of the proposal in lines 1-3. That is, at least in some cases, an inviter or offerer, upon hearing a silence post the invitation or offer, may take this silence as displaying specifically that recipient is having some sort of trouble or problem with the acceptability of that invitation or offer as it stands so far. In other words, a silence post an object such as an invitation or offer may be taken as a *pre-rejection* silence. Now as Pomerantz (1978) further states:

> One domain that may be critically reviewed is the initial assertion's formulation with respect to referential adequacy. (p. 4)

Again, although she was referring to objects such as assertions, her findings are applicable here: an inviter or offerer, on hearing such a silence which he takes as a pre-rejection silence, may review his initial invitation or offer for its possible inadequacies which may be the source of the possible unacceptability of the invitation or offer as it stands so far. And if inviter or offerer then cares to display[4] an attempt to deal with whatever is causing the possible unacceptability of the invitation or offer as it stands so far, one thing he may do following such a post-invitation or post-offer silence is to produce some revision, modification, addition, "correction," etc. of the original invitation or offer, where such a revision or modification would possibly deal with whatever trouble or problem was causing the unacceptability of the invitation or offer as it originally stood. In Instances #5 and #6, the proposal is that the object in line 3 is just such an attempt on the part of inviter to deal with some sort of trouble, inadequacy, problem, etc., with the invitation as it originally stood in line 1:

INSTANCE #5. (NB 43, p. 150)

Invitation	1	C:	Well yih c'n both sta:y.
	2		(0.4)
Revision	3	C:	Got plenty a roo:m,

INSTANCE #6. (NB 38, p. 92)

Invitation	1	B:	C'mon down he:re,=it's oka:y,
	2		(0.2)
Revision	3	B:	I got lotta stuff,=I got be:er en stuff'n

These objects in line 3, i.e., the modifications or revisions of the invitation, are the products of the inviter's analysis of the possible trouble or inadequacy of the invitation as it stood in line 1. That is, up to this point in the sequence, recipient has said nothing. Again, Pomerantz (1978) points out:

> What the "trouble" may be is not specified or indicated as such, in and through the gaps, qualified turn starts, etc.; that indeed is a product of such a search or critical review. (p. 4)

Now the sorts of objects which are used in this sequential position, i.e., following a post-invitation silence, and which I am terming modifications or revisions, may come from different classes of objects and may be doing very different sorts of interactional work such as inducing, giving reasons why recipient should accept, dealing with possible objections recipient may have about the invitation or offer, adding more details of what the invitation or offer involves, etc., but sequentially, they have the following features in common: first of all, they display that the inviter or offerer is taking the silence as a pre-rejection silence and is attempting to deal with this possibility of rejection by producing some revised or modified version of the invitation or offer, where this next version might now make it possible or desirable for recipient to accept. Secondly, these revised or modified versions provide a next place for recipient to do some sort of response, such as an acceptance. That is, Jefferson (1978), in talking about instances in which the recipient of a story, rather than doing something such as an appreciation of the story at its end, instead is silent or produces tangential talk, states about such cases:

> Storytellers do not explicitly challenge or complain of tangential recipient talk (as they do not complain of recipient silence). Instead, they propose that the story was not yet completed by offering a next story component. Upon completion of that component, a next point occurs at which the story can be responded to, . . . and thus, at least an opportunity for, and perhaps an invitation to, a different order of response—in the case of tangential talk, a more fitted response—is provided by an added story component. (pp. 233–234)

Similarly, in Instances #5 and #6, if an inviter or offerer gets no response (such as an acceptance) after the original invitation or offer:

Invitation C: Well yih c'n both sta:y.
→ → (0.4)

then in doing a modified or revised version of the invitation or offer, a next place is provided for a response, possibly but not necessarily an acceptance[5] (in the instance below, the revised version of the invitation gets a weak rejection):

Invitation C: Well yih c'n both sta:y.

(0.4)

Revision C: [Got plenty a' room,
B: [Oh I-

(·)

→ → B: Oh(h)o(h)o please don't tempt me,

B. Post-invitation rejection.

Just as an inviter or offerer may take a post-invitation silence as a display that recipient was having some sort of trouble with the invitation or offer as it stood, where this trouble was specifically with issues of the acceptability of the invitation or offer, so an inviter or offerer may take an *actual* rejection as a display of some sort of trouble that recipient is having with the acceptability of the invitation or offer as it was originally put. And again, if inviter or offerer cares to display an attempt to deal with this possible trouble with his invitation or offer, he may then produce some sort of revision, modification, "correction," etc., of the invitation or offer following this actual rejection of its first version. In Instances #8 and #9, there is an initial invitation or offer, followed by a rejection, and this rejection in turn is followed by inviter's or offerer's producing some sort of modification or revision of the original invitation or offer:

INSTANCE #8. (V-II)

Invitation A: . . . you c'n ahl come up here,

(0.3)

Rejection B: Nah that's alright wil stay down he[re,
Revision A: [We've gotta color T. V:,

INSTANCE #9. (Computer)

Offer A: Oh I was gonna sa:y if you wannid to:,=˙hh you could meet me at U.C. B: an' I could show yih some a' the other things on the compu:ter, (·) maybe even teach yuh how tuh program Ba:sic er something.˙hhh

(0.6)

Rejection B: Wul I don' know if I'd wanna get all that invo:lved, hh˙ hhh![(˙hh)
Revision A: [It's rilly intresti:ng:. (0.2) I

showed Tom how tuh pro- (·) how do: uh:
program a: ˙hhh the computer doo: make a ra:ndom
number cha:rt, eh heh! ˙hh! An' that rilly turned
'im o:n,

Sequentially speaking, the doing of such a post-rejection modified or revised invitation or offer provides a next place for another response, possibly acceptance (but, of course, possibly another rejection). That is, if an inviter or offerer does not get acceptance after the initial version of the invitation or offer:

Initial Version A: . . . you c'n ahl come up here,
→ → B: REJECTION

Initial Version A: . . . maybe even teach yuh how tuh program Basic er something.
→ → B: REJECTION

then the doing of a revised or modified invitation or offer provides a further place for recipient to respond, possibly with an acceptance, but also possibly with another rejection:

Initial Version A: . . . maybe even teach yuh how tuh program
Ba:sic er something. hhhh
Rejection B: Wul I don' know if I'd wanna get all that
invo:lved, hh˙ hhh! [(˙hh)
Revised Version A: [It's rilly intresti:ng:.
(0.2) I showed Tom how tuh pro- (·) how
do: uh: program a: ˙hhh the computer doo:
make a ra:ndom number cha:rt, eh heh! ˙hh!
An' that rilly turned 'im o:n,
(·)
Acceptance → → B: Hih! huh! huh! huh! (·) ˙hhhh! ((sniff))
We:ll,=how 'bout if I do meet you in the
computer center tomorrow then.

Initial Version A: . . . you c'n ahl come up here,
(0.3)
Rejection B: Nah, that's alright wil stay down he[re,
Revised Version A: [We've
gotta color T.V.:,

Rejection	→ → B:	˙tch ˙hh I know but u- we're watching the Ascent 'v Ma:n, ˙hh en then the phhreview: so: y'know wil miss something if we come over.

C. Revisions or modifications following weak agreements.

Following an invitation or offer, recipient may sometimes produce what Pomerantz (1975) calls a "sequentially weak agreement form," such as "hm," "uh huh," "yeah," etc. She says about such weak agreements:

> While they occur in agreement sequences . . . they also occur in disagreement sequences, for example as passes past possible disagreement points. Given the relevance of agreement/disagreement, the production of weak agreements may be disagreement-implicative. (p. 82)

Generalizing her findings to invitation or offer sequences, in which the relevance is acceptance/rejection, then a weak agreement following an invitation or offer may be taken by inviter or offerer as possibly pre-rejection. Again, inviter or offerer may take this possible pre-rejection as coming from some sort of trouble recipient is having with the acceptability of the invitation or offer as it stands. And again, if inviter or offerer cares to deal with this possible trouble, he may then revise or modify his invitation or offer in an attempt to perhaps make it now acceptable to recipient. In Instances #10 and #11, there is an invitation and a request, each followed by a weak agreement, then followed by inviter's and requestor's doing some sort of modified or revised version of the initial invitation or request:

INSTANCE #10. (SBL 27, p. 250)

Invitation	A:	So I jus' wan' duh tell yih if you'd come we- we're inviting the kinnergarden teachers too becuz we think it's a good chance tuh get tuh know the mothers.
Weak Agreement	B:	Uh huh.=
Revision	A:	=˙hh So if yer free*:. (·) It's et the youth hou:se.

INSTANCE #11. (NB 48, p. 201)

Request A: Uh will you call 'im tuhnight for me.=
Weak Agreement B: =eYea:h,
(·)
Revision A: Plea:::se.

Again, as in the instances of revisions or modifications following a silence or an actual rejection, the doing of a revised or modified invitation or offer following a weak agreement provides a next place for recipient to do some further response, possibly, but not necessarily, an acceptance. In Instance #10, the revised version gets a weak acceptance:

Revision A: =˙hh So if yer free*:. (·) It's et the youth hou:se.
(·)
Acceptance B: We:ll? (·) ez far ez I kno:w, (0.5) I will be.

In Instance #11, the revised version gets a more emphatic agreement:

Revision A: Plea:::se.=
Agreement B: =eYe:ah.

D. Extension of invitation or offer beyond first possible completion point.

Jefferson (1973) has shown that speakers have the "technical capacity" to precisely place their talk at such places as the possible or actual completion point of an utterance. Now with respect to objects such as invitations and offers, recipients, in doing acceptances, can and do place their acceptances at first possible completion point, or as in the case of Instance #13, in the middle of the word which is a possible completion point:

INSTANCE #12. (SBL 5, p. 18)

Request A: We:ll, will you help me [out.
Acceptance B: [I certainly wi:ll.

INSTANCE #13. (TC shopping)

Proposal A: Hey maybe some Saturday we c'd have the guys watch the kids ('n we c'd) go Christmas

shop[ping.
Acceptance B: [eYeah:.=Right.=
Tommy's gonnuh: be all for that.[6]

In these instances, acceptance was done either at first possible completion point or even a little before. Now there is some evidence that if inviter does not hear acceptance at first possible completion point, he may take this as possible pre-rejection:

INSTANCE #14. (TC 10)

A: Uh: ↑would it be: alright if we came in a little early or (·) uh::
would that upsetchu[r
B: [I: don't think so.

In this instance, requestor, upon not hearing acceptance at first possible completion point (i.e., after "early"), seems to be taking this lack of acceptance as possibly displaying that recipient might be going to reject the request. Now in Instance #14, requestor is doing what might be called a marked version of displaying that the absence of acceptance at first possible completion point is being taken as pre-rejection, but in other cases, inviters and offerers may use what might be called unmarked forms: rather than specifically questioning recipient about the acceptability of the offer or invitation, as was done in Instance #14, they instead modify or revise the offer or invitation by extending it beyond one or more possible completion points:

INSTANCE #15. (NB 52, p. 266)

P: Oh I mean uh: you wanna go t'the store er anything over et the
Market Basket er anything?

INSTANCE #16. (NB 38, p. 85)

B: Wanna come down'n have a bite a lunch with me:?=I got some
be:er en stuff,

In each instance, first possible completion point is in fact not the end of the utterance: in Instance #15, the components "er anything," "over et the Market Basket," and "er anything" follow the first possible completion point ("store"). In Instance #16, the first possible completion point "lunch" is followed by the additional components "with me" and "I got some beer en stuff." Now Jefferson (1973), in analyzing the utterance "You want sumpn to do Carol?", states about such tag-positioned components (i.e., those occurring after a first possible completion point):

> A question that invites its recipient to do a task may be well-constructed if it orients to such issues; if, for example, it designs its components to make it possible to scrutinize the elapsed time between question and answer for a recipient's willingness or reluctance, not merely to speak, but to take up the task. (1973, p. 73)

Similary, in Instances #15 and #16, the addition of the tag-positioned components may be providing a place for inviter or offerer to monitor for whether or not there is a response such as an acceptance. Then, in not hearing acceptance at this point, i.e., at first possible completion point and in overlap with the tag-positioned component, inviter or offerer may then add yet more components onto the invitation or offer, modifying it in an attempt to make it now perhaps more acceptable to recipient.

III. Revised or Modified Rejections

E. Rejection finalizers.

Just as the doing of an invitation, offer, request, proposal, etc., sets up that in the next turn a sequentially appropriate next object can be either an acceptance or a rejection, so the doing of a rejection in turn sets up that in the turn following it, a sequentially appropriate object can be either something which displays that inviter or offerer either is or is not going to go along with, "agree with," "accept" the rejection. Furthermore, as it was argued in Part II that inviters and offerers may modify or revise their invitations and offers to deal with possible or actual rejection, it will similarly be proposed that *rejectors,* when faced with either the possibility or the actuality that inviter or offerer is *not* going to go along with the rejection, may revise or modify their rejections in an attempt to get inviters and offerers to go along with the rejection.[7]

Now a first consideration must be the following: what sorts of objects display that inviter or offerer *is* going to go along with, "agree with," or "accept" the rejection? Consider the instances below:

INSTANCE #17. (Cookout)

```
Invitation    A:  Why don't we get [together ↑Fri:dee ni:ght,=
              B:                   [Uh.
              A:  =An' have a cookout er sumpin.
                                 (·)
              B:  F:riday ni:ght. [hh
              A:                  [See see (watsch) up on yer schedule.
                                 (0.5)
              B:  Fri::day ni: [ght.
              A:               [Ya:h) we thought thad be °a good
                  (night).°
                                 (·)
              A:  °(night tuh do tha:t)°
              B:  °Friday night.°
                   (12.5)  ((B is off phone speaking to third party))
              B:  We:- uh:: kymmm! ˙hh [h
              A:                       [(                  [   )
Rejection     B:                                           [ha- had
                  received an invitation: ˙hhh to: uh: ((sniff)) °have
                  dinner with some people in Los Angeles [::.°
      → →     A:                                         [°↑O:↓o::h.°
```

INSTANCE #18. (V-II)

```
Invitation    A:  I ca:lled um to see if you want to uh
                                 (0.4)
              A:  C'm over en watch, the Classics Theater.
                                 (0.3)
              A:  Cindy'n Bob 'n I,=
              B:  =She Sto [ops t'Conquer?
              A:           [(  )-
                                 (0.4)
              A:  Yeh.
                                 (0.3)
Rejection     B:  Mom js asked me t'watch it with her, h=
      → →     A:  =Oh. Okay,
```

INSTANCE #19. (V-II)

Invitation A: Y' c'd all c'm up'n have apple crisps?
(0.2)
A: Is that any temptation.
(·)
Rejection B: ˙hh No: Annie really it's not.=Cindy's not even over: hh˙ here yet.
→ → A: Oh I see.

INSTANCE #20. (Trip)
I
Offer A: You wan' me bring you anything?
(0.4)
Rejection B: No: no: nothing.
→ → A: Aw:kay.
(·)
B: Thank you.
(·)
A: Awkay buh bye:

INSTANCE #21. (NB 36, p. 45)

Offer C: ˙hh Hey I gotta good trip if he wans tuh go:,=it's on a Mondee though ken 'e go on tha[t,
Rejection A: [No he's goin' with th' Gas Compny 'e's all booked up so that'll be enough fer him.
(0.6)
→ → C: Oh:.

INSTANCE #22. (SF II)

Invitation A: 'f we have a game you wanna come on out?
(0.2)
Rejection B: ˙k ˙hhhhh uh:: give me a ca:ll?=A:nd uh ah'll letche kno:w.hh=I: don't thi:nk the:t ah'll be financially: uh:: stable,=˙hh [hh= enough to really p'ticipa:te,=
A: [Mm hm.
B: =In thee uh festivities,
→ → A: ↓Oh.

In each instance, the rejection is followed by an object (arrowed in each instance) such as "oh," "oh I see," "okay," or "alright." It will be argued that such objects, when they occur post a rejection, are displaying that in some way inviter or offerer is going along with, "accepting," or "agreeing with" the rejection.

Now at the point in the sequence at which there has been an offer or invitation followed by a rejection, there are two conflicting "proposals" outstanding: (1) that what the invitation or offer proposes be the outcome of this segment of interaction and (2) that what the rejection proposes be the outcome of this segment of interaction. And at this point in the sequence-so-far, i.e., where there have been just an invitation or offer and its rejection, it is still in question as to which of these two "proposals" will in fact be the outcome. That is, the mere doing of a rejection does not mean that it will be the outcome; at this point in the sequence, it still has the status of a proposal. Now by doing an object such as "all right," "okay," "oh," or "oh I see," what inviter or offerer is displaying is that he *is* going to go along with what the rejection proposes, i.e., that it rather than the invitation or offer be the outcome of this segment of interaction. Furthermore, inviter or offerer, in producing such an object, also thereby displays that he is "conceding" his proposal, i.e., "conceding" that his invitation or offer be the outcome. What this in turn means is that the doing of an object such as "oh," "okay," "allright," etc., post a rejection displays that for the time being anyhow, inviter or offerer will do no further objects which would push for acceptance, such as revised or modified invitations or offers. This in turn means that the rejection is thereby being taken by inviter or offerer as *final* rejection. For purposes of terminology, objects such as "oh," "oh I see," "okay," and "alright," when they occur post a rejection, will be called *rejection finalizers.* [8]

Parenthetically, that an inviter or offerer has displayed through the use of a rejection finalizer that he is taking the rejection as final does not mean that there will be no further re-issues of the invitation or offer within that interaction. In particular, invitations and offers may be re-done, perhaps in modified versions, if the circumstances under which the rejection was taken as final have changed. In the instance below, there is a series of offers and rather firm rejections:

INSTANCE #23. NB 52, p. 266)

Offer	1	P:	D̲on'tchu want me tuh come down'n getchu
	2		t'morrow en take yih down: duh the beauty parlor,

	3		(0.3)
Rejection	4	A:	What ↓for.=I jus' did my hair it looks like pruh uh
	5		prufhessional.
	6		(0.4)
Offer	7	P:	Oh I mean uh: you wanna go t'the store er anything
	8		over et the Market [Basket er anything?]
	9	A:	[·hhhhhhhhhhhhhhhhhhh] h=
	10	A:	=Well ho[ney (I-)]
	11	P:	[Or Ri] chard's?
	12		(0.2)
Rejection	13	A:	I've bou:ght ev'rythai:ng,
	14		(0.9)
	15	A:	If [you want me tuh go t'the beaudy pahler ah wi:ll,
Finalizer	16	P:	[Oh.
Offer	17	P:	Well I jus' thought maybe we g'd go over tuh
	18		Richard's fer lunch then after I get muh hair fixed.=
	19	A:	=A:ri:ght.

In line 16, offerer produces a rejection finalizer, which happens to occur in overlap with rejector's doing something which indicates that she's backing down from her previous hard line of rejecting whatever was offered and that she's now possibly open to further offers. That is, rejector's saying "If you want me tuh go t'the beaudy pahler ah wi:ll," now changes the circumstances under which the finalizer was produced, and offerer thereafter immediately does yet another offer (lines 17-18). What this instance demonstrates is that rejection finalizers may operate rather locally, such that following a rejection which was taken as final, invitations and offers may be re-done under certain circumstances.

F. Post-rejection revised invitations and offers.[9]

In the previous section, it was proposed that a class of objects termed *rejection finalizers* display that inviter or offerer is taking the rejection as final. Now in contrast, what sorts of objects display that inviter or offerer is *not* taking the rejection as final? A first sort of object which will be considered is just the sort of revised or modified invitation or offer which was examined in PART II:

INSTANCE #24. (V-II)

Invitation	A:	. . . you c'n ahl come up here,
		(0.3)

Rejection B: Nah that's alright wil stay down he[re,
Revision →→ A: [We've gotta color T. V:,

INSTANCE #25. (NB 52, p. 248)

Offer P: Wul lissid- (·) uh:: d'you wah me uh come down'n getche t'[morrow er anythi]ng?
Rejection A: [N o : d e a r.]
(·)
A: No:, [I'm fine.
Revision →→ P: [To the store] er any[thing,

In PART II, it was proposed that these sorts of revised or modified invitations and offers displayed attempts on the part of inviter or offerer to deal with the rejection. That is, the revision or modification of an invitation or offer may be a display by inviter or offerer that the rejection came from some inadequacy with the original invitation or offer, such that if this inadequacy is corrected or remedied through a modified or revised invitation or offer, then perhaps the invitation or offer will now be accepted. It is in this way that the doing of a modified or revised version of an invitation or offer post rejection displays that inviter or offerer is taking that rejection as *non-final.*

Now from *rejector's* point of view, that his rejection is being taken as non-final as displayed through this revised or modified invitation or offer, means that if rejector cares[10] to get his rejection taken as final, then one thing he can do post such a revised or modified invitation or offer is in turn to do some sort of modification or revision *of the rejection:*

Initial Version of Rejection B: Nah that's alright wil stay down he[re,
A: [We've gotta color T.V.:,
Modified Version of Rejection B: ˙tch ˙hh I know but u- we're watching the Ascent 'v Ma:n, ˙hh en then the phhreview: so: y'know wil miss something if we come over.

Initial Version of Rejection A: No: dear.
(·)

	A:	No:, [I'm fine.
	P:	[To the store] er any[thing,
Revised Version of	A:	[·hh I've
Rejection		got evrything bought dear,

Such a modified or revised rejection provides a next place for inviter or offerer to do a rejection finalizer. That is, if rejector does not get a rejection finalizer after the original version of the rejection, then the doing of a modified or revised rejection now provides a next place for inviter to do a rejection finalizer:[11]

Initial Version	B:	Nah that's alright wil stay down he[re,
	A:	[We've gotta color T. V:,
Revised Version	B:	·tch ·hh I know but u- we're watchin:g the Ascent 'v Ma:n, ·hh en then the phhreview: so: y'know wil miss something if we come over.
Finalizer → →	A:	°'khay°

G. Post-rejection silence.

In the previous section, it was proposed that a first kind of object which rejector may take as displaying that inviter or offerer is not going to take the rejection as final was a revised or modified invitation or offer post the first version of the rejection. Now a second kind of object which rejector may take as displaying that inviter or offerer is possibly not going to take the rejection as final is a silence following a first version of a rejection:

INSTANCE #26. (NB 47, p. 181)

Offer	B:	I':ll: take er in Sun[dee.=
	A:	[·hhh=
Rejection	A:	=OH:: NO:: Portia.
→ →		(0.2)

INSTANCE #27. (NB 47, p. 181)

Offer	B:	Er: we c'n: take 'er: uh: (0.2) (·hh) to the bus staysh- uwell let's see well I: don't go to work until three:,
		(0.2)

Rejection A: Oh no I wouldn't ask yuh tuh do that Portia,
→ → (0.3)

INSTANCE #28. (SBL 25, p. 239)[12]

B: Wuh listen then we're jus' gonna s- ah uh Sam en I are gonna stay home,=then,
(1.0)
A: W:hy:: [:.
Rejection B: [nNo:, (·) becuz now that's reediculous.
→ → (1.0)

Now in PART II, it was proposed that a post-invitation or post-offer silence is sometimes taken by inviter or offerer as a display that recipient is having some sort of trouble with the acceptability of the invitation or offer, such that following this silence, inviter or offerer may produce some modified or revised version to deal with the possibility of rejection. Similarly, it is being proposed here that a rejector, on hearing a silence post his rejection, may sometimes take this silence as a display that inviter or offerer is finding the rejection inadequate in some way for purposes of being taken as final rejection. And again, if rejector wants to deal with this possibility, then following such a post-rejection silence, he may produce some sort of modified or revised version of the rejection:

INSTANCE #26.

Initial Version A: =OH:: NO:: Portia.
(0.2)
Revised Version A: Oh m[y Go::d n]o: Portia.
P: [eeYea::h.]

INSTANCE #27.

Initial Version A: Oh no I wouldn't ask yuh tuh do that Portia.
(0.3)
Revised Version A: That's (just) too much tuh go tuh work honey.
(0.4)
P: Well no: actually uh: Sundee we could take 'er over d' the bus station,

INSTANCE #28.

Initial Version B: nNo, (·) becuz now that's reediculous.
(1.0)
Revised Version B: So wil draw stra:ws in the neighborhood. (·)
Or Sam 'n- I think Sa:m en I 'ed better
we'll stay ho:me.=
A: =Ple:ase don't do tha:t becuz it was a:ll set u:p.

Again, as with those instances in which a revised rejection was done post a revised invitation or offer, here in these instances in which a revised or modified rejection is done post a silence, this modified or revised version provides a next place for inviter or offerer to do some sort of response, possibly a rejection finalizer, but also possibly some further revision or modification of the invitation or offer, as in Instances #27 and #28.

I. Extension of rejection past first possible sentence completion point.

In Instances #26–28, a first version of a rejection was followed by a silence, and it was proposed that this silence in some cases is taken by rejector as displaying that inviter or offerer may not be taking the rejection as final. That is, the post-rejection silence provided a "space" for rejector to monitor for whether or not his rejection was being taken as final. In Instances #26–28, the silences were two-tenths of a second or longer. Now in this section, it will be proposed that other kinds of objects (i.e., other than silences two-tenths of a second or longer) also may provide "spaces" for rejectors to monitor for whether or not their rejections are being taken as final. The first set of objects is in the following instances:

INSTANCE #29. (SBL 10, p. 28)[13]

→ → A: ˙hh Well you know (eh-) seven days a week is just too much
for me, (·) I cahn't do it with the children.

INSTANCE #30. (SBL 10, p. 40)

Invitation B: And uh i:f you'd care to come over and visit a
little while this morning I'll give you a

```
                       [cup of coffee.=
                A:     [·hhhh!
Rejection → →   A:     =Uh huhh!=Well that's awfully sweet of you I
                       don't think I can make it this mo:rning,=·hhhh
                       uh:m
                                   (0.3)
                A:     I'm running an a:d in the paper a:nd uh: ·hh I
                       have to stay near the pho:ne.
```

INSTANCE #31. (NB 52, p. 248)[14]

```
Offer           B:     To the store er any[thing,
Rejection → →   A:                        [·hh I've got evrything bought
                       dear, (·) ·hhh en I:: gotta great big Johnson pie
                       even bought the(b) (0.4) whip cream tuh throw
                       on it.
```

In the arrowed utterances above, first possible completion point is in fact not actual utterance completion by virtue of the fact that there is an additional component beyond this first possible completion point, i.e., a tag-position component: (Tag-positioned components are in capitals)

> Well that's awfully sweet of you I don't think I can make it THIS MORNING,
>
> Well you know (eh-) seven days a week is just too much FOR ME,
>
> I've got evrything bought DEAR,

Now as Jefferson (1973)[15] suggests, the doing of such tag-positioned components may be providing a space for speakers to monitor for certain things. In the cases under consideration here, the doing of such tag-positioned components may be providing a space for rejector to monitor for some response, such as a rejection finalizer. Furthermore, in Instances #29-31, note that the tag-positioned component is followed by either a micropause and/or inbreath. That is, the total amount of space here in each instance provided for rejector to monitor for some response, such as a rejection finalizer consists of a tag-positioned component *plus* a micropause and/or inbreath:

	Well you know (eh–) seven days a week is just too
Monitor Space→ →	much FOR ME (·)
	I don't think I can make it
Monitor Space→ →	THIS MO:RNING,=˙HHHH
	I've got evrything bought
Monitor Space→ →	DEAR, (·) ˙HHH

Jefferson (1973) also points out that such tag-positioned components are systematic loci for overlap, i.e., for other speaker to start talking. Now in some cases, a rejector in not hearing a response, such as a rejection finalizer, in this monitor space provided here by the tag-positioned component plus micropause and/or inbreath, may take this as a display that inviter or offerer is passing up the chance to start talking at this point (i.e., in the monitor space), and rejector in turn may take this as a display that possibly inviter or offerer is not going to take the rejection-so-far as final. In an attempt to deal with this possibility, rejectors may subsequently add further components, i.e., they may extend their rejections:

Rejection	Well you know (eh–) seven days a week is just too
Monitor Space	much FOR ME (·)
Extension	I cahn't do it with the children.
Rejection	I don't think I can make it
Monitor Space[16]	THIS MORNING,=˙HHHH
Extension	Uh:m (0.3) I'm running an a:d in the paper and a:nd uh: ˙hh I have to stay near the pho:ne.
Rejection	I've got evrything bought
Monitor Space	DEAR, (·) ˙HHH
Extension	en I:: gotta great big Johnson pie even bought the(b) (0.4) whip cream tuh throw on it.

These extensions may be considered revisions or modifications of the earlier part of the rejection, insofar as they are attempting to deal with the possibility that inviter or offerer is not going to go along with the rejection in its earlier form and insofar as they provide a next place for inviter or offerer to do some sort of response, such as (but not necessarily) a rejection finalizer. In Instance #30, the extension gets this rejection finalizer:[17]

A: I'm running an a:d in the paper and a:nd uh: ˙hh I have to stay near the pho:ne.=˙hh [hh
→ → B: [Alri:ght,

In Instances #29-31, the monitor space consisted of a tag-positioned component *plus* a micropause and/or inbreath. In the instances below, the monitor space (in capitals) consists only of tag-positioned components:

INSTANCE #32. (V-II)

Invitation A: Y' c'd all c'm up'n have apple crisps?
(0.2)
A: Is that any temptation.
(·)
Rejection B: ˙hh No: ANNIE REALLY IT'S NOT.

INSTANCE #33. (V-III)

Offer B: Dih you wan' ( ) a ride ho:me?=er ( )=
Rejection A: =Oah no.=UH-UH

INSTANCE #34. (NB 36, p. 56)

Proposal C: Why 'onche get that nay- uh::: Revlon nai: [l::
Rejection A: [˙hhh=W'l that's not therapeutic CLARA R:ILLY

Examining Instance #32 in detail, the first monitor space is "Annie" and it could be that in not hearing a response such as a rejection finalizer here, rejector adds the next component "really." This next component further provides a monitor space, and again, in hearing no response, rejector adds the further component "it's not," which again provides a further monitoring space. Now in not hearing a response such as a rejection finalizer in any of these spaces, rejector then adds:

Rejection ˙hh No:

Monitor Spaces	Annie really it's not.=
Extension	=Cindy's not even over: hh˙- here yet.

This extension "Cindy's not even over here yet" is a modification or revision of the rejection insofar as (1) it is an attempt to deal with the possible unacceptability of the rejection-so-far, and (2) it provides a further place for a rejection finalizer to be done:

Extension	B:	. . . Cindy's not even over: hh˙- here yet.
Finalizer	A:	Oh I see.

A similar argument can be made for Instances #33 and #34:

INSTANCE #33.

Rejection	A:	Oah no.=
Monitor Space	A:	=Uh-uh.=
Extension	A:	=I ws just (telling you about it) so you wouldn't wor[ry.
Finalizer[18]	B:	[Oh thank you.

INSTANCE #34.

Rejection	A:	W'l that's not therapeutic
Monitor Space		Clara r:illy
Extension		it says on the (0.4) thi:ng,=uwhen (you)- (·) uh: this p'roxide is: uh: kind of a
		(0.2)
	A:	˙hh[hhh
	C:	[Whaddih yuh mean uh uh doctors use it.

Instance #34 also illustrates the other sequential possibility post an extended rejection: that that extended rejection will still not be taken as final, and that the proposer instead may do something which indicates that he is pushing for acceptance of his proposal.

In Instances #32-34, the space for rejector to monitor for a response such as a rejection finalizer was provided by one or more tag-positioned components. Now it may be that speakers can monitor for lack of response in an even "tighter" space. First of all, Jefferson (1973) and Jefferson, Sacks, and Schegloff (1979) have shown that speakers have the capability to monitor and respond not just word by word, but also syllable by syllable, and in the case of laughter, particle by particle. Second, speakers can and do come in with responses during a word which is a possible completion point and which is intonationally stretched:

INSTANCE #35. (SBL 22, p. 201)

A: Why can't i dist make those things I made before:.=Does it
    have tuh be so ni: [ce.
B: [Heavens no.=Make 'em up.

INSTANCE #36. (SBL 28, p. 260)

A: Maybe I'll ca:ll you i:f I decide I c'n go [:.
B: [Oka:y:.

Now in the instances of rejection below, the word which is a possible first completion point is stretched intonationally:

INSTANCE #37. (SBL 17, p. 118)

Offer B: Dih yuh need any ca:rds I have (·) I have a couple
    decks thet'v never been [opened.]
Rejection → → A: [·hhhhhh] hh So have I:,

INSTANCE #38. (SBL 17, p. 115)

Offer B: (Uh) you don't need a ↑fo:rk.
Rejection → → A: Uh uh no:.

INSTANCE #39. (V-II)[19]

Rejection B: ˙tch ˙hh I know but u- we're watchin:g the Ascent
→ → 'v Ma:n, ˙hh en then the phhreview:

Now it may be that speakers have the capability to monitor so closely and precisely that these rejectors here, upon not hearing a response such as a rejection finalizer, in overlap with the stretched component, take this as displaying that possibly inviter or offerer is not going to take the rejection-so-far as final. Then, to deal with this possibility, rejector may add some extension which is a modification or revision of the rejection-so-far, and which provides a further place for inviter or offerer to respond, possibly with a rejection finalizer:

INSTANCE #37.

Rejection	A:	So have I:,=
Extension	A:	=I got couple (of [new one] s)
Finalizer	B:	[A w r i] ght honey,

INSTANCE #38.

Rejection	A:	Uh uh no:,=
	B:	=[No.
Extension	A:	=[That's- that's the reason I made this kind of thing I di:d.
	B:	Uh huh.

INSTANCE #39.

Rejection	A:	˙tch ˙hh I know but u- we're watchin:g the Ascent 'v Ma:n,
1st Extension	A:	˙hh en then the phhreview:
2nd Extension	A:	so: y'know wil miss something if we come over.
Finalizer	B:	°'khay°

J. Weak agreements post a rejection.

In part II, it was pointed out that occasionally an invitation or offer may be followed by a weak agreement such as "hm," "mm hm," or "yeah." Similarly, occasionally a rejection may be followed by a weak agreement:

INSTANCE #40. (NB 45, p. 171)

Offer	M:	C'n I: add anything fuh you::?=
Rejection	A:	=˙hh Oh: honey thanks I think I:: I'll let Sam go.=[Maybe he'll get some fi:sh.
	M:	[(↓eYes).
		(·)
Weak Agreement	M:	eYe:s.

INSTANCE #41. (Beer party)

Request A: Brad 'n I: 'n To:mmy: (·) y'know wunnered ir
we c'(n) come over later.=Do we haf tu pay any
initialization fee er somethin' [tuh get ( )
B: [hhhhhh!
(·)
B: tsk! (·) Hm:::.=How much later dih you
wanna come ove[r.
A: [Oh I don' know.=
A: =What's the schedule over there.
(·)
Rejection B: Wuh see the trouble i:s, (0.5) i:s uh (0.8)
(there's) not a ↑whole lot, (·) a:nd ˙hhh it was
the whole (end) of our dorm fe:es.
Weak Agreement A: M:mm::.

In each instance, a rejection is followed by a weak agreement. Now if it is the case that in certain environments, a weak agreement may be disagreement-implicative (Pomerantz, 1975), then a rejector, on hearing a week agreement post his rejection, may take it that inviter or offerer is possibly not going to take the rejection as final. And again, if rejector wants to deal with this possibility, subsequent to the weak agreement, he may produce some sort of modified or revised rejection, where this modified or revised rejection provides a next place for inviter to respond, possibly with a rejection finalizer:

INSTANCE #40.

Weak Agreement M: eYe:s.
(·)
Revision A: I'll plan on tha:t.
Finalizer M: A:lright de:ah.

INSTANCE #41.

Weak Agreement A: M:mm:[:.
B: [˙hhhhh So::, (·) uh::,
(1.5)
Revision B: I:: efer now: anyway hih! hih! yer not- ˙hh eh-
(·) eh- nuthin' personal'r anything b't yer not
invited becuz the rest uh the dorm will throw
yuh out. [hh
[

Finalizer A: Ri::ght. (·) I see.

IV. Summary

This paper has examined how the doing of an object such as an invitation or offer sets up that in the next turn a sequentially appropriate object is either an acceptance or rejection. A variety of objects were described which inviters and offerers may take as actual rejection or pre-rejection, and it was proposed that in the face of such actual or possible rejection, inviters and offerers may in some way revise or modify their invitations and offers, where such revised or modified versions provided a next place for recipient to respond, possibly with an acceptance. Similarly, the doing of a rejection also sets up that in the turn following it, a sequentially appropriate object is something which will display that inviter or offerer either is or is not going to go along with the rejection, i.e., either is or is not going to take it as final. A variety of objects were described which rejectors may take as displaying that inviter or offerer is taking the rejection as non-final. It was proposed that, when faced with either the possibility or the actuality that inviter or offerer is taking the rejection as non-final, rejectors may then revise or modify their rejections to deal with this.

NOTES

1. There are other possibilities of course, such as counterinvitations, equivocations, postponements, evasions, etc., but this paper will examine only acceptance and rejection.

2. The terms "inviters and offerers" and "invitations and offers" will be used as a shorter version of "inviters, offerers, requestors, proposers, etc.," throughout this paper.

3. Sections A, B, and D were condensed from a paper given at the SSRC/BSA International Conference on Practical Reasoning and Discourse Processes, Oxford, England, July 2–6, 1979. A complete treatment on revised and modified invitations and offers will appear in Atkinson and Heritage (1984).

4. It should be emphasized that dealing with a troublesome invitation or offer by its producer may be entirely a pro forma matter. That is, the producer of an invitation or offer may or may not care whether or not his invitation or offer gets accepted, but in some cases, perhaps certain rules of etiquette or politeness call for a display by the inviter or offerer that he does not care that his invitation or offer is accepted.

5. By virtue of the fact that another sequentially appropriate object after a revised or modified invitation or offer is a rejection, a modification or revision

thereby provides a next place not just for doing acceptance but also for doing rejection.

6. Note the immediate revision in the acceptance from "eYeah:" to "Right." This revision may come about because, as was pointed out in Section C, objects such as "yeah" may be taken as weak agreements and thereby as, if not pre-rejection, at least perhaps not whole-hearted acceptance.

7. Again, as in the case of modified or revised invitations and offers, the doing of a revised or modified rejection to deal with the possibility that inviter is not going to take the rejection as final may be purely a pro forma matter. In some cases, rules of etiquette or politeness may call for a show that rejector "really" wants his rejection to stand; on the other hand, doing a revised or modified rejection may in some cases be a way for the recipient of an invitation or offer to test the sincerity of that invitation or offer.

8. It should be noted that the objects I am terming "rejection finalizers" may also be doing other kinds of sequential or interactional work and that they obviously come from different classes of objects. For example, "Aw:kay" as in Instance #20 is obviously a pre-closer. Objects such as "oh" are also used to display understanding after a possible earlier misunderstanding, and they are also used to concede arguments or disagreements. Nonetheless, while these objects may be doing other sorts of sequential and/or interactional work, when they occur in this specific place, i.e., after a rejection, they have in common the feature of displaying that the just-prior rejection is being taken as final rejection.

9. Anthony J. Wooton, University of Cork, England, has also done work on extended request-rejection sequences in his paper "The Management of Grantings and Rejections by Parents in Request Sequences." In his paper, he goes into much greater detail about the specific wording of rejections and re-rejections than I have here, and the reader is therefore referred to his paper.

10. Again, it should be emphasized that this may be a mere display of caring to get the rejection taken as final.

11. Of course, the doing of a modified or revised rejection does not always lead to the doing of a rejection finalizer in next turn. In some instances, offerer or inviter may not do a finalizer, such that rejector may then produce a further revision or modification. For a detailed consideration of just this sort of occurrence in Instance #25, see Section I.

12. The first two lines of Instance #28 are a rejection of an invitation made either before the segment of the call on tape or made in a previous interaction. Incidentally, "Why" is yet another sort of object which displays that the inviter or offerer may not be taking the rejection as final. This object will not be analyzed in this paper, but a further instance of it is displayed below:

Rejection	A:	No that's a hell of a long trip.
		(0.5)
→ →	P:	Why::.
		(·)
Revision	A:	Oh no I wouldn't think of it dear.

13. This is a re-rejection of a job offer made earlier in the call.

14. See Instance #25 for the earlier part of this offer sequence.

15. See Section D for the relevant quotation from Jefferson (1973).

16. I am not considering "uhm" (0.3)" to be part of the monitor space. That is, "uhm" displays that A is already starting a next object, and the proposal here is that she is doing so by virtue of not having heard inviter starting up in the monitor space "this mo:rning,=˙hhhh." Furthermore, Harvey Sacks (1972) characterizes "uh" as displaying "I'm taking the floor" and also as displaying that thereby a silence which follows "uh" is part of that speaker's turn. I.e., in this case, "uhm (0.3)" is the start of the extension.

17. If a rejector does not get a finalizer following a first extension, he may subsequently do a further extension, which is what happens in Instance #31:

1st Extension	A:	en I:: gotta great big Johnson pie even bought the(b) (0.4) whip cream tuh throw on it.
		(1.0)
2nd Extension	A:	˙hh [hhhh En] I got the boi:led onion in the-
	P:	[°eYe:ah°]
		(·)
	A:	˙hh the package uh frozen creamed onions en I'm just hav'n stuff celery en olives 'n etc.

18. Although this object "oh thank you" is obviously doing some sort of interactional work unrelated to the rejection, such as acknowledging that speaker A was doing B a favor in calling, it is nonetheless a rejection finalizer by virtue of the fact that it does the sequential work of displaying that the just-prior rejection is going to be taken as final rejection and that therefore no re-issues of the offer are going to be done.

19. This is an instance in which a first monitoring space, consisting here of the stretch on "Ma:n," plus inbreath is bypassed, and therefore rejector extends the rejection with "en then the phhreview:". It is this second monitor space, i.e., the stretch on "phhreview:" that I am now considering. See Instance #24 for the earlier part of this sequence.

REFERENCES

Atkinson, J. M. and J. C. Heritage, *Structures of Social Action,* Cambridge: Cambridge University Press, 1984.

Jefferson, Gail (1973), A case of Precision Timing in Ordinary Conversation. *Semiotica,* Vol. 9, No. 1, pp. 47–96.

——— (1978), Sequential Aspects of Storytelling in Conversation. In James Schenkein, Ed., *Studies in the Organization of Conversational Interaction.* New York: Academic Press, Inc., pp. 219–248.

———, Harvey Sacks, and Emmanuel Schegloff, (1979), Notes on Laughter in the Pursuit of Intimacy, manuscript.

Pomerantz, Anita (1975), *Second Assessments.* Unpublished Ph.D. dissertation, University of California, Irvine.

____ (1978), A Sequential Analysis of Interpreting Absences, manuscript.
Sacks, Harvey (1971), unpublished lectures, University of California, Irvine, March 11 lecture.
____ (1972), unpublished lectures, University of California, Irvine, Spring, Lecture 3, pp. 14–16.
Wooton, Anthony J. The Management of Grantings and Rejections by Parents in Request Sequences, manuscript.

TRANSCRIPT SOURCES

The following instances are from Gail Jefferson's transcripts: 8, 18, 24, 39.

The following instances are from my parasitic retranscriptions of Jefferson's transcripts: 1, 3, 4, 5, 6, 7, 10, 11, 12, 15, 16, 19, 21, 22, 23, 25, 26, 27, 28, 29, 39, 31, 32, 34, 35, 36, 37, 38, 40.

The following instances are from my transcriptions: 2, 9, 13, 14, 17, 20, 33, 41.

All names of persons in all instances are fictitious.

Elementary Properties of Argument Sequences

Jeff Coulter

The examination of several interaction sequences which can be characterized as "arguments" (or, minimally, disagreements between parties in talk) reveals some structures whose form (or logic) is analyzed here.

The elementary form, in two party talk, is characterized as an argument sequence with two pair parts: declarative assertion and counterassertion. Its expansion into a four part structure can take the form of (1) declarative assertion; (2) disagreement; (3) solicit and (4) counter-assertion. Both of these can proceed next to a backdown/reassertion or next assertion by prior speaker. Movement within or out of the argument can be achieved by a next assertion which is hearable as a shift or change of topic. A major design feature of counter-assertions is described in terms of the property of "contrastive matching to prior assertion."

First speaker, following second speaker's counter assertion, can produce a backdown, or minimally, a silence hearable as backdown-implicative. This latter may lead to an explicit backdown. Thus, as Coulter argues, there is a preference for explicit backdowns are terminations for an argument sequence.

The presence of other parties introduces possibilities of techniques for latching into the argument and producing alignments which manifest themselves in topic expansions.

Two basic variants on the assertoric form are noted by Coulter as questioning challenges and story complaints. Multi-

component and multi-turn possibilities emerge here and the second party's response now can be examined for how it is organized to counter the first party's assertions, e.g. a contrastive counter assertion.

Further argument types are considered under the heading of open textured argument environments wherein participants negotiate and dispute criteria for selection and applicability of topics and categories. This latter possibility indicates that arguments can evolve out of whatever resources are available to participants as they interpret and assess the argument-relevant character of their talk.

This paper opens the topic of argument in discourse for further inquiry and suggests its richness not only in terms of multi-party complexities but also for the study of how utterance components may be "shaped" or transformed into argument relevant resources.

In what follows, I shall attempt to describe some fundamental, structural properties of arguments as they arise in the course of ordinary social interaction. As I understand it, following the broad program of the late Harvey Sacks, a "structure" of human interaction, analytically described, can take the form of an *ordered optionality system.* Starting with any sequentially initial or opening illocutionary action, there are "illocutionary environments" or "opportunity spaces"[1] arising subsequent to each completed or interrupted utterance. What sort of (illocutionary) action may be performed in such an opportunity space is constrained by standards of appropriateness and intelligibility furnished by the linguistic culture. The optionality system for any type of sequence (complaint sequence, request sequence, argument sequence, etc.) is a system which reflects these standards and renders them explicit. Of course, to treat a sequence of interaction in this way is to assume that the apparent orderliness of interaction is, indeed, systemic. However, this has proven to be a productive assumption to make, and it informs the approach adopted in this paper without foreclosing on the possibility that it will turn out to be too strong a claim in the long run.

The options that are actually adopted in any given conversational interaction cannot be assigned probability frequencies for the simple reason that the universe of possible instantiations of any given sequence class is unknown (and unknowable: it is indefinitely large). Consequently, the study of any particular instantiation of a sequence class (e.g., arguments) must be motivated not by an interest in empirical generalization to the class but by an interest in the *a priori* relations between illocutionary actions and illocutionary spaces provided by the culture under investigation.

In the data presented below, we shall be focussing upon some elementary structural properties of an emerging argument, extracting various components from it for close scrutiny, and importing additional instances to buttress the analysis for those cases in which the structural properties might not appear immediately transparent to the intuition. I shall not attempt to *define* "argument": it will suffice if the instances analyzed below in a step-wise explication can be given such a hearing. If they cannot, or cannot without strain, be grasped as instances of argumentative interaction, then I shall be explicating only my idiolect. However, even if that were true, the abstract properties of the sequence(s) might still stand under some different vernacular sequential characterization. What counts here is, primarily, the specification of *abstract* interactional properties.

The Data

A.

(3.0)

1. John: It BEGAN by talking about whether they should be rooming together
2. Paul: Yeah
3. Sheila: Yeah
4. John: But what you're really talking about is that you're really worried about the two of them that they sleep away the day
5. Paul: Right
6. Sheila: Mm hmm
7. John: than the time depressed. Why not work directly on that point

(1.0)

B.

8. Mary: Well ya know I mean I hate to bring this up again I feel as though I'm being very redundant but when I start going to school again I will be waking up very early and you know evidently will be retiring a little earlier as well - but this is like a few days' off and I-I do need my rest

9. John: Come on=
10. Mary: =I do=
11. Sheila: =[It's more than two weeks] (off) from work
12. Mary: =Uh-[honest

C.
13. John: For what?
14. Mary: What do I need my rest for? U-eerh ta get my system going in the right way in the right-
15. John: -I think ya need some exercise to get your system going
16. Sheila: That's correct - also the more you rest the more slowed down you feel you sleep twelve hours a day ya gonna re:eally feel dead for the rest of the day
(2.0)
17. Sheila: 'f ya sleep eight hours you're gonna feel a lot more alive
18. Mary: Oh no not eight - I've never gotten along on eight hours sleep
(1.5)
19. John: You-you've no-never gotten along very well on twelve either
20. Mary: Yes I ha:ve
21. John: No you haven't
(1.0)
22. John: After twelve hours of sleep you've come down here and sit your little ass down and listen to records and that's it for the rest of the day
(10.5)

D.
23. John: And O.K. to address it to the issue at hand you're only reinforced by Joe's behavior, 'coz every chance you get damnit you go up there and sleep too
24. Mary: I know ( )=
25. John: =The other day you were [in your room]
26. Mary: [I know] (yeah)
27. John: N'd you'd just got up at eleven o'clock and you were back in bed at one and I asked you why you were in bed . . at two an' you said you were depressed an' I said O.K. you can be depressed standing up now ouda bed'n' I had to come back up-up an hour later to do the same thing

28. Mary: Is this a house or a hospital anyway?
(2.0)
29. Paul: Both
30 Mary: Both?
31. Paul: Mm hm
32. John: W-wrong it's a house . . I'd do the same thing for my brother if he were in bed since I don't have any sisters I have to put it on that level
(2.0)
33. Mary: So I would do the same thing if I were in a hospital
(1.0)
34. John: Well, O.K.
35. Mary: -(as if I'm sick) ( ) I'm depressed
36. John: (I mean) uh-uh I don't feel like a custodian
(1.5)
37. John: ya know
38. Mary: Yee:eah?
39. John: But I'm not gonna see someone come up with a weak excuse like I'm depressed I'm gonna sleep away, no way, I wouldn't let my best friend do that
40. Mary: Mmmmm
(3.0)

(The argument continues with Mary asking: "What is this big thing on sleep anyway?" . .)

Assertoric Sequences in Arguments

An argument, as it arises in conversational interaction, characteristically comprises two or more disputants articulating adversary positions (or "theses") with respect to some topic, including at least an exchange of assertion and counter-assertion with some attendant expansion. We shall be dealing here, for the most part, with Declarative Assertions and assertoric expansions, taking the transcription-data to constitute a series of instantiations of quite general, abstract structures of interaction.

The major distinguishing feature of a Declarative Assertion (and Counter-Assertion) is that it is designed to make some *point* to be addressed by one or more interlocutors. I am treating Declarative Assertions and their sequentially co-ordinated turn-types of Counter-Assertion and Reassertion as the basic illocutionary phenomena because I think that we can agree that an utterance counts as a Declarative Assertion if, in its sequential environment, it occasions *more than* an Acknowledgment. In this respect, a distinction may be drawn between Declarative Assertion and Simple Assertion. Rather than attempt a stipulative definition of either type, I shall claim the following simple instances as type-specific in the hope that the reader's intuitions work along similar lines as my own:

Declarative Assertion: A: You're always sleeping in late!
Counter-Assertion: B: I wuz up at eight this morning

and:

Simple Assertion: A: The mail's come
Acknowledgment: B: Fine

Of course, Declarative Assertions are vehicles for the lamination of illocutionary forces such as "accusation," "suggestion," "excuse," etc., but because in many instances such conversational objects are equipotentially discernible as, respectively, "complaint," "command," and "justification," contingent upon the local assignability of presuppositions of certain sorts,[3] I shall attempt in this paper to restrict the problem of turn-type identification by considering Declarative Assertion (and its variants) as the basic sequential object.

A first observation about the data concerns the minimal structure for Declarative Assertion. This takes the form of an adjacency-pair[4] with alternate second-pair-parts, in which the production by any opening speaker of a Declarative Assertion occasions either an Agreement, a Disagreement Token or a full-fledged Disagreement which I am here calling a Counter-Assertion.

Thus:

First Pair-Part: Declarative Assertion
Second Pair-Part: Agreement/Disagreement Token/Counter-Assertion

In the data, two simple adjacency-parts of Assertion/Agreement operate in tandem order (Sequence A):

1. John: It BEGAN by talking about whether they should be rooming together
2. Paul: Yeah

(3. Sheila: Yeah)
4. John: But what you're really talking about is that you're really worried about the two of them that they sleep away the day
5. Paul: Right
(6. Sheila: Mm hmm)

John's initial Declarative is a Formulation[5] (utterance 1.) which is hearably expansion-implicative due to its opening turn-component ("It BEGAN by . . "), and, following its Confirmations (Agreements), it gets expanded in utterance 4., again with subsequent Confirmations (Agreements). (It should here be noted that I am making no clear distinction between an Agreement Token such as a "Yeah" or "You're right" and a more elaborate form of Agreement; such a distinction and its analytical exploitation would take us beyond the focus of this paper.)

Turning to Disagreement Tokens, the following interesting property is observable: following Declarative Assertions, simple Disagreement Tokens may operate as Pre-Counter-Assertions or as Counter-Assertion implicative, thereby expanding the sequence beyond the adjacency-pair boundaries into one involving an insertion-expansion with the familiar feature of mirror-embedding.

For example:

Dec. Assertion:	1.	A:	Well, he had all the chances and didn't make much of 'em
Disagreement Token (Operative as) Pre-Counter-Assertion:	2.	B:	That's not really true
Solicit:	3.	A:	Oh? Why not?
Counter-Assertion:	4.	B:	For a start, y'c'd hardly blame im for iz wife's illness and that's when the rot started . . .

Another such sequence:

Dec. Assertion:	1.	A:	What a bizness! The guy just can't be trusted
Disagreement Token (Operative as) Pre-Counter-Assertion:	2.	B:	I disagree

Solicit:	3.	A:	Huh? RE:EALLY?
Counter-Assertion:	4.	B:	He's a very smart operator but basic'ly a reliable person. ( )

It is evidence in favor of treating Disagreement Tokens in such sequences as Pre-Counter-Assertions to find them occasioning in next turn objects which function as Solicits do in Pre-Announcement, Pre-Invitation and Pre-Offer sequences.[6] Thus, turns designed to employ only a Disagreement Token (such as "That's not really true," etc.) make conditionally relevant[7] in next turn the production of a Solicit-object which is then (structurally) satisfiable by a Counter-Assertion.

Most Pre-objects operate as first-pair parts of the adjacency pair: Pre-(Item) plus Solicit, positioned *prior to* some Base Sequence they foreshadow (and can thereby forestall). Thus, consider the following:[8]

PRE-ANNOUNCEMENT SEQUENCE:

Pre-Ad-Pair	Pre-Announcment:	1.	A:	Guess what!
	Solicit:	2.	B:	What?
Base Ad-Pair	Announcement:	3.	A:	I got an 'A' on my paper
	Assessment:	4.	B:	Oh, that's GREAT!

PRE-INVITATION SEQUENCE:

Pre-Ad-Pair	Pre-Invitation:	1.	A:	Busy tonight?
	Solicit:	2.	B:	No
Base Ad-Pair	Invitation:	3.	A:	Wanna take in a movie?
	Acceptance:	4.	B:	Why not.

PRE-OFFER SEQUENCE:

Pre-Ad-Pair	Pre-Offer:	1.	A:	I got some of those candies you like
	Solicit:	2.	B:	Marvellous!
Base Ad-Pair	Offer:	3.	A:	Want some?
	Acceptance:	4.	B:	Yes indeed!

Note the *tandem* structure of the Pre- and Base Sequences; in the case of Pre-Counter-Assertion plus Solicit, the Pre-Sequence must be *embedded into* the Base Sequence of Declarative Assertion/Counter-Assertion rather than occurring prior to such a Base Sequence. In another respect, however, Pre-Counter-Assertions share a property with other pre-objects in that they can preface their Base forms in *same* turn. Just as one can find, e.g., "collapsed" pre-announcements plus announcements in same turn (as in: "Guess what? I got an 'A' on my paper"), the same holding true for the other pre-types outlined above, so also can one locate cases in which a Pre-Counter-Assertion (Disagreement Token) can preface a Counter-Assertion in same turn, as in:

1. A: Seems to me the President's got a lot on his plate right now
→ 2. B: Not at all - when you consider what Nixon had to deal with he's got a light load

As second pair-parts to Declarative Assertions, Agreements structurally work to close assertoric sequences on same topic. However, Disagreement Tokens and Counter-Assertions operate to expand the sequence on same topic. There can thence develop a tertiary structure describable as follows:

First Part:	Declarative Assertion
Second Part:	Counter-Assertion
Third Part:	Backdown/Reassertion/Next Assertion

Or, in the case of sequences involving inserted Pre-objects:

First Part:	Declarative Assertion
Pre-Second Part (1):	Disagreement Token (as Pre-Counter-Assertion)
Pre-Second Part (11):	Solicit
Second Part:	Counter-Assertion
Third Part:	Backdown/Reassertion/Next Assertion

Backdowns (from prior positions or theses advanced in assertoric form) are topically, even sequentially, terminative, whereas Reassertions are sequentially expansive in that they can take additional Counter-Assertions. However, Reassertions are not to be thought of simply as repeat formulations of prior assertions; the notion refers to the recycling of a position or thesis and not to the recycling of an utterance, although clearly some sterile arguments can get generated by utterance-reassertions alone. The "third part" opportunity space or illocutionary environment is examinable by speaker-hearers to see whether what fills it counts as a Backdown from prior position, a Reassertion of prior position, or a Next (i.e., New) Assertion which shifts the focus of the topic, changes topic or introduces something wholly extraneous, in which latter case the turn may be Misplacement Marked with a construction such as "incidentally" or "By the way . .", etc.[9]

Once a Backdown has been produced in third position, further Counter-Assertions are dispreferred. This may be evidenced by noticing utterances 21-28 in the data. Mary produces a Backdown in utterance 24 following John's multi-component Counter-Assertion across lines 21-23. John presses beyond Mary's Backdown, however, in utterance 25, and even beyond Mary's Second Backdown in utterance 26 (although it is possible that it was not heard as such due to some overlapping). Having completed his now over-built Counter-Assertion in utterance 27, John is met with a challenge from Mary in her utterance 28: "Is this a house or a hospital anyway?"

Backdowns need not be explicitly articulated: an assignable silence post an (Expanded) Counter-Assertion may be heard to constitute a Backdown. However, Explicit Backdowns may be preferred over Backdown-Implicative Silences. An interlocutor may be pressed by his co-conversationalist until an Explicit Backdown is achieved, even after a Backdown-Implicative Silence has arisen between them. Note utterances 21-24 in the data:

Counter:	21. John:	No you haven't
		(1.0)
Expanded Counter:	22. John:	After twelve hours of sleep you've come down here and sit your little ass down and listen to records and that's it for the rest of the day
Backdown-Implicative Silence:		(10.5)
Second Expansion on Counter:	23. John:	And O.K. to address it to the issue at hand you're only reinforced by Joe's behavior, 'coz every chance you get damnit you go up there and sleep too
Explicit Backdown:	24. Mary:	I know ( ) =

Let us now turn to consider some of the (orderly) complications which arise when a third interlocutor latches into an argument sequence already underway.

Latching into Argument Sequences

The data presented in the transaction consists of five parties (one of whom is silent throughout), and, although for the most part it is John and Mary who are engaged in argument, two additional speakers, Sheila and Paul, affiliate themselves to the ongoing argument at certain junctures.

Our problem, then, is to give some account of third- and *n*-party latchings into developing sequences of argument. In Sequence B, lines 8 through 12, we can locate a first attempt by Sheila to join the argument. Mary's utterance (line 8) constitutes a first Declarative Assertion which enunciates her position on the topic at hand (her sleeping away the day). John's utterance (line 9) works to challenge the prior assertion in such a way as to presuppose that it cannot be seriously meant, and in this way his "come on" operates sequentially as a Counter-Assertion rather than a simple Disagreement Token. It gets, in its turn, Mary's utterance 10 which is built across Sheila's self-selected utterance 11 to form a Reassertion. Sheila's self-selected contribution is disattended by Mary in favor of her completion of her Reassertion. Had it been attended to it, Sheila's utterance would have constituted a Latched Counter-Assertion working together with John's initial Counter in utterance 9.

In Sequence C, Sheila finds a way to latch into the argument by producing, in line 16, an affiliated utterance initiated with a simple Agreement Token, "That's correct," to which she adds, without gap or overlap, the remaining components of her utterance. Her successful intervention provokes a pause, and she proceeds to self-select once more at line 17 to build upon her prior utterance-components. Sheila's positioning of her contribution to the argument immediately adjacent to John's Counter-Assertions, and her use of a clear Agreement Token in turn-initial position, affiliate her position to that of John against Mary. As an affiliated or Latched Counter-Assertion, it alters the projected sequence, requiring Mary to orient to it as a New Assertion in the conversation. Mary now opts for a Counter-Assertion in line 18, and John follows up with a Reassertion of *Sheila's* position in his utterance at line 19, albeit particularized for Mary herself instead of left as pointed general advice as it had been in Sheila's Latched Counter. Here is position co-production at work, with the co-producers (John and Sheila) now responsible (or ascribably responsible) for the same argumentative stance vis-a-vis Mary until further notice.

Latching is characteristically a self-selection phenomenon rather than something conversationally invited by one or both disputants in an argument, although on some occasions an explicit current-speaker-selects-next technique may be employed to align some third party to a current position being articulated by one of the disputants.[10] One method for achieving the orderly transition from a two-speaker argument to a three-speaker argument via third-speaker self-selection, and one which Sheila employs in her first successful Latched Utterance at line 16, is to confine oneself to *a topical expansion on the just-prior utterance whilst preserving its point.* The maximization of orderliness in position co-production may be achievable by minimizing the novelty (for the argument) of the resources used in constructing the initial Latched Utterance. The introduction of potentially problematic new materials in a first Latch can derail the attempt at co-production of the case; there is a strong sense in which the producer of the ongoing case is treatable as responsible for *any* Counters latched to his own *unless he disaffiliates at the earliest turn.* Failure to do so may bind the one latched onto as concurring in the position advanced in the latched utterance.

Two Variants on the Assertoric Format for Arguments

Returning to the data, it may readily be noticed that the structural descriptions so far outlined will not suffice for "blocking out" the entire argument (i.e., for specifying the co-ordinated turn-types on an utterance-by-utterance basis). A detailed inspection of the transcription reveals the operation of at least two variants on the assertoric format for argument development, variants which may be documented further by considering additional data.

These two variants may be referred to as the "Questioning Challenge" and the "Story-Complaint." Instances of the former would include the following:

Questioning Challenge Form of Counter:	13. John:	For what?
Dec. Assertion as Answer (Post an Understanding Check):	14. Mary:	What do I need my rest for? U-eehr ta get my system going in the right way . .

Questioning Challenge Form of Counter:	28. Mary:	Is this a house or a hospital anyway?
	(2.0)	
Dec. Assertion as Answer:	29. Paul:	Both.
	(11)	

From other materials, we find the following:

[Adato: VII: 9-23:3]

Dec. Assertion:	1. Jay:	Marijuana is very cheap
Questioning Challenge Form of Counter:	2. Stan:	Very cheap et fifty cents a joint? en a dollar a joint? is very cheap?
Dec. Assertion as Answer:	3. Jay:	You - About a - eh about a third of a joint gets you high.
Questioning Challenge Form of Counter:	4. Stan:	So?
Speaker Transition Space:	(1.0)	
Dec. Assertion Expansion:	5. Stan:	The difference is thet [(chu need'm so much)

and, in the next extract, the Questioning Challenge is employed as the format for Counters across six turns:

[Adato: V: 6-12]

Questioning Challenge Form of Counter:	10. Jay:	Who shall we leave the institutional decisions to. Johnson?
	(untimed pause)	
Beginning of Expansion:	11. Jay:	[[(Johnson-)
Dec. Assertion as Answer:	12. Sy:	(That's what) they elected (im for),
	(untimed pause)	
(Compound) Questioning Challenge Form of Counter:	13. Jay:	(But) is that what we elected (im) for? Did - did we elect im for the

		Vietnam war?
	(untimed pause)	
Dec. Assertion as Answer:	14. Sy:	We elected him, to decide fer us. If we don'like iz decisions we:: c'n vote fer somebuddy else.
	(untimed pause)	
Questioning Challenge Form of Counter:	15. Jay:	Who. Nixon?

Apart from the instance in the "Marijuana" extract where Stan self-selects following a speaker-transition space to produce a Declarative Assertion, the sequences take the form of potentially chainable adjacency-pairs; the "Vietnam" extract shows how extended a chain can be made by participating interlocutors.

The "Story-Complaint" format is a multi-component assertion built to advance a more complex position than could fit into a unit-component Declarative Assertion, and it features the grounds for the position therein being advanced. An instance from the main transcription runs as follows:

Story-Component:	25. John:	The other day you were [in your room]
Second Backdown:	26. Mary:	[I know] (yeah)
Story-Complaint:	27. John:	N'd you'd just got up at eleven o'clock and you were back in bed at one and I asked you why you were in bed . . at two an' you said you were depressed an' I said O.K. you can be depressed standing up now ouda bed 'n' I had to come back up-up an hour later to do the same thing

Another instance of the Story-Complaint would be as follows:

[Adato: V: 6-12:4]

Story-Complaint:	Jay:	OH HELL. I mean y'know Vietnam's a prime example of that, 'n every damn politician kno:ws thet that's the case. We've been pouring in-so much money fer so called, economic reform in Vietnam. A:nd uh::

people ferinstance like Lorry Sherman who
usetuh work fer the Agriculture Department
y'know uh:: some years ago, y:know went
there en found thet there wasn't o:ne bit of
- refo:rm being done. In fact, there's:::--
retrogression -- in that respect.

Not all multi-component assertions are Story-Complaints, and one conventional, though by no means invariant, distinguisher is that Story-Complaints package *one* point, while multi-component assertions may package several points in the same turn. A recurrent method for dealing with the multi-component assertion not built as a Story-Complaint is for the next speaker to separate the *last* component for treatment in his turn rather than attempt to mirror the series of points in a stepwise rebuttal, although clearly the latter may occur.

An additional, and highly conventional, design format for Counter-Assertion deserves separate attention.

The Contrastively-Matched Counter

The simplest, indeed archetypal, instance of this object is to be found in the main transcription at line 21, John's "No you haven't" positioned after Mary's "Yes I ha:ave." However, its properties may become more complex as Declaratives are rebuilt into Counters in adjacent turns according to the design convention of contrastive matching. Indeed, contrastive matching enables a speaker to produce a symmetrical utterance which accomplishes *two* functions simultaneously, viz., to rebut the prior Declarative Assertion's point and to advance an alternative position. Our data are rich in this device, and the following is a set of instances:

Seq. C, lines 14 & 15:

14. Mary: . . . . U-eehr ta get my system going in the right way in the right-

→ 14. John: - I think ya need some exercise to get your system going

Seq. C, lines 18 & 19:

18. Mary: . . . . I've never gotten along on eight hours sleep

(1.5)

→ 19. John: You-you've no-never gotten along very well on twelve either

Seq. C, lines 20 & 21:

20. Mary: Yes I ha:ave
→ 21. John: No you haven't

Seq. D, lines 32 & 33:

32. John: .... I'd do the same thing for my brother if he were in bed. .
(2.0)
→ 33. Mary: So I would do the same thing if I were in a hospital

I have located only one further instance from other materials, although it is intuitively clear that this is a routine argumentative device:

8. A: I don't like the way ya keep going' on about it
→ 9. B: An I don' like the way ya keep doing it when everybody's asked ya not to . .

Contrastively-Matched Counters include some turn-initial re-orderings, obligatory pronomial transformations and, critically, one or more major transformation on a category or category-phase occurring in the prior turn which alters it in the paired Counter to its contrastive category. That contrastive category is contrastive for the context created by the talk in its local setting and takes the burden of the Counter's function as an argumentative device. The category "rest" in utterance 14 becomes "exercise" in utterance 15. The phrase "on eight" becomes "on twelve" in utterance 19. "Yes" in utterance 20 becomes "No" in utterance 21. The phrase "for my brother if he were in bed" in utterance 32 becomes "if I were in a hospital" in utterance 33. In the auxiliary instance, "goin' on about" in utterance 8 becomes "doin'" in utterance 9.

This constructional matching feature of many Counters may be preferred by a speaker to the extent that he will redesign his Counter already underway and project a different turn construction so as to accommodate a match. A clear instance is in line 19 in the second instance above:

19. John: You–you've no–never gotten along very well on twelve either

Here, John self-corrects his "no" (sounding like the first part of "not") to "never," and from that point engages in constructional matching with the category-transformation already noted. It is quite possible that John envisaged in mid-production the possibility of producing an unseemly phonemic string, "not gotten," and sought to avoid it, but he did so in favor of a match and his noticing the possibility presupposes his attention to Mary's use of "gotten" and his interest in using the term himself.

Categorical "Open Texture" as an Argumentative Resource

Many main and subsidiary sequences in extended arguments feature negotiations and disputes (sometimes left unresolved) over the criteria for the applicability of some particular category, its scope of application, or its local relevance to the domain of discourse. Such sequences are made possible in virtue of a property of linguistic categories designated by Waismann as their "open texture";[12] their unsusceptibility to formulation in terms of a set of necessary and sufficient conditions for their correct use in all contexts of invocation. Argument environments are replete with evidence to support the contention that "criteria for correct use" are tied to communicative purposes, and are manipulable in ways not pre-specifiable independent from such purposes. Moreover, categorial invocations of various kinds are implicative for the assessment of argument-positions so far not explicitly articulated in the discourse, as they make relevant the ascription of tacit commitments and orientations to their users.

In the ensuing extract, Jay is pursuing his position on the central topic of the argument with George about the advances in the technological means for mass destruction:

[Adato: IV: 8-18]
22. Jay: (. . . . .) You en me don't have the use a'that technology, (1.9)
23. George: ( )
24. Jay: Johnson, Rusk et'all, (i,i) uh, Nixon et'all, (0.9) uh have, or, are in position to use, that technology,
25. George: I don'know what
(9.7)
26. George: We use the photo machines here,
(1.6)
27. Jay: We're talkin' about- you- (1.9) I, I just referred to the uh, technology of d'struction.

(2.4)
28. George: Okay we c'n use rifles, 'n shotguns,
(0.9)

A mutually known topic-relevant category ("technology" is used by Jay in utterance 22 (and not for the first time), whose scope of applicability is delineable by reference to the topic but which *could* encompass objects not tied to this particular topic. In seeking to undercut Jay's claim advanced in his utterances 22 and 24 about the exclusivity of those who are in a position to use "that technology," George invokes an object-set ("photo machines") which could legitimately instantiate "technology" but not for *this* domain of discourse. By employing a disjunctive criterion for what counts *here* as "using that technology," George could be heard either as off-topic and/or as seeking to ironicise Jay's claim about an exclusivity of use. Jay's specification of the *type* of technology he is referring to (in his utterance 27) as the technology of destruction still permits George to specify yet *another* disjunctive instantiation at utterance 28 with his reference to "rifles, 'n shotguns," continuing his effort to undercut Jay's initial exclusivity-of-use claim. Eventually, yet a further particularization is required from Jay in order to establish the pre-requisite common frame of reference for the topic to be pursued, and he provides this further on:

[Adato: IV: 8–18:2]
30. Jay: Well I w'z making an obvious ref'rence? (0.7) to, nuclear POWer:::.

Of course, there are still further possibilities which George could exploit in the service of undermining Jay's position; for example, he could (perversely or as a delaying strategy) constitute Jay's reference to "nuclear power" as a reference to nuclear-power plants which generate electricity for millions rather than to nuclear weapons which are *direct* means for mass destruction. However, at this point the elaboration of possibly alternative specifications ceases and the argument follows a different trajectory. It does so, however, not because some ultimately self-evident "meaning" has imposed *itself* upon George but because other matters assume relevance for him at that juncture.

Consider now Mary's utterance 28 in our main transcript and the side-sequence[13] it generates:

28. Mary: Is this a house or a hospital anyway?

(2.0)

29. Paul: Both
30. Mary: Both?
31. Paul: Mm hm
32. John: W-wrong it's a house . . I'd do the same thing for my brother if he were in bed since I don't have any sisters I have to put it on that level

(2.0)

33. Mary: So I would do the same thing if I were in a hospital

(1.0)

Mary's Questioning Challenge in utterance 28, positioned after John's prior Counter, works to raise a doubt about John's rights to (have) behave(d) in the ways he has recounted. Its sequential embeddedness enables the utterance to be heard not as some kind of off-topic request for information, but as a challenge articulated in a very subtle rhetorical format. One method for dealing with Questioning Challenges which leave open, or which provide for, an answer in the form of a Counter-Challenge, is to opt for just such a return. However, the return-utterance must be informed by some analysis on the part of its producer of the implications or presuppositions of the Questioning Challenge to which it is addressed.

Mary's utterance 28 appears to project, as a preferred answer, the first locational category in her contrast ("house") which she may presume is the appropriate category for their mutually-known organizational context of speaking. As residents of a "halfway house," her interlocutors may be expected to orient to "house" as indeed the correct designation of their context, but were they to accede to this, then they would perhaps find themselves committed to accepting incumbency in locationally-bound categories ill-fitted to their critique of Mary's conduct.[14] Under some different designation of their location (e.g., "hospital," which Mary provides as a contrast-category), their setting-appropriate membership categories may carry entitlements for their critique of Mary but at the cost of opening themselves to the argument that, in fact, they are located in a halfway *house.* Thus, Mary is setting them a categorial puzzle with a preferred solution, one that would favor her by disenfranchising them from rights or entitlements to pursue their critique so vigorously. Organizational locations bespeak a local distribution of membership categories with their bound rights and duties, such that "house" implicates "family members" whereas "hospital" implicates "custodians," "doctors," and similar more professionalized designators with *their* conventional implications for appropriate conduct. Mary's tacit assumption appears to be that family members would not or should not behave towards her as John et al. do, whereas hospital staff might have such a right in dealings with a "patient." An instance in which a similar challenge appears, although in this case by employing membership categories themselves rather than implicating them via some other categories, would be the following:

A: What are you, my insurance agent or my psychotherapist?
B: Your agent
A: Well start acting like it: I'm not paying you for psychoanalysis

Note that here, as in Mary's utterance 28, the preferred answer appears as the *first* category in the contrast. However, following Mary's turn, Paul self-selects with a *dis*preferred answer in saying "Both" (an ellipsis for: Both a house and a hospital), thereby providing for the fullest range of possible membership categories as relevant to their interaction, neatly under-cutting her with a Counter-Challenge which forestalls her exploitation of a categorial resource ("house") in the development of her point. Mary then produces another Questioning Challenge in utterance 30 in the form of a (Repeat-type) Understanding Check confirmed by Paul in his subsequent turn. John now disaffiliates immediately in utterance 32 (his earliest opportunity to do so), and characterizes their locational context as a "house," but then proceeds to display his right to have said what he did by reference to the familial membership categories of "brother" and "sister," both of which are categories in the Membership Categorization Device "Family"[15] which is tied to the location-category "house." Whereas Paul was concerned to diffuse the impact of Mary's challenge, John has found a way of taking it up. Mary's Contrastively-Matched Counter in utterance 33 switches the issue neatly by invoking the contrastive category "hospital," which she had earlier introduced as the dispreferred one, in the service of excusing/justifying *her* conduct which has been the topic of the argument.

In the subsequent discourse, John invokes a membership-category more fitted to "hospital" than "house"; he notes that he does not feel like a "custodian" in his Disclaimer (utterance 36). Indeed throughout the whole sequence, the equivocality of the location-term—a halfway house—with respect to its proper placement under the auspices of the alternative categories introduced into the argument, "house," and "hospital," becomes *itself* a tacit resource for identity-negotiation.

Conclusion

The analytical observations collected in this paper do not exhaust the materials under discussion, but they are sufficiently abstract to constitute the elements of a "production model" for arguments in social interaction as a class of communicative events in the culture. Any production model of this sort will specify aspects of the ordered turn-options endogenous to the sequence-type under examination, as well as features of turn-construction.

This report is to be understood as a contribution to the formal description of the informal logic of the culture;[16] the logic which organizes the co-production of recognizable "arguments" is a part of the culture or, better, its hitherto uncodified dimensions.

ACKNOWLEDGMENTS

This paper is based on a public lecture, Basic Structures for Arguments in Interaction, delivered to the Third Annual International Institute in Ethnomethodology and Conversation Analysis held at Boston University, July 1978. I am grateful to the Institute participants for their helpful comments. I am especially indebted to Gail Jefferson who very kindly supplied me with additional materials, some of which have been incorporated here. All data extracts headed "Adato" come from her corpus. Responsibility for what has been made of the data rests with me.

NOTES

1. I am treating these concepts as equivalent for present purposes. The latter notion was developed by Harvey Sacks.

2. The transcription is continuous but divided by straight lines into segments demarcating manageable sequences. I am grateful to Neil Wilson for making available to me his "Halfway House" research tapes from which this data has been extracted with his permission, and to Tim Anderson for his initial and perceptive transcription. This version is based upon my own hearing, using Anderson's transcript as a reconciliation source. The symbology throughout is taken from Gail Jefferson. For a full account of the contemporary notation system used in this work see the Appendix in this volume and also Schenkein (1978).

3. For a consideration of *belief*-presuppositions in particular, and their role in practical comprehension, see Coulter (1979).

4. For discussion of this notion and its properties, see, *inter alia,* Schegloff and Sacks (1974).

5. For some discussion of formulations see Heritage and Watson (1979).

6. For an extensive examination of "pre-sequence objects," see Sacks (1967) and Terasaki (1976).

7. This notion was developed by Schegloff (1972).

8. These examples are adapted from ones given in the discussions of pre-sequence phenomena by Sacks (1967) and Terasaki (1976).

9. On the notion of "misplacement markers" and their properties, see Schegloff and Sacks (1974).

10. On speaker-selection and its orderliness in conversation, see the extensive analysis by Sacks, Schegloff and Jefferson (1974).

11. Notice that in these sequences, each next Questioning Challenge is occasioned by the answer given to the prior.

12. See Waismann (1965).

13. For some discussion and exemplification of "side sequences" and their properties, see Jefferson (1972).

14. On categorization, see Sacks (1972).

15. On MCD's, see Sacks (1972). On the notion of "category-bound" activities, entitlements and obligations, etc., see Sacks (1974) and Watson (1978).

16. For the distinction between "formal" and "informal" logic, see Ryle (1954). The relevance of these and other distinctions drawn by ordinary language philosophers to the eneterprise of sequential analysis is discussed in Coulter (forthcoming).

REFERENCES

J. Coulter, Beliefs and practical understanding, in G. Psathas (Ed.), *Everyday Language.* New York: Irvington Publishers, 1979.

——, Contingent and *a priori* structures in sequential analysis, in J. M. Atkinson (Ed.), *Papers from the Oxford International Symposium on Practical Reasoning and Discourse Processes,* forthcoming.

J.C. Heritage and D.R. Watson, Formulations as conversational objects, in G. Psathas (Ed.), *Everyday Language.* New York: Irvington Publishers, 1979.

G. Jefferson, Side sequences, in D. Sudnow (Ed.), *Studies in Social Interaction.* New York: Free Press, 1972.

G. Ryle, *Dilemmas.* Cambridge: Cambridge University Press, 1954.

H. Sacks, unpublished lecture, School of Social Science, University of California at Irvine, November 1967.

——, An initial investigation of the usability of conversational data for doing sociology, in D. Sudnow (Ed.), *Studies in Social Interaction.* New York: Free Press, 1972.

——, On the analyzability of stories by children, in R. Turner (Ed.), *Ethnomethodology.* Baltimore: Penguin, 1974.

H. Sacks, E. A. Schegloff and G. Jefferson, A simplest systematics for the organization of turn taking for conversation, in J. Schenkein (Ed.), *Studies in the Organization of Conversational Interaction*. New York: Academic Press, 1978.

E. A. Schegloff, Sequencing in conversational openings, in J. A. Fishman (Ed.), *Advances in the Sociology of Language,* Vol. 11. The Hague: Mouton, 1972.

E. A. Schegloff and H. Sacks, Opening up closings, in R. Turner (Ed.), *Ethnomethodology*. Baltimore: Penguin, 1974.

J. Schenkein (Ed.), *Studies in the Organization of Conversational Interaction*. New York: Academic Press, 1978.

A. Terasaki, Pre-announcement sequences in conversation, Social Science Working Papers, Orange Book Series, No. 99, 1976.

F. Waismann, Verifiability, in A. G. N. Flew (Ed.), *Logic and Language*. New York: Anchor, 1965.

D. R. Watson, Categorization, authorization and blame negotiation in conversation, *Sociology,* Vol. 12, No. 1, January 1978.

The Organization of Talk, Gaze, and Activity in a Medical Interview

George Psathas

The sequential organization of talk, gaze, and bodily activities is examined to discover patterns which represent interactional phenomena. Video tape recordings of a medical history interview between a student optometrist and a patient are examined to show the ways in which gaze of speaker and hearer are related to utterance production, turn transition points, and other activities, particularly those of the interviewer.

Gaze is found to be sensitive to turn transition points as well as being capable of being used by one participant to direct the other's gaze.

By being able to establish the relevance of objects in the setting and directing the other to monitor bodily activities of the interviewer occurring within turn-transition spaces, competent interviewers are able to "direct" the activities of the interviewee in ways which suggest modes of "influence" or "control" of the interaction. The sequentially organized patterns which are discovered show that bodily activities can come to have interactional significance which cannot be discerned from the examination of utterances alone.

The ways in which talk and gaze are organized in interaction represents topics which have thus far drawn little attention from researchers studying interaction. Only with the use of video or filmic recording techniques has it become possible to capture the details of these relationships and demonstrate that particular interactional patternings occur.

The research of Kendon (1965, 1967, 1970, 1973), Markel (1975), Erickson (1975), and Goodwin (1979, 1981) represent notable contributions[1] to the study of these relationships as do the important observations of Goffman (1963, 1971, 1974).

This study will focus on the relation between talk and gaze but include an additional element, namely, bodily activities occurring in the setting which are displayed and recognized as relevant to the interaction by the participants. The data on which these observations are based are drawn from initial medical history-taking interviews between a student optometrist and a clinic patient,[2] referred to hereafter as "doctor" and "patient." I first want to note some important features of these interviews in order to show the context within which the observed patterns occur.

A predominant feature of the interview is that one participant, the doctor, asks questions and the second, the patient, provides answers. (See Frankel, this volume.)

The question-answer sequence, as Sacks (1967) has noted for conversation, appears to operate with two basic rules: in two-party conversation, if one party asks a question, when the question is completed, the other party takes a turn at speaking, offers an answer to the question and no more than that.

A: Q
B: A

A second rule which operates is that the person who asked the question can talk again, having a "reserved right to talk again" after the one to whom the question was addressed has answered. In using this "reserved right" another question may be asked:

A: Q_1
B: A_1
A: Q_2
B: A_2 etc.

This rule is called by Sacks the "chaining rule." Together with the first rule it provides for the occurrence of an indefinitely lengthy string of Q-A sequences with speaker change occurring from Q to A.

In the one interview we shall examine in detail (transcribed by

Richard Frankel) many such Q-A sequences occur. In fact, virtually the entire interview consists of such "chained" Q-A structures. The doctor adds an element in most of the interchanges, an acknowledgment token, such as "mmh hmh," "okay," "awright," and the like so that more accurately we can characterize the Q-A interchanges as:

Doctor: Q_1
Patient: A_1
Doctor: Acknowledgment$_1$, Q_2

An instance is quoted in detail from Interview 3:

Q_1 17. D: hhh Oka:y,=an' how lo:ng have yih noticed this' been happening=
A_1 18. P: =Oh:, quite awhile now
(0.5)
Ack_1Q_2 19. D: Uh hu:h, °hh (0.3) a:nd (0.2) couple a' months:,
(0.4)
A_2 20. P: Oh: much longuh then//that.
Ack_2Q_3 21. D: Okay °hhh An:d what is yer occupation?
A_3 22. P: Dry cleaning,

In this series, three Q-A sequences occur in succession with each of the doctor's questions being preceded by a minimal acknowlegment of the patient's answer. When this pattern is not followed, a close variation of it is found. In this instance the doctor prefaces his next question with a repeat of the patient's prior answer.

A_3 22. P: Dry cleaning,
→ 23. D: Dry cleaning, °Oka:y fi:ne. °hhh A::nd how is yer vision at distan:ce,
24. P: Pt. (0.2) uh fairly good. (0.2)

In three series in the interview, the doctor's question is not preceded by an acknowledgment of the patient's prior answer.

52. P: nNot that I c'n//recall
→ 53. D: Flashes of//li:ght]?
54. P: N:::]
55. ( ): ((clears throat))
(0.6)

56. P: No::,
→ 57. D: Things flo:ating in yer (·) vision?
(0.3)
58. P: Uh//casionally, Yea:h]

Another pattern is for the doctor to repeat the patient's prior utterance in the interrogative and to receive a confirmation from the patient. This sequence may be characterized as question-answer-repeat answer (serving as understanding check) and then confirmation/disconfirmation.

Question	12. D:	Is this when yer (·) uhm, looking at (·) distant thi:ngs?// er like when yer doing (nearly).] =
Answer	13. P:	No:t distance. up close,] =
Repeat answer (understanding check)	14. D:	Up clo:se?
Confirmation	15. ::	Yea:h

Or, the repeat of the patient's answer may not elicit an utterance (here an examination of the videotape may show that the patient gave some non verbal sign of agreement):

Interview 3

34. P: Uh:: I'd say, (1.1) ah don' know about a year and a half.
→ 35. D: A year and a half? (0.4) Oka:y and hh (4.2) when w'z yer last eye exa:m, (0.4)

Patients, throughout the four interviews we have examined, never ask a question except for one instance which may be considered a request for a repeat or clarification:

4. D: (°hhh) Awright first of a:ll c'n you tell me why you made an appointme:nt t' have yer eyes examined at this ti:me, hh
(0.8)
→ 5. P: wh:y?
(1.0)
6. D: D'-are you having trou//ble with yer visio:n)?

Thus far, the pattern is quite striking. The doctor produces questions; the patient produces answers. Question-answer sequences are chained together throughout the interview.

We have focused solely on the utterances produced by both parties and now want to extend our analysis to include additional information available to us by virtue of the fact that these interviews were videotaped. The videotapes reveal that gaze direction and other bodily activities are also organized in ways which are integrated sequentially into the on-going and developing pattern of the talk.

The first additional element we shall consider is gaze direction. Goodwin (1979) has been able to show that in a multi-party situation, the production of a single utterance by a speaker may be shaped, in the course of its production, by the ways in which the speaker's gaze meets or does not meet the gaze of his recipients. As a fine example of recipient design, Goodwin is able to show that the content of the utterance is modified by the speaker and fitted to the recipient who reciprocates the gaze.

Our data show that gaze direction is organized in various ways in relation to utterance production. I will delineate some of these patterns and examine how gaze direction is organized by both speaker and hearer a) within turns and b) at turn-transition points.

In order to understand the following data extracts, the symbols for gaze direction (explained more fully in the Appendix) must first be noted. Since there are only two participants we will consistently notate the doctor's gaze direction with symbols placed above the utterance and the patient's gaze direction with symbols placed below the utterance. We are interested in only four aspects of gaze direction:

————————	gaze directed to the other's face	) stationary gaze
- - - - - - - - - - -	gaze directed elsewhere	)
. . . .	gaze moves toward the other's face	) moving gaze
, , , , , , , , , , , ,	gaze moves elsewhere	)

The Organization of Gaze

I. Within speaker's turn

A. For speaker

1. Speaker's gaze *moves* within speaker's turn. (Patient's gaze direction is noted below the line)

Interview 1, Segment 1

5. Patient: I do a lotta reading an my eyes
p -

6. have been (++) I think wh't ch'd call
p -

7. prob'ly tired lately
p . . . . . ________

Speaker's gaze is away from hearer's face, looking in a downward direction, and as the utterance nears completion, begins to move up toward the doctor's face ("prob'ly"), reaches the face and remains there until the utterance is completed. ("tired lately").

2. Speaker's gaze *does not move* within speaker's turn (Doctor's gaze direction is noted above the line)

Interview 1, Segment 3

____
1. Doctor: D'you ever see double?

Here speaker's gaze is on recipient's face at the start and throughout the turn and does not move *within* the turn.

B. For hearer

1. Hearer's gaze *moves* as speaker is speaking, i.e., within speaker's turn.

Interview 1, Segment 2

1. Doctor: How far d'you feel you haftuh hold yer (++)
p ____

2. your: book before (++)
p________ , , , , , , , ,

3. you c'n really focus
p - - - - - - - - - - - - - - -

Hearer moves gaze away from speaker's face at "before" and focuses on his hands which he has raised in front of him through speaker's utterance of "you c'n really focus."

2. Hearer's gaze *does not move* as speaker is speaking, i.e., within speaker's turn. (Doctor's gaze is noted above line.)

Interview 1, Segment 1

```
                d ________________________
5.  Patient:    I do a lotta reading an my eyes
                d ______________________________
6.              have been (++) I think wh't ch'd call
                d ______________
7.              prob'ly tired lately
```

Throughout the speaker's utterance, recipient gazes at speaker's face. Thus, within speaker's turn we have discovered that each party may or may not move their gaze. It cannot be said that gaze is either fixed or not fixed within a speaker's turn and we shall next note the ways in which both parties' gaze may be sensitive to turn transition points before going on to consider how gaze may be coordinated for the two.

What we are able to say at this point is that, considered separately, each party's gaze, within a speaker's turn at talk, does not, in itself, promise to reveal how gaze may be co-ordinated *within* utterance production.

Turning next to turn-transition spaces, we will note that for both speaker and hearer, gaze is sensitive to the beginnings and endings of utterances as speaker change occurs. We will note one pattern:

II. At turn-transition spaces

A. At utterance completion, hearer's gaze is at speaker's face *and* speaker's gaze is at hearer's face–we shall refer to this as mutual gaze.

Interview 1, Segment 1

```
                d ______________
7.  Patient:    prob'ly tired lately
                p . . . . . ________
```

At the last words of the patient's utterance ("tired lately") they are in mutual gaze although, just prior to this, patient's gaze was elsewhere.

B. As next utterance is begun, former hearer, now current speaker, moves gaze away and former speaker, now current hearer, holds gaze on speaker's face.

Interview 1, Segment 1

```
                    d ___________________
7.  Patient:        prob'ly tired lately
                    p . . . . . __________

                    d __________ - - - - - - - - - - - , , , ,
8.  Doctor:         mmh hmh, 'hh have you: uhm
                    p ______________________________
```

In this instance the speaker change is immediate, with no gap between and no overlap of speech from one speaker's turn to the next. We can characterize this pattern, IIAB, as *mutual gaze at turn transition points.*

However, sometimes the turn transition point is marked by a noticeable silence or space without either person speaking. These spaces, or gaps, nevertheless may involve changes in gaze direction by either or both parties.

III. Within turn-transition spaces

A. Within the turn-transition space, the speaker who has just comleted an utterance may continue to gaze at the hearer's (next speaker's) face. See below.

Interview 1, Segment 3

```
                    d ______________________________
1.  Doctor:         D'you ever see double? (+ + + +)
                    p ____________________________ , ,
```

Within the (0.4) gap, the next speaker (patient) shifts gaze away from the other's face after having been in mutual gaze.

Then, as next speaker (patient) begins his utterance, his gaze is away from the hearer and returns within the next turn transition space so that they are in mutual gaze again (see lines 2, 3 and 4, Interview 1, Segment 3).

As the patient completes his "no" he moves his gaze back to the

Interview 1 Segment 3

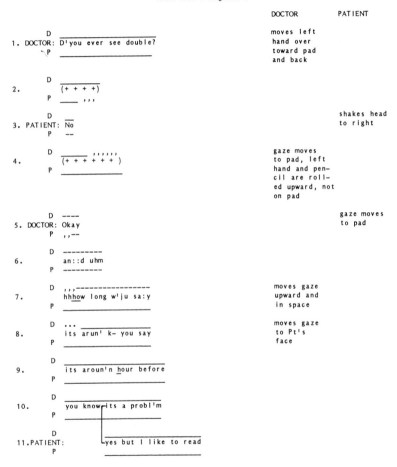

```
                                                                DOCTOR          PATIENT

           D  ______________________                            moves left
1. DOCTOR: D'you ever see double?                               hand over
           P  ______________________                            toward pad
                                                                and back

           D  _________
2.            (+ + + +)
           P  _____ ,,,

           D  __                                                                shakes head
3. PATIENT:   No                                                                to right
           P  --

           D  ______ ,,,,,,                                     gaze moves
4.            (+ + + + + + )                                    to pad, left
           P  ______________                                    hand and pen-
                                                                cil are roll-
                                                                ed upward, not
                                                                on pad

           D  ----                                                              gaze moves
5. DOCTOR:    Okay                                                              to pad
           P  ,,--

           D  ---------
6.            an::d uhm
           P  ---------

           D  ,,,-----------------                              moves gaze
7.            hhhow long w'ju sa:y                              upward and
           P  ____________________                              in space

           D  ... _______________                               moves gaze
8.            its arun' k- you say                              to Pt's
           P  ____________________                              face

           D  ______________________
9.            its aroun'n hour before
           P  ______________________

           D  _____________________
10.           you know┌its a probl'm
           P  ______________________
                      │
           D          │   ______________________
11.PATIENT:           └yes but I like to read
           P              ______________________
```

doctor and holds it at the doctor's face during the (0.6) gap (line 4). As the doctor moves her gaze away prior to speaking and directs it elsewhere, the patient also moves his gaze in the same direction while the doctor begins her "okay." The patient's gaze movement lags slightly behind the doctor's and can be seen as "following" the doctor's gaze direction.

The within turn-transition space movement of gaze is therefore to be seen as sequentially related to the movement of gaze just prior to and just post the transition space.

The pattern we have identified here, Interview 1, Segment 3, may be characterized as mutual gaze by speaker and hearer at the completion of speaker's utterance (line 1), a shift out of mutual gaze (produced by next speaker) during the transition space (line 2), a continued absence of mutual gaze (produced by next speaker) during next speaker's utterance (line 3) and a return to mutual gaze after next speaker's utterance completion (line 4). This involves the first speaker, now hearer, in maintaining gaze direction at the other's face throughout (lines 1, 2, 3, and part of 4 until just before she speaks again).

This pattern seems to involve a "monitoring" by hearer of the speaker's face so as to be available for mutual gaze when speaker completes his utterance. Then, as hearer becomes speaker, his gaze moves, while the hearer enters into the same pattern of monitoring.

Goodwin (1979) claims that hearers look at speakers more than speakers look at hearers. Particularly within the turn, as Goodwin argues, persons have different rights to look at each other: the speaker is expected to gaze only at a gazing hearer while the hearer may gaze at either a gazing or non-gazing speaker.

The preferred sequencing, says Goodwin,[3] is for hearer to bring gaze to speaker before speaker brings gaze to hearer. Sequencing in the opposite direction would produce a situation where speaker is gazing at a non-gazing hearer. Kendon (1967) finds that speaker looks away at the beginning of his utterance while hearer gazes toward the speaker there. Our observations for two party interaction relate such a gaze pattern to the fact that hearer has just completed a turn at talk and brought his/her gaze to hearer at that completion point. Returning gaze at the other's face as the other now begins to speak enables him/her to be available for the speaker's return utterance—and (eventual) return of gaze.

There are two matters of interactional significance that may be facilitated by such a pattern. The first is that speaker, by moving his gaze direction to the hearer, may signal a turn completion point. That is, at that point where mutual gaze is joined the speaker may be said to be projecting the impending turn completion.

Secondly, this type of gaze direction may also be used to select the next speaker, a matter perhaps of greater significance in a multi-party situation.

For hearers, the pattern suggests a monitoring of the speaker to discover both of these matters which may not be apparent in the utterance type itself, i.e., *when* the speaker's utterance will be or has been completed and *who* is to speak next. We will not discuss here the possibility that additional non-verbal cues are being provided by the speaker which can also serve to signal these matters, e.g., facial movements, breath patterns, etc.)

In the predominant utterance types found in these data, i.e., questions and answers, the doctor's questions project noticeable turn completion points both syntactically and semantically. They are of the form involving such interrogative signifiers as "how," "when," or "what" and are constructed with noun-verb inversions, "have you . . . ," "do you . . . ," "would you . . . ." Thus the following recur frequently:

"have you ever . . . . "
"d'you remember . . . ."
"how do you feel . . . ."
"how long would you say . . . ."
"how far do you feel . . . ."
"do you ever feel . . . ."
"when w'z yer last . . . ."

Such utterances can be monitored by hearers for their projected completion points, i.e., the question's terminal point.

Thus, we are suggesting that gaze may be patterned in particular ways for particular utteraance types. In the two-party interview situation, gaze can be used by speaker to signal a turn completion point and the question-answer format provides a specific interactional structure within which a number of additional interactional features may be intertwined.

What must be noted about the two-party situation is that each person is being monitored by the other through the use of gaze. There are no other potential speakers present. Gaze can be used in particular ways since the other is fully present, in a face-to-face orientation, and all gestures and bodily activities can be monitored rather closely.

There are two uses of gaze which are to be considered next. The first is the use of gaze, together with other actions, to *establish the relevance of physical objects* for the interaction then underway and the second is the use of gaze to *direct the other's gaze.*

Uses of Gaze

I. Establishing an object's relevance

In the first segment to be examined, Interview 1, Segment 1, we find that as the doctor starts her first utterance her gaze moves to what appears to be a clip board and pad of paper attached to it (hereafter referred to as "the pad").

As she begins her question (line 2) she begins to move her gaze toward the patient's face and holds her gaze there until the completion of the utterance (line 3).

Following the patient's answer she begins her second utterance, lines 7-9, and as she completes her acknowledgment of the patient's answer, she moves her eyelids, then her head and her gaze, down to the pad. She returns her gaze up to the patient's face only when she is well into her next question (line 8).

The glance to the pad can be interpreted as a search for the next item or question, i.e., the pad may contain a list of items about which information is to be obtained. Whether there are any questions on the pad or not does not have to be known by us as observers. The look to the pad is organized sequentially in such a way that by preceding the asking of a question, the patient (and we, as observers) can interpret it as having relevance for the interview. The pad's relevance, once established, may then be drawn upon as a resource in the management of other aspects of the interview, as we shall see.

II. To direct the other's gaze

The second use of gaze is to direct the other's gaze to an object or activity and thereby provide for the other's monitoring of that object or activity. (The uses of such monitoring will be discussed in a later section of this paper.)

In this segment, Interview 1, Segment 2, the doctor "catches" the patient's gaze as he completes an utterance and then "moves it" to the pad where she then proceeds to write (lines 4-9).

The brief mutual gaze in line 5 is sufficient to "catch" the patient's gaze and move it, by line 7, to the pad.[4] The doctor is able to hold a (1.1) second gap in line 7 as she moves her pencil to the pad and a

Interview 1 Segment 1

		DOCTOR	PATIENT
	D ----------------------------------	gaze at pad	lids down
1.	DOCTOR: Okay Mister Carroll, 'hh uh:m (+++)	lifts lids	gaze at floor
	P ----------------------------------		or pad
	D ....______________________________	gaze at Pt. left hand	
2.	what is yer(.) k- chief reason fer	holds pencil moves hand	
	P ----------------------------------	off pad to side of pad	
	D ____________________________________		
3.	coming in fer yer examination tihday		
	P ------------------------------------		
	D ________	gaze at	gaze down
4.	(++++++)	Pt's face	at floor
	P --------		or pad
	D ______________________________		
5.	PATIENT: I do a lotta reading an my eyes		
	P ------------------------------		
	D ____________________________________		
6.	have been (++) I think wh't ch'd call		
	P ------------------------------------		
	D ____________________		lifts lids
7.	prob'ly tired lately		and head up
	P .... ___________		gaze at Dr's face
	D _________------------ ,,, -------	moves lids down, head	
8.	DOCTOR: mmh hmh,'hh have you: uhm (++++++)	down, gaze to pad	
	P ___________________________________		
	D ------- .... _________________________	lifts head up, gaze	
9.	'hh-beh-hev you ever worn glasses before?	at Pt's	
	P ____	face	
	D ______		
10.	(++++)		
	P ______		
	D _______________________________,,		blinks, gaze at Dr., moves
11.	PATIENT: u- uh: quite a few years ago. (+++)		lids down then up to
	P __ ,,,, -----------.... __________		gaze at Dr's face

Interview 1 Segment 2

```
                                                                    DOCTOR            PATIENT
               D  _______________________________________________
1. DOCTOR:     How far d'you feel you you haftuh hold yer (++)
               P  _______________________________________________

               D  __________________ ,,                             gaze moves        raises hands
2.             Your: book before (++)                               to Pt's           in front
               P  __________ ,,,,,,,,,,                             hands             of body

               D  --------------------                              gaze at           gaze at palms
3.             you c'n really focus                                 Pt's hands        raised in
               P  --------------------                                                front of body

               D   ----------
4. PATIENT:    'bout here
               P   ----------

               D  _____,,                                           brief mutual      gaze at Dr's
                                                                    gaze, lifts       face
               (++++++)                                             head, lowers
               P  _____                                             lids, moves
                                                                    gaze to pad
               D  ----
6. DOCTOR:     Okay,
               P  ____

               D  ----------------------------                      lifts left        gaze at Dr's
7.             (+ + + + + + + + + + + +) uhm::                      hand moves        face lowers
               P  _________________ ,,,,, ------                    pencil and        down to pad
                                                                    hand to pad
               D  ----------------------------------------
8.             (+ + + + + + + + + + + + + + + +) you: uh-(.)        moves pencil
               P  ----------------------------------------          on pad

                  ....____________________________                  lifts pencil      raises lids,
               D                                                    raises head,      gaze at Dr's
9.             when you when yer eyes get tired                     gaze at Pt's      face
               P  .... ___________________________                  face

                  _____ ,,,,
               D
10.            d'you ever
               P  __________

               D  -------------------------------------             gaze away
11.            feel: (.) that uh: 'hh you-u (you'll)                behind Pt or
               P  _____________________________________             in space

                  ... _______________
               D                                                    moves head up,
12.            y- yer vision blurs:?                                body back
               P  _______________________
```

(1.5) second gap in line 8 while writing on the pad. The patient's gaze is not directly on the pad and the writing until line 8. At this point he is able to monitor the activity of writing until line 9 when the doctor lifts her gaze and stops writing as she begins her next question.

There are assuredly other instances in which another party's gaze may be directed by the use of one's own gaze. We are not arguing that only if mutual gaze first occurs would it be possible to direct the other's gaze. We are arguing only that this pattern is found in these data and that there is a complex sequential organization involving speech, gaze, and activity which requires description and analysis.

The Organization of Talk, Gaze, and Activity

Having established that gaze patterns are discernable we will now try to show how talk, gaze, and a monitorable activity such as writing on the pad may be sequentially organized in accomplishing particular interactional tasks.

A noticeable feature of two party conversation is that there are silences, both within speaker's turn and between speaker's turns. Researchers of conversational and interactional analysis have routinely noted these silences and timed their length. Conversationalists display a close awareness of such spaces. Their talk is generally non-overlapped and can flow quite smoothly from one speaker to another, across turns, with no timeable silence occurring.

We should offer first a few possibly clarifying distinctions to refer to the absence of talk: a silence is a space in the talk where no discernable verbal sounds are being uttered. Silences, when they occur within a speaker's turn at talk and are preceded by and followed by the same speaker's utterances, are called "pauses." When they occur in turn-transition spaces, they shall be referred to as "gaps."

If a gap occurs, it may or may not be clear whose turn is to be next. In the two party situation either party may take next turn if the gap is not otherwise sanctionably or noticeably claimed by one of the parties. A claim on the space may be expressed or implied in a number of ways.

One way of making a claim is based on the *form* of the prior utterances. We have already noted that a question asked by A allows A to claim the next turn at talk after the answer is provided by B. The doctor, in these data, "chains" questions in series. The completion of the answer by the patient to the first question is then the appropriate place for the doctor to continue with the next question.

Interview 1, Segment 1

6. Patient: prob'ly tired lately

7. Doctor: mmh hmh, 'hh have you: uhm (++++++)

8. 'hh-beh'hev you ever worn glasses before?

The doctor, in line 7, follows the patient's answer (line 6) to the first question with no gap and produces an acknowledgment before going on to the next question.

Where a gap does occur, as in the next segment, it could be heard as a space "owned" by the next speaker, doctor, because the completed utterance is an answer to the prior question.

Interview 1, Segment 2

4. Patient: 'bout here

5. (+++++)

6. Doctor: Okay

Thus, a (0.5) second gap occurs before the doctor produces her acknowledgment. This space can be considered as "owned" by the next speaker.

However, we have access to additional information from the videotape and can see how the doctor uses her gaze, the pad, and the activity of writing in these turn-transition spaces not only to establish that the gap is hers, but by directing and holding the patient's gaze, to provide a visually monitorable activity which can be interpreted by the patient as relevant to the prior utterance.

We will refer to the details of Interview 1, Segment 2 in the following argument.

The patient has just finished answering the prior question by using a hand gesture (line 4), placing both hands in front of him, palms facing him, as though holding a book, to show how far he has to hold his book before he can really focus. The doctor's gaze is at his hands until he completes his utterance "'bout here." Then, as he lifts his gaze to the doctor's face, they are in brief mutual gaze; the doctor lifts her head, lowers her eye lids and "directs" the patient's gaze down to the pad.

Her gaze moves to the pad in the (0.5) second gap (line 5). She acknowledges his answer with an "okay" and then "produces" a (1.1) second silence (line 7). The silence, however, is filled with the activity of lifting the left hand and the pencil and placing both on the pad where she then proceeds to write during a (1.5) second silence (line 8) just after a brief utterance "uhm." During the (1.5) second silence the patient's gaze is now on the doctor's pad and hand, monitoring the movement. The doctor begins her next utterance with "you: uh-(·) when you," two beginnings which are recycled into "when yer eyes get tired d'you ever feel: (·) that uh: 'hh you-u (you'll). y- yer vision blurs?"

She has raised her head up from the pad as has the patient and they reach mutual gaze as she says "when you" (line 9) with the patient (hearer) continuing to look at her face throughout her utterance until completion. The patient's (hearer's) monitoring of the activity of writing could be considered the equivalent of the monitoring of the face during the act of speaking. Conceivably, just as the eyes and the mouth may communicate that an utterance is about to reach completion, so may the hand and the instrument it contains be monitored to ascertain when the writing is completed.

The doctor's apparent difficulty in producing the next question—there are three self-initiated repairs—may be related to the difficulty of making written note of the answer to the last question while searching for the next topic and also beginning to speak the next question.

The gap (line 5) in the turn transition space is thus found to be *filled* with the bodily action of lifting the head, lowering the lids, and attempting to "move" the patient's gaze to the pad. We cannot characterize this space as *empty* though it may be devoid of speech production.

The close examination of those spaces within a speaker's turn which are characterized as "silences" or "pauses" can also be shown to include bodily activities which are monitorable by co-participants for their relevance to the interactional production of the interview.

For example, in line 7, the (1.1) second silence within the doctor's turn at talk is filled with the activity of lifting the hand with the pencil to the pad and writing on the pad during the next (1.5) second silence (line 8).

We would argue that the manner by which the doctor is able to move the patient's gaze to the pad as she takes up the activity of writing is an interactional accomplishment designed to hold the "utterance-free" space. Once the pad has been established as an object of relevance for the interview and once the activity of writing, sequentially placed just after the patient's answer, is established as an activity also of relevance for the interview, the doctor-interviewer is able to utilize the object and the activity in holding the next turn at talk. Here, the object (pad) and the activity (writing) are not in themselves used to communicate though we can conceive of instances where they might be so used, e.g., when a person writes a note for the other to read as it is written, or draws a direction map for the other to use in getting to a place. The recipient (hearer, viewer) may visually monitor these actions as they are being performed. Similarly, speakers may use gestures to communicate and, as these gestures are performed, modulate the pace of speech production and fill pauses in the talk with gestures.[5]

In the interviews under study in this research we have found that utterance-free spaces (pause, gap) can be held for a considerable length of time while writing is performed. Interview 2, Segment 1 provides an instance where a (12.5) second gap is filled by the doctor's writing on the pad (lines 7–12).

This particular segment is revealing in another way. After (7.0) seconds the doctor's hand lifts at the wrist slightly as there is a noticeable pause in the writing and slight movement of the hand across the page.[6] At just that point the patient's gaze lifts from the pad to the doctor's face. This may reflect the viewer's anticipation of becoming a hearer and that the doctor will begin to speak. She can be said to be "preparing" to gaze at the doctor's face.[7] But he continues to write for an additional (4.5) seconds and the patient moves her gaze back to the pad and the writing.

The sensitivity of the viewer's gaze to the other's activity strongly indicates that the activity, writing, is being monitored for its interactional significance. The completion of the writing could be the place when speech will resume and the doctor's next utterance be produced.

The activity of writing can also be seen to have a pace, course, and structure of its own, perhaps as complex as talk, since the writing instrument may be raised between words or to dot i's and cross t's, to move across the page to the next line, or, if a questionnaire is being filled out, to move to relevant places on the page.

Conclusion

These data have enabled us to show that interactants are capable of sequentially organizing utterance and gaze in ways that are particularly

Interview 2 Segment 1

		DOCTOR	PATIENT
1.	D ________________ DOCTOR: (You havin' trouble) seeing in distance P ________________		
2.	D ______________________________ PATIENT: in the distant and uh close up P ,,,,,, ------- ...... ________		gaze moves away then back to Dr's face
3.	D ____ DOCTOR: both P ____	head lifts then moves down	
4.	D ____ PATIENT: both= P ____		nods head
5.	D ________ ,,, ------- DOCTOR: (distant and up uh–)= P ,,,,,,,, -----------	gaze moves to pad	
6.	D --- PATIENT: yes ---		head lifts up lids move down gaze to pad
7.	D - (+ +) P -	writes on pad moves hand and pen	
8.	D - (+ +) P -		
9.	D - (+ +) P -		
10.	D - (+ +) P - - - - - - - - - - . . . ____________	Dr's hand lifts slightly from pad	brief lid raise to Dr's face
11.	D - (+ +) P , , , - - - - - - - - - - - - - - - - - -		
12.	D - (+) P -		
13.	D - - - - - (+ + + + +) P - - - - -		
14.	D ------------ .... ________ DOCTOR: when was your last eye exam? P .... __________________	pencil still on pad, gaze moves to Pt's face	lifts lids gaze at Dr's face

sensitive to turn-transitions. Gaze can be used to display a co-participant's attention to speaker as well as to direct the other's gaze to other features in the setting or other activities.[8]

Once these patterns are established it is possible for additional matters of interactional significance to be produced.

In the instances noted here, it is possible for an object such as the pad to be made relevant for the interview and for the activity, such as writing on the pad, to be so organized sequentially in relation to the talk, that it is itself monitored for its interactional significance.

We are now in a position to comment on the matter of silences in utterance production in interaction. Silence is an auditory phenomenon, discernible as the absence of speech. But in the face-to-face situation where two parties are mutually aware of each other, each is able to monitor the other's bodily actions as well as all objects in proximity. The closeness of the two participants to each other makes it possible for movements of the head, eyelids, gaze, arm and hand and for objects such as pads and writing instruments to be displayed and sequentially organized in their use with the on-going speech production so as to achieve *interactional* significance. That they have such significance is clearly displayed by the interactants, repeatedly, in numerous places within the interview data presented here.

Thus, the presence of silences (pauses, gaps) or, alternatively formulated, utterance-free spaces in interaction does not necessarily mean that no actions of *interactional* significance are being produced or monitored auditorally, visually, or even tactually by the parties. Spaces may not be "empty" but filled–and it is possible to discover what they are filled with by examining video or filmic records. That bodily actions may have a sequential organization of their own goes without saying; but, they may also be fitted to the on-going talk in particular ways and for particular purposes. Our argument therefore is that utterance-free spaces in the face-to-face interaction situation need to be studied to discover the varieties of interactional phenomena being produced by co-participants.

The general implications of the findings presented here are that in the face-to-face situation where each person is able to monitor the other both auditorily and visually it is possible for gaze to be used to facilitate turn transitions, to direct the other's gaze (attention) and to coordinate gaze with other activities so as to enable turns at talk to be held across silences (gaps) of considerable length.

The activities displayed in such silences which are capable of visual monitoring by the other can be interpreted by the other as interactionally relevant. The activities themselves may come to be constituted as action-within-the-turn. As such, they may be monitored for their internal temporal organization, their meaning-units, and their spatial contours, as well as for their nested (or laminated) organization with talk and the turn taking system.

Interactionally relevant activities achieve a displayed and accomplished relevance in and through their connectedness with such other elements as gaze and talk.

The discovery and analysis of the sequential structures of gaze and bodily actions as interactional phenomena in their own right and in their connections to talk requires further detailed study.

ACKNOWLEDGMENTS

I wish to thank Richard Frankel for his considerable assistance in making detailed transcriptions of these interview materials and generally for the innumerable insights he provided over the course of several years while at Boston University. I also wish to acknowledge the contributions of other members of the Interaction Research Group at Boston University, particularly Jeff Coulter, Tim Anderson, David Helm, Paul Jalbert, Jay Meehan, Amy Neustein, Tracy Paget, Marty Sawzin and Earl Taylor.

The materials upon which these analyses are based are a series of five initial interviews between optometry students and their clients. The tapes provided the data base for an ongoing series of weekly meetings among members of the Interaction Research Group for two semesters during 1979-80. Thanks are hereby expressed to Dr. David Greenberg of the New England College of Optometry for his kind permission to reproduce the data in transcribed form.

NOTES

1. Goodwin (1979), in an excellent and detailed analysis of a single sentence, shows how the sentence is formed by the speaker in relation to the particular others present and toward whom the speaker is gazing.

This work serves as a major starting point for the present study. Goodwin provides an insight into how speaker's utterances may be shaped according to whom they are in eye contact with as they are speaking in a multi-party situation.

His study is concerned with the way in which the speaker's gaze direction, in the course of production of a sentence, is related to the content of the utterance. Specifically, he finds that as the speaker in a multi-party situation produces his utterance, he moves his gaze from one party to another. As each recipient is gazed at, the direction of the recipient's gaze is also noted. Goodwin finds that the speaker does modify his utterance as his gaze locates particular others. This is shown by the analysis of the modification of the utterance as different recipients are located by the changes in the speaker's gaze. When recipients do not make eye contact with the speaker, the speaker may re-start, use pause, or other such devices, in an attempt to gain such contact.

A speaker may move his gaze and achieve eye contact with other recipients as the utterance is produced and shaped for each particular recipient. (This conforms with the notion of recipient design as developed by Sacks and others.)

In contrast to Goodwin's work we can quote from Markel (1975, p. 195). "Everyday experience indicates that when engaged in a conversation, if you are going to look at your partner, you have to look in the direction of the face. Looking away is all right, but looking at any other part of the body is not acceptable, and is likely to disrupt the flow of conversation."

This is illustrative of the kind of anecdotal observation found in many studies which do not examine, in detail, the sequential organization of interactional phenomena.

A somewhat more detailed examination of the relation of gaze and talk is reported by Kendon (1973) when he describes a multi-party situation:

> Typically both speaker and direct recipient are oriented towards one another. As a rule, they repeatedly scan each other; from time to time their eyes meet. This orientation of head and eyes towards another, with intermittent aiming of the eyes directly at the other, is one of the principal ways in which a person signals to whom his messages are directed . . . in "aiming the eyes" what we characteristically observe is that the speaker's head repeatedly returns to the same position and then pauses. When not looking at his addressee he looks up or down or to the side, but not at anybody else. When he addresses several others at once, his repeated positioning will be replaced by a repeated scanning of those who constitute the recipients of the address. The movements of his head have a systematic relationship to the organization of his utterances.
>
> . . . so far as the listener is concerned, if he is the direct recipient of the address, he may be distinguished from the others in the gathering by a heightened *congruency of posture* with that of the speaker; his head is usually slightly "cocked" to one side, and his visual attention is far more consistent than that of other listeners. Also the direct recipient, unlike other listeners, tends to *exhibit a particular set of gestures,* such as head nods, and their vocal equivalent ("I see," "uh huh," etc.—sometimes

> known as attention signals) are placed at specific points in relation to the speaker's behavior.
>
> It has also been shown that a speaker and his direct addressee tend to show a *coordination of bodily movement* that we do not find between speakers and listeners who are not directly addressed. It has been observed that the direct recipient may pick up some aspect of the speaker's movements and move in a similar fashion in synchrony with him. (Kendon, 1970:52-53)
>
> . . . the rather conspicuous mirroring of movement . . . does not occur continuously. It is usually observed both at the start and again towards the end of an utterance. Our hypothesis is that in matching another's movements the listener signals that he is giving his full attention to the speaker. However, once this has been established the recipient needs only to remain in a listening posture and to display intermittent attention signals. Where . . . the recipient replies next we tend to find conspicuous movement relationships at the end of the interchange as well. This may both signal clearly to the speaker that the listener wishes to speak himself and it may also facilitate the precise timing of the entry of the other into the role of speaker rather as when a musician conspicuously beats time just before it is his turn to play.

Kendon (1970:61) continues:

> the way a speaker patterns his gaze in relation to his speech could function as a cue serving to regulate the behavior of his interlocutor. In looking away the speaker signals his intention to continue to hold the floor and thereby to forestall any attempt at action by his interlocutor. In looking at partner, if he does so briefly in mid-utterance, he signals merely that he is going to continue. If he looks at his partner in a sustained fashion as he finishes speaking this acts as a cue to the other to begin speaking.

2. The interviews studied are between a student optometrist and a clinic patient and involve history taking prior to an eye examination. We refer to the student optometrist as "doctor" and the clinic patient as "patient" though the nature of the interview and the lack of medical status of the student suggest a more appropriate designation would be "interviewer" and "interviewee." Nevertheless, from the perspective of the participants, the interview is one of medical history taking and occurs in the context of a health care facility. By referring to the parties as "doctor" and "patient" I do not intend to imply that this encounter is similar to encounters between medically trained practitioners and their patients. The focus of the paper is on the organization of interaction in the encounter and not on the medical or non-medical status of the parties.

3. Goodwin (1979) proposes that two rules operate: "1) the gaze of a

speaker should locate the party being gazed at as an addressee of his utterance (p. 99) and (2) when a speaker gazes at a recipient he should make eye contact with that recipient." (p. 106)

"Rule 2 also establishes a preferred sequencing for the gaze of the parties at turn beginning, with the hearer expected to bring his gaze to the speaker before speaker brings his gaze to hearer. Sequencing in the opposite order produces a situation where the speaker is gazing at a non-gazing hearer. The implication of this rule is consistent with the finding of Kendon (1967, p. 33) that a speaker looks away at the beginning of his utterance, while the hearer gazes toward the speaker there." (p. 117)

4. We are claiming that this space, or pause in the talk, is not necessarily "owned" by the doctor since she has just acknowledged the patient's answer in line 6. The minimal acknowledgment of the patient's answer could allow a speaker change again, i.e., the patient could speak. But, the manner in which the gaze is used and the space filled with an activity (writing) are utilized to convey to the patient that what the doctor is doing is part of her next turn in the interaction.

5. Kendon (1965) discusses gestures which accompany speech in considerable detail and speaks of gesticulation units and phrases. A gesticulation unit is maked by the beginning and ending of a set or series of complex movements which conclude when the limb, for example, returns to the rest position which marked the approximate starting point of the gesture. Within a gesticulation unit (G-unit) there may be several phrases which may be manifestations of "idea units" expressed in the verbal utterances being produced by the speaker-gesticulator.

Kendon (1965:359) argues that

> phrases of gesticulation that co-occur with speech are not to be thought of either as mere embellishments of expression or as by-products of the speech process . . . (they) are rather alternate manifestations of a process by which ideas are encoded into patterns of behavior which can be apprehended by others as reportive of those ideas . . . (It) is as if the process of utterance has two channels of output, one, speech; two, bodily movements.
>
> Phrases of gesticulation tend to appear a little in advance of their associated speech phrases and their preparation begins sometimes well in advance . . . the temporal priority of gesture may partly be due to the fact that for a given idea to be expressed in words it must be strung out over time whereas the same idea may be expressed in gesture in a single movement . . . Speech production may be interfered with (the pause) while gestural encoding is more readily accomplished than verbal encoding and may be faster for this reason.

Kendon (1965:363) concludes that

> gesticulation is a second product of the process of utterance. In the kinesic channel, movement patterns do not appear to have properties like the lexical and syntactic character of spoken

> language though they appear to share, in the dynamics of their organization, some of the prosodic features of speech.

He discusses briefly some gesticulation patterns related to intonation, speech content, object depiction, encoding of abstract features of discourse, e.g., themes, and framing units of discourse organization, though he does not claim that gesture is an invariable accompaniment of speech.

The bodily activities we are noting in the data presented in this paper are not part of the utterance production process. The writing on the pad is a separate action with an intrinsic significance and structure. However, it contains a series of actions which are sequentially organized in relation to utterance and gaze and therefore can be examined for their *interactional* significance.

6. Erickson (1975, p. 186) notes that "proxemic shifts occur very frequently at the beginning and ending segments of interaction that can also be identified by changes of speech content and style and by changes in the interaction process. This suggests that proxemic shifts may function as indicators of situational shifts and topic changes in interaction."

However, Erickson does not examine the sequential organization of proxemic shifts or their relation to utterances. Moreover, proxemic shift is a coder's category which lumps together various bodily movements ("body as a whole is moved, upper or lower half of the body, a few body parts move forward or back a large distance, and a few or single body part move forward or back"), and does not examine, in particular instances, the meaning of such movements as they would be interpreted and responded to by interactants (members).

7. An alternative interpretation is that the patient monitors the writing and sees that it will continue. She then uses the space to "steal a glance" at the doctor's face. Whichever interpretation may be made, both depend on the patient's visual monitoring of the doctor's writing activity which continues throughout the utterance-free space.

8. Frankel (1981) has identified one use of talk to draw recipient's gaze *away* from a relevant object in a medical physical examination. In that instance, the pediatrician, just prior to bringing his hands into contact with the patient's (child's) body, begins an utterance which is a question. At the onset of the physician's talk, the child's gaze is drawn to the physician's face and away from the hands. The child maintains eye contact until the conclusion of the question, then, as his answer begins to be formulated, moves his gaze to his mother seated at the side of the room, formulates his answer assisted by a prompt from his mother, and returns his gaze to the physician's face. The physician's hands, in the meanwhile, have been placed on the child's body and are engaged in physical contact examining the child.

The physician's use of a question (talk) and his own gaze (directed to the child's face) rather than the child's body or to his own hands works to shift the child's gaze from the physician's hands to his face.

In the instance examined here we have noted that speaker's gaze is used together with talk to draw the recipient's gaze *toward* the object and activity toward which the speaker orients his/her *own* gaze. Although a question may be formulated by the speaker (doctor) as his/her own gaze is directed to the pad (and writing activity), recipient's gaze does not orient to the speaker's face until speaker moves his/her face upward and gazes directly at the recipient.

REFERENCES

Erickson, F., One function of proxemic shifts in face-to-face interaction, in A. Kendon, R.M. Harris, and M.R. Key (Eds.), *Organization of Behavior in Face-to-Face Interaction.* The Hague: Mouton, 1975, 175–187.

Frankel, R., Are interviews conversations? It depends., paper presented to the First Annual Conference on Ethnomethodology and Conversation Analysis, Konstanz, West Germany, April, 1980.

____, The laying on of hands: Aspects of the organization of gaze, touch and talk in a medical encounter, paper presented at Annual Conference on Culture and Communication, Temple University, April, 1981.

____, Talking in interviews: A dispreference for patient initiated questions in physician-patient encounters, this volume.

Goffman, E., *Behavior in Public Places.* Free Press, 1963.

____, *Relations in Public.* New York: 1971.

____, *Frame Analysis.* Cambridge: Harvard University Press, 1974.

Goodwin, C., The interactive construction of a sentence in natural conversation, in G. Psathas (Ed.), *Everyday Language.* New York: Irvington Publishers, 1979, 97–122.

____, *Conversational Organization: Interaction between Speakers and Hearers.* New York: Academic Press, 1981.

Kendon, A., Gesticulation, speech and the gesture theory of language origins, *Sign Language Studies,* 9, 1965, 349–373.

____, Some functions of gaze direction in social interaction, *Acta Psychologica,* 26, 1967, 22–63.

____, Movement coordination, *Acta Psychologica,* 32, 1970, 1–25.

____, The role of visible behavior in the organization of social interaction, in M. von Cranach and I. Vine, *Social Communication and Movement.* London and New York: Academic Press, 1973, 29–74.

Markel, N. R., Coverbal behavior associated with conversation turns, in A. Kendon, R.M. Harris, and M.R. Key (Eds.), *Organization of Behavior in Face-to-Face Interaction.* The Hague: Mouton, 1975, 189–197.

Psathas, G., (Ed.), *Everyday Language,* Irvington Publishers, N.Y., 1979.

Sacks, H. unpublished lectures, School of Social Science, University of California at Irvine, 1967.

Sacks, H., E. A. Schegloff, and G. Jefferson, A simplest systematics for the organization of turn-taking for conversation, *Language,* 50, 4, 1974, 696–735.

Talking in Interviews: A Dispreference for Patient-Initiated Questions in Physician-Patient Encounters

Richard Frankel

This paper examins turn-taking during medical interviews and suggests that: (1) the turn-taking system for casual conversation does not always represent a model for the interview; (2) the medical interview is restricted with respect to turn types and speaker identity; and (3) that these restrictions amount to a dispreference for patient initiated questions and patient initiated utterances in general.

The data from ten tape-recorded medical encounters in ambulatory care visits between adult patients and physicians in general internal medicine are analyzed to show that less than 1 percent of all utterances by patients occurred in first position conversational slots. The vast majority of physician initiated utterances were questions, and subsequent to a patient response were followed by another question.

The types of patient initiated utterances utilized were found to be of four types:

1. *Sequentially modified questions. The question asked by the patient is prefaced by a query or a noticing.*
2. *Questions in response to solicits by the physician. The solicit warrants new information from the patient by forecasting a new phase of the interview and the close of the on-going sequence.*
3. *Initiations at boundaries marked by announcements or interruptions. Patients initiate at boundary points marked by announcements or interruptions as well as*

through the use of claims to having been asked about the matters they introduce.

4. Initiations in the form of multi-component answers.

Virtually all these types of patient initiation can be shown to be sensitive to the interactional constraints operating in the encounter, namely, the distribution of speaker rights and obligations (physicians initiate sequences and topics) and utterance type in relation to the speaker (physicians ask questions–patients respond).

A Characterization of the Problem

In their pioneering work on the organization of turn-taking for naturally occurring conversation, Sacks, Schegloff and Jefferson (1974)[1] provided the first comprehensive and systematic account of the mechanisms by which parties engaged in casual conversation arrange their speech production activities in an orderly and coherent fashion. For Sacks et al., conversation is one of an indefinite collection of activities for which turn-taking is a central organizational resource. One subset of the collection is referred to as "speech exchange systems" and includes "talking in interviews, meetings, debates, ceremonies, and conversations."[2]

This paper introduces some considerations of turn-taking during interviews and suggests that (1) the turn-taking system for casual conversation does not always represent a model organization for interviewing behavior, (2) talking in interviews is but one of an array of organized activities which constitute an encounter, (3) the array is organizationally systemic and interactive, with talk combining and being combined with other members of the collection to produce behavior organized by reference to tasks and activities unique to interviewing, (4) the characterization of talk in interviews as turn organized and turn bound must be viewed in light of other activity "systems" within which that talk operates and interacts.

Recent linguistic and sociolinguistic studies of the interview have suggested either directly, Labov & Fanshel (1977), Coulthard & Ashby (1975), Cicourel (1974), or indirectly, Churchill (1978), Shuy (1976), Kendon (1977), Scheflen (1973)[3], that interviews are essentially conversational in nature. Two implications from such studies as these are: (1) that casual conversation provides a model solution for problems which arise in the interview, and (2) the better we understand the rules of casual conversation, the better we understand interview behavior. To date, neither case has been made convincingly (i.e., on empirical grounds), although the assumption which treats the basic mechanisms of conversation and interviewing as one and the same phenomenon is pervasive.[4]

Sacks et al. (1974) propose, among other systemic features of conversational speech exchange that the order, size, length, content, and distribution of speaking opportunities is variable and relatively unconstrained in terms of pre-specification. By contrast, other speech exchange systems are claimed to differ from conversation along a dimension which moves from casual talk toward ceremony, where the salient feature of ceremony is the relatively large degree to which pre-specification of the types, content, and distribution of speaking turns operates. Interviews are cited as one example of a speech exchange system falling somewhere between conversation and ceremony. Thus, "The turns an 'interview system' organizes alternatingly are 'questions' and 'answers.' In (this) as well as other speech-exchange systems, the turn-taking organization employs, as part of its resources, the grosser or finer pre-specification of what shall be done in the turn it organizes."[5] Although an element of pre-specification has been introduced as a limiting condition on the types of speech activities which may appear in an interview system, for instance, little if any insight is gained as to how such a system is administered and what the distribution of rights, duties, and obligations concerning these delimited activities might be.

Our studies of the fine structure of medical interviews indicate not only that the items sequenced by a turn-taking system for interviews, namely questions and answers, are restricted but that in the administration of such systems routine restrictions also appear in terms of the assignment of turn format types to speaker types. In short, these restrictions amount to a general dispreference for client/patient initiated queries as evidenced by the distribution of patient initiated utterance-types across a corpus of recorded interviews.

The data for the study consist of 10 tape-recorded ambulatory care visits between adult patients and long term practitioners in general internal medicine.[6] These encounters provide a basis for assessing routine communication structure in ambulatory settings, as well as allowing for comparison between the interviewing behaviors of established practitioners and student physicians.

Theoretical Considerations

Questions, it has been noted, primarily by researchers interested in the analysis of single sentences, may be treated as structures which indicate that a speaker is doubtful, uncertain, or uninformed about what s/he is saying.[7] Within the wider domain of speech processes that move across sentences and across speakers, questions have been identified as turns or utterances which perform various sorts of tasks in requesting of a hearer, for instance, that s/he clarify, reiterate, confirm, supply information, and/or repair the content and sense of previously provided talk.[8] Finally, from the point of view of the structural organizations involved, it has been observed that questions and the speech which follows them are bound or packaged together both in terms of the order of elaspsed time which obtains between the completion of a question and the beginning of a next utterance, and also in terms of the degree of "fittedness" which utterances subsequent to questions display.[9] As has been elaborated by Sacks in his work on the organization of conversational activity, questions and responses are linked in time and structural organization via a set of conventional rules that provide the resources and constraints upon which subsequent actions are seen as appropriate or not. From a sequential point of view then, questions may be seen as one component of a formatted device for limiting, obliging, and in some cases demanding, what the conditions for subsequent actions will be. Sacks has termed these devices "adjacency pairs," and has shown their basic structure to apply to a number of utterance types in addition to questions.[10]

While the work questions accomplish in isolation or as adjacency pair components is interesting, little emphasis has been placed upon overall structural constraints which might limit the distribution of turn types to particular speaker types, or the effects such constraints might produce over the course of an encounter. As a consequence, the basic interactional properties of the medical interview remain unknown and the question of which model of speech exchange best describes interviews remains unanswered.

Sack's (1966) early notion of a "chain rule," consisting of speaker's maxims for linking questions to answers, and sequences of questions and answers to one another, states "When you are asked a question, respond with a direct answer, and then give the floor back to the questioner."[11] The chain rule describes a state of affairs in which each speaking turn is limited to a single speech activity, one question or one answer. Logically, it also limits speaker types to turn types since in a standard two-party interview, a response amounts to a return of the floor to the questioner who may, if s/he choses, continue the exchange by initiating another question. Presumably, where questioning is the major on-going activity of one speaker and answering the activity of another, that is, where turn-type incumbency is limited or constrained, the chain rule will very nearly describe the organization and distribution of the talk. Such fixed relations between speakers and the types of turns they employ also describes a speech exchange system in which one party (a questioner), recurrently imposes upon another party (an answerer), a set of sequential obligations, the net effect of which is to create a type of deference structure.[12] In terms of the array of speech exchange systems proposed by Sacks et. al. (1974), talk organized strictly according to the "chain rule" would appear much more like ceremony than casual conversation.

In casual conversation, on the other hand, speakers and the types of turns they employ are free to vary for entire conversations, topics, and utterances. There is no necessity for one party to remain a questioner and another an answerer. Additionally, since questions represent only one of a variety of paired formats sequenced by a turn-taking organization, far greater variation is realizable both in terms of the distribution of turn-types and the speakers who fill them. And while it is the case that certain conversational structures such as stories display distributional properties in terms of repetitive use (turns taken in constructing a story "round," for example) the repetitions are generally available as individual options rather than generalized requirements.[13] Finally, in casual conversation, the chain rule is modified by the fact that turns at talk may legitimately contain more than one type of speech activity: a single conversational turn can unproblematically contain an answer plus a question, two answers, or a non-response plus a response in combination.

The "chain rule" was originally proposed as an abstract model of relationships between utterance types; not as a characterization of particular types of encounters. However, it is apparent that an encounter organized strictly according to the "chain rule" would systematically limit the participation options of each of the parties. Such limitations, as noted by Sacks, Schegloff, and Jefferson (1974), are more characteristic of ceremonies than casual conversation. In operational terms, one could apply the "chain rule" as a "test" of the degree of ceremony or deference contained in one or a class of encounters.

In addition to the "chain rule" for questions which instructs a recipent to provide a direct answer and then turn the floor back to the questioner, at least three other conventional variants of the "chain rule" may be noted. One, which has been analyzed by Schegloff (1968) and termed an "insert" sequence" demonstrates how, following a question, a second question can legitimately follow without dis-integrating the sequence.[14] Jefferson (1972) has also developed an analysis in which large scale activities can warrantably be interposed between the initiation of a two part sequence such as question-answer and its conclusion. These "side" sequences as Jefferson has characterized them occur in a wider variety of sequence types than Schegloff's "insert" sequences which are restricted to the Q-A type exclusively.[15]

Another routine possibility for responses to questions is that the turn they occupy contains more than a single speech activity.[16] Thus, a speaker in responding to a direct question may, after providing a direct answer, append a question of his or her own to that answer. Schematically, such a sequence appears as follows, where the outermost brackets indicate a single turn composed of two different unit types, an answer, and a question.

A: Q
B: [[A] + [Q]]

Although in principle, the question operating as a second element of B's turn need not be joined or fitted to A's question or the response it has gotten, such instances, where they do occur in conversation, tend to operate as techniques for initiating, controlling, or competing for topic. In any case, regardless of the degree of disjunction, the appearance of a question in a same turn that contains an answer to a previous question obliges the original speaker of the question to, at least temporarily, become an answerer before s/he can again return to asking questions.[17]

In those situations in which a value is placed upon being a questioner rather than an answerer, both parties may attempt to manage control of the situation by appending questions to any answer turn.

Thus:

A: Q
B: [A] + Q
A: [A] + Q
B: [A] + Q etc.

In this case, although questions and answers are still "chained" together, it is not by the alternation of individual speakers bound to individual turn-types. Instead, each speaker requires the other to become an answerer *before* s/he can resume questioning. Strategically then, this organization may be seen to be composed of a set of complementary "moves" which first satisfy and then place similar sequential obligations upon the prior speaker. The order of obligation introduced here is deliberately accented, by placing a value on Q's as utterance initial moves, to demonstrate how turn and speaker type variability produce the possibility of complementary solutions to issues of constraint or obligation.

In addition to a single turn containing both a response to a question plus a question, a third routine turn shape involves producing an answer component to which a second answer component is appended. Here, as well as with the "response plus question" turn-type, there is no necessary relationship which must obtain between the two answer components; a second answer component may elaborate the sense or scope of a first and thereby, seek to expand the domain of the original question, or it can introduce information disjoined from the first answer component.

The basic format for this turn shape is:

A: Q
B: $[[A_1] + [A_2]]$

It is worth noting that in interviews at least, and it is probably true for some types of free-ranging conversation as well, the order of obligation posed by appending a second answer component to a first, while operative, appears considerably weaker in terms of the constraints it places upon the previous speaker to formulate a response which is sensitive to the additional information that has been provided. For example:

Dr: And did this make you ill?
Pt: Yes, it did. One by one everyone in my family became ill. My thought was that we were all somehow prone to this particular bug.
→ Dr: Do you smoke?

Here the additional information provided by the patient is simply not taken up by the physician/interviewer as he moves to his next question. In so doing, s/he is provided with an option rather than an obligation in terms of how additional components of the previous turn are to be handled.

More frequently, additional information supplied as a second component to an answer turn yields a type of response which has characteristics of both "insert" and "side" sequences. In these cases the interviewer or questioner will, in his or her next turn, initiate a query or series of queries regarding the additional information, at the completion of which he will return to his or her original line of questioning. Schematically, these sequences are organized as follows:

A: Q_1
B: $[[A_1] + [A_2]]$
A: Q'
B: A'
A: Q_2

In comparison with the "answer plus question" response, the multi-answer type response not only provides an option as to which portion of the information will be retrieved in the next turn, it does so without obliging the questioner to become an answerer.

To summarize thus far: in a speech exchange system in which turn-type and speaker type are free to vary it should make little difference as to the type of device used to enter new information onto the floor. However, where the constraints upon speech exchange reduce or minimize the types of turns each party can use appropriately, the kinds of turn organizations being proposed as routine solutions for entering new information onto the floor become valued as more or less preferred. In a system, for example, which "alternatingly" distributes questions to an interviewer and answers to a respondent (Labov and Fanshel for example (1977), define an interview as ". . . a speech event in which one person, A, extracts information from another person, B, which was contained in B's biography"), the techniques whereby new information can be and is placed on the floor are of real consequence in terms of the course, direction, and acceptability of the encounter to the speaking parties.[18]

It is being suggested that speech exchange systems such as medical interviews are unlike free-ranging conversation, in part because of the routine restrictions placed upon speakers and the types of turn organizational formats they conventionally employ during an encounter.

Data Analysis

Perhaps the strongest evidence for a dispreference for patient initiated questions comes from a gross comparison between the number of physician initiated and patient initiated sequences. In all, 3,517 utterances were transcribed for the 10 interviews, of which 30 were considered to be sequences initiated by patients; 17 of the 30 involved "normal" troubles such as requests for clarification, information, etc., and are thus not included in the analysis. In total, less than 1 percent (.09 percent) of the utterances produced by patients occurred in first position conversational slots.[19]

The vast majority of the physician initiated utterances were questions and were followed, subsequent to a patient response, with questions thus creating the type of Q-A chains in which turn type and speaker type are restricted to an ABABA format for turn exchange.

The Q-A chains themselves seem to display characteristic shapes in terms of internal design and discreteness from one another. The chains might be likened to topical divisions in casual conversation (in fact, from a medical point of view, they are thought of as body system reviews) and in combination, form larger units or phases which compose the encounter.[20] The chains themselves apparently have some properties which restrict patient responses. One type of typical chain currently under investigation is composed of a full question initiated by the physician, followed by a series of items or particles which, by reference to the initiating utterance as a shifter or topic marker tie the items in the chain together as a series of affiliated actions.[21]

For example:

→ A: Does anybody have tuberculosis?
B: No, not that I know of
A: Heart disease
B: No
A: Diabetes
B: No
A: High blood pressure
B: My father had that
→ A: Did you ever have whooping cough
B: Yes
A: Scarlet fever
B: No

In this fragment, each of the arrows indicates a division in the questioning chain, the divisions being marked by the use of a full question format followed by a series of items which compose that local chain. The chain's completion occurs at the point at which another complete question occurs. It seems to be the case that the reduction of information provided beyond the initial question in the chain also operates to reduce the amount of information which is relevant for the patient to supply. That is, in the presence of a question particle or token, which is itself a reduced form of and affiliated to the chain initial utterance, the appropriate response is shaped both by the organization of the chain as composed of questions and answers and also the shape or form that the questions take. Thus, there are perhaps some structural grounds for claiming that the shape of a questioning chain and the obligations it engenders can be connected in terms of techniques for controlling information reduction and expansion in the medical interview. In this case, the reduction rule seems to amount to a shaping of response appropriateness by reducing the questioning format to a token or list item.

Types of Patient Initiated Utterances

In the collection of patient initiated utterances, we found speakers employing questions in response to questions, and also employing them in response to non-questions such as announcements, instructions, etc. We found patients using questions solicited by physicians and in those instances in which solicits were not present, questions appeared at sequence and segment boundary points. Finally, we did find some instances of patients supplying answers to questions and appending a question or a request for permission to ask a question to their response turns. More characteristically, however, new information supplied by patients was supplied in the form of a response turn with multiple answer components.

In terms of patients initiating direct questions, we found no instances of a topically disjunctive question positioned either at a phase completion boundary or after a physician initiated question. That is, in 3,517 utterances, there were no "free standing" patient initiated questions. As powerful sequential devices for entering new information onto the floor the relative scarcity of questions among all patient initiated utterances is striking. The types of patient initiated utterances break down as follows:

1. Sequentially modified questions.

In two cases, Samples 1 and 2 below, direct questions were initiated by patients. However, in both cases the question itself appeared only after being prefaced by a request to query in one instance and a noticing in the other.

Sample 1

443 Dr: Very good. (0.4) very good=lemme see yer ankle.
(2.2)
Dr: Pt. ˙hhh VERY GOOD
→ Pt: I wanna ask yih som'n.
Dr: What's that.
(0.6)
Pt: Pt. ˙hh (0.5) I have - (0.6) (this) second toe (·) that was broken. (0.4) But I wen' to the p'diatrist (·) becuz I couldn' find a doctor on th' weekend. (0.4) En he said it wasn' broken.=it was. So it wasn' (·) taken care of properly ˙hh N' when I'm on my feet, I get a sensation in it.=I mean is there anything (th't) c'n be do:ne?
Dr: How long ago d'ju break it
Pt: Mmh two years.
Dr: Yih c'd put a metatarsal pad underneath it . . .

Sample 2

813 Dr: It's okay, (1.3) Okay y'c'n grab th' sides again if yih want to, (1.7) Pull against the sides. (0.5) that's it,
Dr: Fine.
(3.2)
→ Pt: That's pretty int'resting.=How come you do that examination (·) sitting u:p? (0.2) I mean pt. ˙hh
Dr: We're gunnuh do it lying down also
Pt: Oh rea:lly.
Dr: Yeh.

Both cases seem to illustrate a principle for reducing or delaying the impact of placing a direct question onto the floor in sequence initial position. That is, in a structural location in which a direct question could go without qualification were it unconstrained, what is being noticed about the current examples is the sequencing of prefatory materials as a device which displays a speaker's orientation to the force of initiating direct questions.

Two additional features are worth noting: first, each of the patient initiations is preceded by a substantial gap (1.1) and (3.2) seconds respectively, and second, each of the questions follows a request for, and acknowledgment of, action by the physician.

Since it is known that gaps in some instances represent a discontinuity in the routine exchange of turns at talk, and that responsibility for such discontinuities are routinely assignable on the basis of the completeness of a last speaker's utterance, it seems reasonable to suppose that the force of a direct question in this environment is further heightened by virtue of the fact that last speaker (the physician) has produced a warrantably complete utterance. However, it is also the case that in confirming a prior request for action with an assessment token "Pt. ˙hhh VERY GOOD," and "Fine," the physician has also brought to a close the segment in which (minimally) the request, its response and confirmation have been operating. Thus, in addition to the lack of cases in which direct questions appear without modification, Samples 1 and 2 provide further evidence that a dispreference for direct questions exists and that it is particularized in terms of an orientation to sequential placement within utterance construction.

2. *Patient initiated questions in response to solicits.*

As indicated, although the overwhelming sequence-type for medical interviews is Question-Answer, and the most frequent combining form of the type is a Q-A chain, both the linkage of sequences into segments, and segments into phases involve characteristic organizational "shapes." A series of single lexical items referring backward to an initial question is one such segment shape. And, as in the case of that shape, it is typical that several may be strung together to form a line or direction to the questioning. While there is some evidence to suggest that patients will occasionally comment on the activity composing these segments, it is rare that these comments take a question form. Thus,

Dr: Have you ever had Smallpox
Pt: No
Dr: Diptheria
Pt: No
Dr: Scarlet Fever
Pt: No
Dr: Rheumatic Fever
Pt: No, but my sister did.
Dr: All right.

→ Pt: I want you to know everything
Dr: Have you ever been operated on

Other types of segments are less straightforwardly linked and, in particular, in what is routinely a concluding phase of the encounter in which diagnostic conclusions, prescriptions, and instructions are presented to the patient, each turn exchange may operate or be marked as a segment. It is interesting to note that this phase of the medical encounter contains the fewest question initiations by physicians and the largest number of questions and utterance initiations by patients.

DATA SET 1: Sample 1

Log 1-90999

225 Dr: An'then (·) if y' pain gets worse er isn't at all relieved
I'd like t'know about that.
→ Pt: Shure. (0.2) Right.
Dr: OKa:y?
Pt: ˙hh NOW ORDINARILY I use alot a suppositories.
(0.3)

Sample 2

Log 10750

457 Dr: I think we c'n letchu stay on just the Digoxin. Yih c'n
stop th//at ev] ery eight hour stuff. Yeah.
Pt: This].
(1.4)
→ Dr: Awright?=
Pt: =Now// I wz to:le t'take one tablet a day.
Dr: (I think-)
Dr: Ye:s.
(0.3)

Sample 3

Log 1-05366

333 Dr: It's a little harder tuh- the urgency is a little greater

when yer–

(0.7)

Pt: Not//inna hospital=
Dr: Mmh hmh
Dr: =Right
Pt: I know.
→ Dr: OKay?=
Pt: = uh://:
Dr: If you wanna come in this//room n'ca:ll?]
Pt: I have Blue] Cross.
Dr: Good.=Y'got yer card with you,=bring yer bag with you,

Sample 4

Log 45246

→ Dr: There anything else y'wanna show me while yer in here.=
Pt: =Uhm, (0.2) No but let me j'st ask you if y'think I have (·) va– a vaginal infection at all becuz– it's– a l'l kinna so:re. Uh– An at– in a way that it doesn't ordinarily (//).
Dr: How long hez that been

.
.
.

Dr: Well. I'll give yih a prescription too.

Data Set 1 illustrates the physician's use of two types of markers used to forecast an upcoming shift in topic or direction. In Samples 1, 2, and 3, the physician has appended a disjunct marker, "OKa:y?" and "Awright?," to previous utterances, which contain elements of evaluation and instruction.

In marking or forecasting an upcoming shift, at least three tasks are accomplished. First, a sequential boundary point is established; second, a sequential option is provided for a recipient to either acknowledge and agree to closure, or to re-open or continue the previous sequence by supplying additional information; third, the device itself operates by requesting or soliciting an aknowledgment of completion or continuation of the sequence, thereby preserving a turn type and speaker relationship.

Such a device is termed a "solicit," and may represent a methodic orientation to routinely restricted patient options for placing new information onto the floor since it essentially warrants the appropriateness of patient initiated talk, including questions, at a particular sequential location. It is worth noting that solicits are apparently positionally sensitive in terms of the responses they produce. For example, Samples 1 and 2 both involve announcements of additional information designed to bear upon the segment or sequence marked for closure. In both cases, the solicit appears to operate to connect local sequences in or between segments. In Sample 3, the solicit operates as a "pre-" to closing a larger unit; in this case it is a phase which includes a potential close to the entire encounter. Instead of referencing backward to a prior item, this solicit engenders reference to an item of upcoming relevance, namely, method of payment.

Finally, it is apparent that solicits may take a variety of turn organizational formats, as is evidenced in Sample 4. Here, the solicit is formatted as a direct question, as opposed to a lexical item. As in the case of responses to a solicit, the *form* of the solicit itself may be positionally sensitive, indicating, as in this case, that a shift into a new phase of the encounter is imminent. It is unclear in Sample 4 why the patient's answer first satisfies the conditions for sequence closure, and is then immediately followed by an item appropriate to the solicit. There is no clear-cut evidence that the complaint is "discovered" past the patient's acknowledgment for closure. It is perhaps related to an alternate sense of "while yer in here," that is created using the acknowledgment plus a "new" item.

Given the evidence thus far it seems likely that solicits and other physician initiated devices for warranting patient responses display another formal property in the medical interview, and that is to limit the extent to which subsequent reference to the information contained within the local sequence-in-progress will occur or have relevance. As a rule of thumb, solicits seem to operate as "last calls" for information. Once the items to which they refer have appeared, they are unlikely to appear again. In terms of the ways in which interviews differ from casual conversation along a dimension of ceremony or pre-specification, solicits seem to act as devices for sequencing collections of discrete items for which selection restrictions operate in such a way as to provide transitions from one sequence, segment, or phase to another.

Two other boundary phenomena are worth noting: boundaries marked by announcement, and boundaries created by interruption. In both instances, patients are active in entering new information onto the floor.

3. Patient initiations at boundaries marked by announcement.

DATA SET 2: Sample 1

Log 45246

→ Dr: So this is the one an' I'm gunnuh write dat down.
Pt: Okay, Pt. ˙hhh//let me just ask you one er two other questions cuz I've had (·) SO MANY QUESTIONS ABOUT THIS DIVERTICULITIS WHICH nobody would stop to answer for me wh't you- hez got//me upset.
Dr: No:w,
Dr: (Lemme see) al] l y' aftuh do is invest d'time n'I// give y'the answer.
Pt: Uhm ka:y.

Sample 2

Log 45246

→ Dr: Awright dat's disease//one.]
Pt: Ok] a:y.
(0.3)
Pt: So- wai- yer gunnuh write down Metamucil or Kellogg's All Bran,// an' I'm also still gunnuh avoid (·) n-n- se:eds, probably, en nuts fer the time being ˙hhh now j's tell me one other thing K˙hh how long after you've eaten s'mthing does it cause you trouble (·) so that I c'n at least locate what's causing the trouble.
Dr: Bo:th.
Dr: ˙hh In your gut (·) something causes trouble within, (0.3) Well- it depends if:, this does what I suspect ˙hh that churning will calm down alot.

Sample 3

Log 1-05366

215 Pt: When I ws i:n graduating fr'm high school, they thought I had had uh:m (1.2) tch. (0.3) uh: waddaycallit (0.6)

u-rheumatic fevuh,
Dr: Mmh hm://h,
Pt: Cuz I- showed some signs of uh
Dr: Yeh (t'ha') thet's in yer reco:rd.
(1.0)
((buzzer))
Dr: J'st a moment.
(2.2)
Dr: Yep. ((telephone interruption))
(77.0)
((phone is hung up))
→ Pt: Now- you asked me 'bout the sleeping, (·)//uhm. I am
a light sleeper.
Dr: ˙Mmh yep.
Dr: Mmh hmh

Sample 4

Log 1-05366

232 Dr: De:ep brea//th.
Pt: :hhh
(0.4)
Dr: Out hh
Pt: hhhh
Dr: Again
.
.
.
Dr: Deep
Pt: ˙hhh
Dr: Out
Pt: hhhhh
(1.2)
→ Pt: You ask' me about- uhm. wud I w'z worrying bout=w'right
no:w, I'm (·) worrying about my son 'n his wife getting a
divorce= so I hev things thet're making me uh heh//heh heh
heh]
Dr: We:ll Y]' know hh=
Pt: =Y' Know?
(1.0)

Dr: Y'gotta problem with yer son doncha,
Pt: Ri:ght.
(1.0)
Dr: ˙hh Nothin' we're gonna solve too quickly either is it.
Pt: Noh. cuz they're three children. (16.0) ((sounds of blood pressure being taken))
Dr: J'st pull this thing down. (0.3) No don't take that off j'st pull the sleeves off// (thet's so) I c'n listen t'yer heart. 'at's a girl.
Pt: oh.

Samples 1 and 2 of this data set indicate that much like the solicits, identification or marking of a segment or phase boundary by announcement produces patient response in the form of new information. Notice that in both cases, the announcement is marked disjunctively by "so," and "awright," indicating an upcoming shift. Notice also, that each announcement names or provides a solution to what it completes in its segment or phase. In Sample 1, it is the announcement that what is being said will be written down; in Sample 2, it is that a review of one of several problems has been addressed completely. As in the case of the solicits, the marking of these boundaries sets the occasion for patient initiation and the introduction of new information.

Both initiations have interesting forms: the first, sample 1, contains a token acknowledgment which would otherwise operate as an agreement to close. This is evidenced by the fact that the physician begins what is projectably a new sequence beginning using the disjunct marker "Now." This turn start is overlapped by an addition to the patient's token acknowledgment, the additional component designed to request additional information about the disease being discussed.

The second initiation, sample 2, is also a response to an announced phase or segment completion. Again, there is acknowledgment though partially in overlap. After a short gap (0.3), the patient appends a new component to her turn, its framing in part sensitive to the segment's close—"so-wai-" indicating "more to come"—from the patient. The actual introduction of the new information comes from a question appended to a partial repeat of information provided in the previous segment. In terms of sequential positioning, both the repeated portion of the previous segment, as well as the question's frame, "˙hhh now j's tell me one other thing," may stand as potential resources for mitigating the effect of introducing a direct question onto the floor without particular invitation or warrant.

Samples 3 and 4 illustrate yet another type of boundary problem, that of interruptions external to the interview. In one case, the patient uses the re-entry of the physician into patient-oriented dialog as a warrant for initiating new information on a previous topic. Whether it is information designed to fill in a previously interrupted topic or to reopen an already completed topic is not immediately evident given the fact that the topic in progress just prior to the interruption is not sleep related. Thus, again at a boundary completion point, the patient initiates, framing the information as having previously been invited via "Now- you asked me."

The second sample is similar to the first with the exception that the boundary point is one in which a medical procedure (taking blood pressure) has just completed. The same framing device, "You ask' me about-" is used, although a search of the entire transcript does not reveal any such question having been raised in the current encounter.

These two fragments are particularly enlightening in terms of their design and the ways in which they handle the problem of initiating new information. Evidently, one way of warranting the introduction of new material is to claim to have been asked to supply it, if not in an immediately prior sequence or segment, at least somewhere within the domain of mutual biography. Whether or not the patient was ever asked to supply the information in question is not at issue. What is being noticed is: (a) the structural location at which the choice to initiate has been made, and (b) the extent to which the selection of the device reflects at least an orientation to the conditions under which new information may be appropriately initiated.

We have now seen a series of instances in which patients wishing to place new information onto the floor have done so either through invitation via a solicit, by initiating at an announced boundary point, or by using such boundary points to issue talk under the warrant of having had it requested at some prior point in time. Each of the devices thus far investigated, in addition to solving a general interactional problem, also appears to orient to a set of conditions relative to the use of direct questions to introduce new information. In the case of the solicits, the salient feature seemed to be the preservation of a turn-type speaker-type relationship; for other types of marked boundaries, it was the use of items prior to a question, repeats, requests for permission, etc. which seemed to bear on *how* and with what orientation the question initiations got done.

4. Patient initiations at boundaries marked by interruption.

Each of the above instances has been considered from the point of view of appropriateness as defined by physician oriented opportunities. The final data set examines a class of patient responses which attempt to enter new information in the form of additional turn components appended to an answer turn.

DATA SET 3: Sample 1

Log 99638

149 Dr: Did y'feel sick.
(0.6)
Pt: A little bit.//Ye:s]
Dr: Mmh hmh.] Right. ˙hh Now c'n yih // tell me–
→ Pt: An I wz very white.
(0.3)
Dr: Pale?
Pt: Pa:le.

Sample 2

Log 10750

358 Dr: Dih ih-ih-ih don' give me the reasons tell me whatcha feel like.
((Intercom buzzes))
Dr: (//)
Pt: Weak.
(1.2)
Dr: Yeh.
(1.1)
Dr: Noh:
(1.8)
Dr: Pt. ˙hh I don' ca:re.
((phone placed back in cradle))
Pt: uh::m, I feel uh– a little weak.
(0.8)
Pt: uh:m

(1.7)

Pt: [[I- I've-] I've bih=
Dr: [[Shortness of (breath)?]

→ Pt: =No I don' even have any shortness of breath. I've been (·) trying not t'go up 'n do:wn (·) stairs any more than possible. (0.3) uh:m, (1.1) I don' have much appetite but then I-I- wann'd a show yih I (·) didn't- the other medicine musta fallen out in the ca:r. (0.5) They gave me: this en they also gave me (0.4) uhm something that I take every,

Dr: E-n-n yih lost the other ones?

(0.3)

Pt: No it's in the ca:r.// It fell outa the ba:g.=

Dr: Oh.

Dr: =Yeh I'm gonna change the other one anyway to an// easier form,

Pt: (something t'take) every six hours.

Dr: Right.

Sample 3

Log 99638

121 Dr: Did that hurtche when y' took a deep breath?

(0.4)

Pt: Well that's excruciating. (·)

Pt: [[I still have tha:t.=
Dr: [[( )

Dr: =When yih take a deep breath it's excruciating,

→ Pt: Well it-it-was. (0.6) I think- well lemme tell you this (anyway). En I got that ther:e, (0.5) an n'en (·) then I got something over here on my neck he:re. (1.1) after that I got ay: uhm (1.3) un:m a kin' of a dull headache over my eye. Everything on the left side.

Dr: Please (0.5) nah c'n I go backward. The pain thetche develop (·) he:re en: just below the ribs er at the ribs th//ere. That wz the same character pain thetche had that day.

Pt: Mmh

Pt: Well I think (·) at the beginning it wa:s.

Sample 4

Log 99638

249 Dr: Hev y'brought any phlegm up since this started.
Pt: Noh
Dr: Hev y'had any blood thetche brought up.
Pt: Noh
Dr: Pt ˙hhh// (   )
→ Pt: But hh et- wh- buht//if th- last weekend especially, (0.4) if I had t'burphh or if I sniff:ed=
Dr: Mmh hmh
Dr: =Ye:s=
Pt: =˙hhh uh- nah just in or- even bl- or blew my no:se, either w- either direction ˙hhh uh:m hh the pain wz
Dr: =Agonizing?=
Pt: =Agonizing.
((Buzzer sounds; receiver is lifted))
Dr: Yes
(2.0)
Dr: C'rrect. j'st right on time.
((Receiver placed back on hook))
Pt: The slightest little wiff, en yih- thet yih//don't think about].
Dr: Uhright. C'n] I ask you a question please.
Pt: Y//es
Dr: Are you as sick t'day as y' were Mondee.
(1.0)
Dr: Are you sicker t'day then y'were Mondee.
Pt: Noh. I think I'm better right no:w.

Sample 5

Dr: . . . talk about thē: (·) uh the- the bloating feeling=the discomfort ch' have after dinn:er?
Pt: Yah.=
Dr: =A::h (·) d'you drink mmilk at all with dinner?
(1.1)
Pt: [[Uh, uh not really n:o.]
Dr: (milk related) or is this in any w- any way rela] ted t'milk.

(0.7)

Pt: No I don't really uh- I would say maybe I drink milk once // a day].

Dr: ˙hh C'n you-] (·) do you- w- d'you uh: does this happen when you don't drink milk.

(0.7)

Pt: hhU:hm (0.3) I haven't noted any // relationship (to it) no]

Dr: Pt.˙hh Y'haven't noted any relation] ship.

(0.2)

Dr: [[˙hh Have you-]

→ Pt: ˙hh Ah- ih] i:t it invariably is related to eating salads.= I like salads.

(1.0)

Pt: And whenever I eat salads I (tend to get)

Dr: Oh that's okay=that's interesting // uh:m

Pt: ( )]

(1.2)

Dr: ˙hhD'you d'you does it- this make you burp. u:h when you // (do this)].

Pt: Alot] (·) ye//h

Dr: Oh- (you'd) say y' y'd:o uhm, y'd:o, oka:y.

Pt: Yeah

(0.3)

Dr 2: Doe//z-

Dr: Good

As has been already discussed, multi-component answer turns have both advantages and disadvantages in terms of the options available to a questioner to minimize or ignore its content in subsequent talk. On the other hand, such turns when they are responded to maintain the speaker type-turn relationship with the physician as the questioning party and the patient as the answering party.

It should be noted that this type of device for supplying additional information was used more frequently than any other. It should also be noted that it had the most mixed results in terms of the sequential placement and acceptability of the information involved.

Sample 1 is relatively straightforward. It involves the patient, appending to a potentially already complete answer turn, "A little bit.// Ye:s.," a second answer component built via "an" to be a continuation and elaboration of the first turn component. It is noteworthy that the patient's addition of information occurs well after the physician has begun a turn which projectably begins a new question sequence and perhaps a new question segment. The fact that the physician "drops out" very soon after the patient begins speaking is perhaps connected to an analysis of the patient's utterance as hearably connected to the prior and therefore in need of a more immediate response than completion of a new and competing question would provide. In any event, the added turn component is taken up by the physician, although minimally through the use of an interrogatively voiced lexical item, "Pale?" It is responded to with a repeat of the item providing confirmation and the interview then resumes with the physician picking up his line of questioning once again. I believe this illustrates a type of preferred solution to the problem of entering new information onto the floor, where that information is not specifically requested or made appropriate by the questioner.

Sample 2 illustrates the use of a response turn that contains both an answer to the immediately prior question and then additional information which is not directly related. It is worth noting that the physician's initiating utterance in this case appears as a phrase, "Shortness of (breath)," rather than as a fully formatted question leading one to suspect that he is attempting to reduce rather than engender more information. However, it is equally worth noting that just prior to the patient's shift into providing new and less connected information there is a (0.3) and (1.1) second gap. As has been stated, such gaps frequently play a prominent role in turning the floor back to a speaker who has already produced a potentially complete utterance and who, upon non-response from a co-recipient, continues to speak. Once the additional information has been supplied, the physician initiates questioning relative to the last item mentioned. What is interesting in this case is the fact that the patient has produced a series of possible additions to her initial answer, i.e., going up and down stairs, loss of appetite, loss of medication, a display of medication, and the beginning of a discussion dealing with the patient's regimen. In the face of this flurry of information, the physician's query, "En-n-n yih lost the other ones?" is an attempt to disambiguate the several strands of talk that have been provided. In consequence, the information provided by the patient regarding stair climbing and appetite are by-passed by the physician's announcement of a change in prescription anyway. Clearly, under other circumstances patient responses could be elaborated almost indefinitely, and certainly beyond any reasonable connection with the original question.

Samples 3 and 4 also display the consequences of employing an answer turn to include not only a direct response to the prior question, but attempts to establish some linkage between it (the direct response and therefore the question) and some other set of events, in Sample 3, a linkage between neck pain and other symptoms. Such a combination is treated as unwarranted by the physician who re-issues the question minus the additional patient reference. A similar situation obtains in Sample 4 and 5, in which the patient appends new information not tied directly to the original question or its initial response.

Conclusion

The initial point of interest for the current study was a comparison of the systemic properties of speech exchange for casual conversation and medical interviews. It was found that unlike casual conversation, the talk produced in medical encounters was much more highly constrained in terms of utterance and speaker types. While it would be tempting to conclude from the investigation that "physicians control interviews by asking too many questions," or that "good patients are those who answer questions when asked, but do not ask too many questions themselves," such conclusions would be both unwarranted and incorrect.

Although essentially similar findings have been reported in the literature on interviewing it would be inappropriate to view the issues of control and responsibility in the medical encounter as properties of individuals. Instead, the main thrust of the analysis has been to describe and demonstrate some of the organizational bases upon which speakers and hearers mutually collaborate in constructing communicative events. That the structures through which a particular collection of sequences is realized appear to routinely restrict the range and type of speaking opportunities suggests less that physicians are at fault or patients are at fault for being poor communicators than it does that the presuppositional grounds upon which the communication situation itself rests need to be examined. Only through such examination will methods for training physicians and patients to effectively collaborate in producing and sustaining mutually satisfying encounters be found. An appreciation of the mechanisms involved in the interactive production of speech during medical interviews is a first step in that direction.

ACKNOWLEDGMENTS

Many of the ideas in this paper were first presented in an ongoing series of weekly interaction research seminars held at Boston University during 1978–79. Faculty and graduate students from several Boston area universities participated in these seminars and I should like to name them and express my appreciation to them for the stimulating and often searching comments made during the preparation of this and other research reports. They are: Tim Anderson, Jeff Coulter, Rolf Diamon, David Helm, Paul Jalbert, Richard MacDermott, Jay Meehan, Elliot Mishler, Tracey Paget, George Psathas, Marty Sawzin, and Earl Taylor. This paper was first presented at the First German British Conference in Ethnomethodology and Conversation Analysis, Konstanz, West Germany, April, 1980.

NOTES

1. Sacks, Schegloff, and Jefferson (1974).

2. As Sacks, Schegloff, and Jefferson (1974:730) suggest, turn-taking may be viewed as a central organizational resource for administering a variety of speech exchange systems, with free ranging conversation representing the basic template which other, increasingly ceremonial, types are transformations of. Having thus located a series of systems tied together by successive transformations of a "master" type, it follows that the turn-taking properties of the entire collection will vary linearly. However, it is important to point out that there are "vertical" as well as "horizontal" linkages which characterize the various forms of speech exchange. For instance, medical interviews apparently show the same general dispreference for client initiated questions as classrooms, courts of law, and other types of professional client interaction which vary considerably in other turn-taking dimensions. See Sinclair (1972:88), Atkinson (1979), and Frankel (1977). The feature which links these types of exchange systems is not simply a greater or lesser degree of prespecification in the allocation of turns, but the recognition and expression of culturally bound asymmetries operating between speakers and hearers as well. To illustrate, the notion of a dispreference for client initiated questions speaks to the issue of options generated independently of whether turns are allocated locally or on a proscribed basis. Using the turn allocation vocabulary suggested by Sacks, Schegloff, and Jefferson, it is possible to make an analytic distinction between the ways in which speaking "in" or "out" of turn produces effects on the current or subsequent distribution of turns. This distinction does not extend, however, to the ways in which speaking opportunities employing preferred or dispreferred formats produce continuations or "in line" variations, i.e., locally managed troubles whose manner of resolution does not affect turn allocation of distribution mechanisms per se.

3. The literature on dyadic interaction, and interviewing as one of its major

forms, is extremely diverse both in terms of type and the amount of control exerted over the settings investigated. The studies cited in this report share at least a similar methodological focus upon the use and direct representation of naturalistic settings as a basis for analytic inquiry. Thus, a number of investigations of the interview, but notably the work of Bales (1950) and his students have been set aside since they do not contain any direct contextual or sequential information.

4. Labov and Fanshel (1977:1) are typical of this point of view. In defining their research task, they state, "This book is an attempt to grasp some of the general principles of conversation as they appear in the therapeutic interview, and some of the ways in which conversation is influenced by the particular character of that event." Similarly, while finding notable differences in the ways in which social setting influences responses to questions, Churchill (1978:39) nevertheless treats all forms of question-answer pairing as analytically equivalent in their bearing upon the utility of Sacks' chain rule for conversation.

5. Sacks, Schegloff, and Jefferson (1974:710).

6. I am grateful to Dr. Eric Cassel of Cornell Medical College and Dr. Albert B. Robillard of Michigan State University School of Medicine for making available a variety of audiotape recordings of ambulatory encounters, some fragments of which appear in the text.

7. Within much of linguistics, see Lyons (1969:98), the single sentence, abstracted from actual situations of use, serves as the unit of analysis. Bolinger, for example (1958:2–5) defines a question as a sentence or utterance which has interrogative syntax, intonation, or gestures accompanying it. Bolinger also includes the broader criterion of an answer's occurrence subsequent to an utterance as a means for detecting a question's presence. In general, however, the force or effect questions might have in dialog is not treated as a relevant linguistic problem. To the contrary, the properties of questions are seen as the self contained and self evident linguistic products of individual speaker, irrespective of the communication situation itself.

8. A more recent concern among linguists is to treat sentences or utterances as a type of social activity whose linguistic boundaries are more properly located in discourse, i.e., in a consideration of the force of what a speaker means or intends to convey in an utterance as well as the vehicle by which it is conveyed. See for example Austin (1962) and Searle (1969:22–26). While attention in speech act analysis is still largely focused on an analysis of intentionality as it is expressed in the sentences uttered by an individual speaker, the effect of force of his actions upon a listener are also considered as linguistic evidence bearing on the performative character of speech. A recent paper by Goody (1978:17–43) deals with different forms of Gonja questioning behavior and attempts to analyze them according to their function as speech acts. Goody suggests that Gonja questioning varies along two major dimensions, information and control, but that the force of all types of questions is the elicitation of a response.

9. Sacks (1971) refers to this characteristic as "sequential design," i.e., the propensity for talk subsequent to an initiating utterance to display in its response a hearer's analysis of what the prior utterance "amounted to" not only as a speech act, but as a sequential activity as well. Sacks, Schegloff and Jefferson (1974:728) refer to this phenomenon as a member's "proof procedure" for locating the type and force of a prior utterance. Thus, the activity of speech pro-

duction and exchange is treated as both contingent, see Garfinkel (1967), and as a member's interactional accomplishment. The focus on language use as fully interactional, i.e., mutually participated in and mutually sustained, differs from the traditional linguistic approach and much of speech act analysis in its emphasis upon contextual particulars and more particularly upon the enabling structures which give sense and direction to speech exchange. A recent paper by Goodwin (1979) demonstrates, among other things, the utility of analysis that is sensitive to the particulars of the speech production process itself. Goodwin describes a situation in which a single coherent utterance is adjusted in its production for the particular circumstances of multiple potential hearers, only the last of whom displays the appropriate orientation, gazing at the speaker, for becoming that turn's recipient. Thus, in contrast with speech act analysis which does not consider speech production per se, Goodwin suggests that the assumption of well formedness, i.e., an utterance constructed by a single speaker and directed toward a single recipient when used as a criterion for judging speech acts recovers only a limited number of actual cases. Sacks (1968) makes a similar point in his discussion of collaboratives, single utterances constructed by multiple speakers.

10. Sacks (unpublished lectures 1972) found that the basic properties of adjacency and sequential fittedness which mark a second utterance in relationship to a first, operate for a number of pair types including: greetings, partings, requests, insults, announcements, instructions and complaints. Sacks (1975) also notes that the temporal relationship which holds between adjacency pair members constrains the domain of appropriate response time available to a speaker. In short, lack of a second pair part on the occurrence of a first constitutes a noticeable absence, analyzable by a current speaker as a failure to hear, deliberate non-response, etc. This property of "conditional relevance," as Sacks terms it, provides a rule based criterion for ordering elementary units of social participation in both normal and deviant circumstances, a feature not available in most linguistic grammars.

11. Quoted from Churchill (1978:29).

12. The Compact Edition of the Oxford English Dictionary defines deference as, "Courteous regard such as is rendered to a superior or to one whom respect is due; the manifestation of a disposition to yield to the claims or wishes of another." In the context of this analysis of speaking practices during medical interviews, the concept of deference is limited to the recurring sets of sequential obligations placed upon a recipient with the introduction of a question operating as a first part in a paired sequence, Q-A. Thus, the obligation to respond, insofar as it characterizes and constrains the speaking opportunities of one member of a dyad and not the other, may be treated as a type of sequential deference. One consequence such an arrangment produces for the medical encounter, one which may provide a further distinction between interviewing and casual conversation, is differential productivity of talk. In general, questions are an economical device for inviting more talk than they themselves require to produce. Thus, Matazzaro's (1964) finding of an equalization of turn productivity (length) for astronaut-ground control dialog is not necessarily matched in the medical interview where routinely questions such as, "What seems to be the problem?" receive replies which are far lengthier than the question that engendered them.

13. Sacks (1972) suggests that second and subsequent stories (jokes as story-types apparently function similarly), may be selected by a recipient to provide a

response which demonstrates knowledge, appreciation or understanding of the situation or events portrayed by last speaker. In so doing, a group or "round" of stories may, but need not necessarily, be produced, which will share a single theme or focus.

14. Schegloff found in addition to the proposed two turn base sequence for adjacency pairs a number of conventional possibilities for internal expansion. Thus, between an adjacency pair first part and its eventual response, a number of contingent actions, e.g., requests for information, clarification, etc., can occur routinely, each fitted in such a way as to modify the sense of the first while preserving its basic organization as a sequenced pair.

15. One environment in which both side and insert sequences are regularly generated in the medical encounter involves the use of technical terminology or "jargon." Requests for information or clarification, see Meehan (1981), often accompany physician questions containing technical or jargonistic formulations. In some cases, patient requests operate straightforwardly as insertion expansions; in other cases, the expansions take on "a life of their own," leaving the initial question unanswered or irrelevant. For example,

Log 1-05366

236 Dr: D'you think y'can give me a m- a moment when this happened to yih,
(1.4)
Pt: Uh::m, (0.9) Y'mean did I call you when it first happened?=
Dr: =Mmh hmh
(0.5)
Pt: Let's see hhl cal:led, Frid'y (1.0) Uh::m hhh Y'mean th' shortness of brea:th,
Dr: Ye:p
(0.8)
Dr: Hev y'hed any palpitations?
(1.3)
Pt: Wadda y'mean by a- what is a palpitation= I really don't know.
(0.3)
Dr: Ā- (1.0) pounding // in the chest?
Nu: Faster]
(2.0)
Dr: [[( )
Pt: [[I don' think so=
Dr: =Okay, Right ye //ah.
Pt: I think I've-
(0.6) ((machine sound))
Dr: Awright. j's move yer head over d'th' side there

16. This factor, though noted by several investigators, Shuy (1976:376), Goffman (1976:259), Mishler (1974:101–103) as a routine turn shape has not received systematic investigation, nor has its implications for speech act analysis been outlined. That a single utterance can contain multiple speech acts is clearly important from a sequential point of view since it presents a recipient with multi-

plex and potentially competing possibilities for response. In terms of the distribution of multi speech act turns for speech exchange systems in general, little is known about the systematic effects of limiting or regulating turn allocation or turn type, as apparently occurs in the medical interview and elsewhere. Regarding such effects, it may be that Churchill's (1978:38–44) finding that the chain rule is followed strictly only 12.2% of the time for casual conversation but rises to 24.0% and 34.6% respectively for legal talk (the rates are greater still (54.0%) where direct examination is compared with cross examination), sheds some light on the effects of context on turn types. However, single utterances containing multiple speech acts are not considered directly in Churchill's analysis as a source of variation from the chain rule, and it is thus difficult to pinpoint the exact effect such utterances might have in different contexts.

17. Goffman (1976:259) refers to this type of organization as a "sociable chain," noting in such an arrangement that the party providing a second to some first pair part also provides the first part of the next pair as part of a single utterance or turn at talk. In comparing children's speaking practices with adults', Mishler (1975:101–103) refers to the same type of structure as "arching," and found that while rates of arching did not vary significantly from adults to children, QA chaining as opposed to arching was twice as frequent as a means of connecting paired units.

18. Mishler (1975:106) comments, ". . . if we grant that the asking of an initial question represents an act of control then it appears that this gives the questioner an "edge" in that he/she is more likely to control the beginning of the second cycle of the conversation than is the responder. There is a concordance between these statistical findings and Sacks' norm (the chain rule), but we are interpreting the questioner's reserved right to talk again as an exercise of social power. To ask a question in response to a question is an act of countercontrol and may require that there is a "true" differential in social power where the responder has more real authority or, at a minimum, that there be equality between the speakers."

19. The criteria used in selecting "free standing" first position utterances were as follows: (1) an utterance initiated by a patient that was topically disjunctive, i.e., competed with an ongoing topic, (2) an utterance initiated by a patient at a phase completion boundary which either began a new topic tied back to a previous topic or re-started a just completed topic, (3) an utterance initiated by a patient after a speech relevant pause that entered new information onto the floor either by topic initiation, extension, or modification. In a follow-up study using similar criteria West (1983), found that physicians in a Family Practice setting initiated 91% of the questions asked suggesting that a dispreference for patient-initiated questions exists more generally in the medical consultation process. See Frankel (1984:155–160), for an extended analysis of this phenomenon.

20. See Frankel (in press: 15) for a discussion of "phases" of the medical encounter.

21. A somewhat similar point is made by Ray and Webb (1966) in describing what they term the "question-answer effect," i.e., a parallel tendency for longer questions to receive longer answers and vice versa.

REFERENCES

Atkinson, J. M., Order in Court, London, Oxford University Press, 1979.

Austin, J. L., *How to Do Things With Words,* Edited by J. O. Urmson. New York: Oxford University Press, 1965.

Bales, F., *Interaction Process Analysis: A Method for the Study of Small Groups.* Reading, MA: Addison-Wesley, 1950.

Bolinger, D., *Interrogative Structures of American English.* Montgomery: University of Alabama Press, 1958.

Churchill, L., *Questioning Strategies in Sociolinguistics.* Rowley, MA: Newbury House Publishers, 1978.

Cicourel, A., *Theory and Method in a Study of Argentine Fertility.* New York: John Wiley Publishers, 1974.

Coulthard, M. and M. Ashby, "Talking with the Doctor I," *Journal of Communication,* Summer 1975, 140–152.

Frankel, R., "From Sentence to Sequence: Understanding the Medical Encounter Through Microinteractional Analysis," *Discourse Processes,* 7, 135–170, 1984.

——, "Microanalysis and the Medical Encounter: An Exploratory Study," in D. Helm, W. T. Anderson, and A. J. Meehan (Eds.), New Directions in Ethnomethodology and Conversation Analysis, New York, Irvington Publishers (in press).

——, "Between Client and Server: Aspects of the Organization of Conversational Exchange During Service," Unpublished Doctoral Thesis, The Graduate Center City University of New York, 1977.

Garfinkel, H., *Studies in Ethnomethodology.* Englewood Cliffs, New Jersey: Prentice-Hall, 1967.

Goodwin, C., "The Interactive Construction of a Sentence in Natural Conversation," in G. Psathas (ed.), *Everyday Language: Studies in Ethnomethodology.* New York: Irvington Publishers, 1979, 97–122.

Goody, E., "Towards a Theory of Questions," in E. Goody, (ed.), *Questions and Politeness Strategies in Social Interaction.* London: Cambridge University Press, 1978.

Goffman, E., "Replies and Responses," *Language in Society, 50,* 1976, 257–313.

Jefferson, G., "Side Sequences" in D. Sudnow (ed.), *Studies in Social Interaction.* New York: Free Press, 1972, 294–338.

Kendon, A., *Studies in the Behavior of Social Interaction.* Lisse: The Peter De Ridder Press, 1977.

Labov, E., and D. Fanshel, *Therapeutic Discourse: Psychotherapy as Conversation.* New York: Academic Press, 1977.

Lyons, J., *Introduction to Theoretical Linguistics.* London: Cambridge University Press, 1969.

Matarazzo, J. D., A. N. Wiens, and G. Saslow et al., "Speech Durations of Astronaut and Ground Communication," *Science,* Vol. 143, 1964, 148–150.

Meehan, A. J. "Some Conversational Features of the Use of Medical Terms by Doctors and Patients in Interaction," in P. Atkinson and C. Heath (eds.) *Medical Work.* London: Gower Press, 1981.

Mishler, E., "Studies in Dialog and Discourse: II Types of Discourse Initiated by and Sustained Through Questioning," *Journal of Psycholinguistic Research*, Vol. 4, No. 2, 99–121, 1974.

Oxford English Dictionary, Compact Edition. London: Oxford University Press, 1971.

Roy, M. L., and E. J. Webb, "Speech Duration Effects in the Kennedy News Conferences," *Science*, 1966, *153*, 899–901.

Sacks, H., "The Search for Help: No One to Turn to," Unpublished Doctoral Dissertation, Department of Sociology, University of California at Berkeley, 1967.

____, Unpublished Lecture Notes, University of California, Irvine, Fall 1968, No. 5, 1–9.

____, Unpublished Lecture Notes, University of California, Irvine, 1971.

____, "Adjacency Pair Organization," Unpublished Lecture Notes, University of California, Irvine, Spring 1972.

____, "Second Stories," Unpublished Ms., University of California, Irvine, 1972.

____, "Everyone Has to Lie," in B. Blount and R. Sanchez, eds., *Ritual, Reality, and Innovation in Language Use*. New York: Academic Press, 1975.

Sacks, H., E. Schegloff, and G. Jefferson, "A Simplest Systematics for the Organization of Turn Taking for Conversation, *Language*, Vol. 50, No. 4, 1974, 696–733.

Schegloff, E. A., "Sequencing in Conversational Openings," *American Anthropologist*, 70, 1968, 1075–1095.

Searle, J., *Speech Acts: An Essay in the Philosophy of Language*. London: Cambridge University Press, 1969.

Sheflen, A. E., *Communicational Structure: Analysis of a Psychotherapy Transaction*. Bloomington, IN: Indiana University Press, 1973.

Shuy, R. W., "The Medical Interview: Problems in Communication," *Primary Care*, Vol. 3, No. 3, Sept. 1976, 365–386.

Sinclair, J. McH., and M. Coulthard, *Towards an Analysis of Discourse: The English Used by Teachers and Pupils*. London: Oxford University Press, 1975.

West, C., "Ask Me No Questions . . .' An Analysis of Queries and Replies in Physician-Patient Dialogs" in S. Fisher and A. Todd (Eds.), *The Social Organization of Doctor-Patient Communication*, Washington, D.C., Center for Applied Linguistics, 1983, 75–106.

Some Features of the Elicitation of Confessions in Murder Interrogations

D. R. Watson

This study presents us with the manifold possibilities of discovering important practices and interactional structures in police interrogations of suspects. The interrogation, a speech-exchange system designed to elicit a "confession" from a suspect, involves the co-participants in ways of speaking which can be analyzed by the methods and procedures developed in conversation interaction analysis.

The interaction competence of both parties, as speakers and hearers, is relied upon in the co-production of the confession. The police interrogator organizes his utterances with reference to knowledge-claims in such a way as to upgrade their status as "known" rather than only "suspected" or "believed." The suspect is put in the position of having to deny or repudiate a series of such claims, organized sequentially in a "bloc" of talk by one speaker, and strengthened by the assembly of "facts" which can be commonsensically interpreted as "true."

Suspects can be invited to present their "story," a narrative form which generally involves multiple utterances, extensive information, organized temporally, and leading to a conclusion. But as "invited stories," confessions are expected to produce what the hearer wants to hear, and his intercalations are designed to keep the story complete, relevant and to incorporate elements claimed to be known by the police-interrogator already. Thus, such stories differ from stories initiated by persons in ordinary conversation in that the recipient makes efforts to control the story's production–and also to keep the suspect talking.

The "persuasion" and "power" which might be commonsensically considered as operating to produce the confession are here discussed as matters which can be studied in the ways in which they themselves are interactionally accomplished in the interrogation.

Interrogations constitute a particular form of speech exchange system. However they can at least be regarded as naturally situated and naturally occuring, and the ones we have recorded were not conducted as simulations, "mock-ups," or in experimental conditions and the like but are quite simply real-world interrogations, with all the consequentiality which this implies.

The transcribed data upon which this analysis is based (see data appendix) are drawn from two videocassette recordings of police interrogations of murder suspects, Lewis Strawson and Stuart Riley,[1] in a large North American city. Strawson is accused of having killed and dismembered a young woman and Riley is suspected of three murders. Both suspects confessed, though Riley only confessed after protracted interrogation and an interview with his parole officer. The recordings were made by social scientists and the police officers. Two officers were present though one did the burden of the interrogating.

The interrogations from which the transcripts below are drawn fall under a general and rather indeterminate set of conversations, namely those where the co-participants are jointly oriented to the possible production of a "single" outcome, in this case, a confession or series of confessions. This is not to say, however, that co-participants espouse the same practical interests in that outcome; indeed, some features of the conversation such as the policeman's use of what we might term "persuasive devices" seem tailored to address such perceived or imputed divergences of interest, as we shall see. Nonetheless, one corollary of such conversations is that when the outcome is produced, the co-participants will find in that a warrant to close the conversation.

Another aspect of such conversations is the distribution feature; that is, the confession has to be produced by one of the interlocutors rather than the other; this has great relevance to our later observations concerning invocations of direct experience.

Much of this paper will be devoted to an attempt to show some of the ways in which what we might grossly describe as "persuasion"–

in this case the persuading of a suspect to confess—may be treated as socially organized. I hope to indicate that the notion of persuasion or even persuasive devices may usefully be deconstructed into more generic aspects of the interrogation as a speech exchange system. For the most part, I shall focus upon the many ways in which knowledge is invoked and mobilized in the course of the interrogation. These include avowals, ascriptions, elicitations and displays of specific items of knowledge and the conversational vehicles and formats in which these are incorporated, embedded, and organized relative to each other. This, however, is not to say that knowledge is not used, invoked, or displayed in other places in the conversation than those indicated in this analysis, since, of course, the actual conducting of any conversation involves an immensely complex and sophisticated commonsense knowledge of communicative conventions, procedures and the like. If for present purposes I may be permitted an analytic over-simplification, this more generic knowledge comprises "knowledge how" (of procedure, etc.) rather than substantive "knowledge that" (e.g., that something is the case). It is through this "knowledge how" that substantive items of knowledge are imputed and ascribed. The specific avowals and ascriptions of knowledge to which I shall be referring can, of course, only be coherently accomplished through the operation of that bedrock level of commonsense knowledge, such as knowledge of how to do competent description and sequencing in ordinary talk. I hope at least to indicate that avowals and ascriptions are not only achieved *through* sequencing but can also be central resources *in* the sequential organization and directiveness of conversation. In other words, I wish to suggest that such knowledge-claims can help us understand what goes on before and after, as well as during, the confession(s). Particular orders of knowledge claim can, I feel, serve to assist interlocutors and analysts alike in identifying that a given stretch of talk indeed constitutes a confession, as will be indicated below.

Knowledgc Claims and Their Organization

The first set of knowledge-claims I want to look at is contained in the sequence of talk in the Stuart Riley case (lines 31-3), where the police officer confronts Stuart with a reconstruction which places Stuart at the scene of the crime. The officer prefaces various items of the reconstruction with the particle "We know . . . ."

e.g. ". . . . with the red leather jacket . . . we know you

> borrowed from a friend . . . we also know about the gun in the Morris homicide. . . ."

Let us consider other possible prefaces to these reconstructed items, such as "we *think* you borrowed the jacket," "we *believe* that you fired a shot at Emburey Street," "it is our conjecture that you gave the gun to Jane," "we're speculating that the tape recorder came from the apartment of Charley Dawson," "it's our supposition that. . . .", or the quasi-interrogative form "we were wondering whether you. . . .", and the like. In contrast to the prefatory particle "we know," these other prefaces can be seen to downgrade the claims constituting the account. By comparison with those terms, "we know" can work to upgrade the claims constituting that account. This upgrading can almost by definition intensify the persuasive power, so to speak, of the claims made. As Jeff Coulter (1979:177–82) has pointed out, knowledge-claims as opposed to, for instance, belief-claims, can, through their upgrading work, serve as persuasive devices. Belief-claims, when used in relation to knowledge claims, can work to downgrade a claim or to incorporate guardedness into the making of a claim.

This can be traced out in terms of the sequential organization of the conversation, in that knowledge claims, as opposed to belief claims, suppositions and the like, can, in the most general way, be said to intensify a preference for confirmation rather than for disconfirmation of the claims being made by the officer. Such confirmation can, of course, be highly implicative for a confession. The redoubled relevance of confirmation may be seen to elevate the policeman's claims, accounts, and the like in a hierarchy of preference—in relative terms, the account becomes preferred rather than dispreferred or of equivalent or equivocal status *vis-a-vis* other hypothetically conceivable accounts. Put in terms of Dorothy Smith's (1978:33–7) published paper, the policeman's presentation of his claims as *knowledge* rather than supposition work to "establish" the facticity of his version or reconstruction. While such upgradings by no means ensure that a confirmation or confession will eventuate, it is certainly the case that Stuart Riley later in the interrogation ascribes knowledge to the police and others too when he says, "O.K., I'm gonna stop, seems everybody knows I just did it, that's all."[2]

To specify the sequential aspects of knowledge-claims a little more closely, let us consider some possible projected turn sequences and turn shapes involving different kinds of claim. Had the policeman said to Stuart Riley "we were wondering if you (gave the gun to Jane)," or "we think you. . . .", or "it is our conjecture that. . . .", then a bland or simple denial such as "no I didn't" on Stuart's part might well be enough to terminate the sequence with, at most, a simple "reception" or acknowledgment from the officer in the third utterance of the sequence. If the officer wants to preserve his initial claim rather than simply acknowledge the suspect's denial he is going to have to do special work in that turn—work which might well involve intensification or upgrading of the claim, e.g., according the claim the status of knowledge rather than conjecture.

However, since the officer in fact prefaces his claim with "we know you gave the gun to Jane. . . .", then a simple denial on Stuart's part might well not be enough to override the policeman's "comeback" in third turn; to be sure, a straightforward denial "no I didn't" would simply open up the gambit "we don't believe you, you're going to have to prove that," or even "are you calling us liars?" In fact, we have a case in point in the Strawson data.

P: Did Don come running out at this time?
S: No, I said nothing of any importance to call him out.
P: I mean, I thought maybe (0.5) he might have heard the girl fall.
S: No.
P: Uh-uh (0.5)
S: She fell very lightly.
P: Uh uh uh ha (0.5) alright she was lying on the kitchen floor.
S: Yes she was.

Here the officer's guarded suggestion "I mean, I thought maybe . . . . he might have heard the girl fall" initially brings a simple "no" from Strawson; Strawson only gives a somewhat more extended account ("she fell very lightly") after a receipt token from the officer. It is notable that in neither of his slots in the conversation does the policeman challenge the suspect's denial of his initial suggestion. These rejoinders frequently work through what Harvey Sacks has termed "technical competition" for turns at talk, i.e., sequential negotiations as to who goes second or even third in a particular sequence of discourse. Such negotiations can have considerable "strategic" import.

Stuart, then, is not simply being given the opportunity to confess—instead, it is being indicated to him that if he wants to disavow the policeman's claim, he is going to have to produce far more than the bland denial or contradiction "no I didn't" or some such variant; and it is indeed the case that while there are many potential opportunity spaces for Stuart during the officer's extended utterance, he in fact does not avail himself of these points of entry to either confirm or deny the claims. This is important since denials, repudiations, etc., are best done immediately after such claims, particularly when these claims may be glossed for their accusatory implications. The policeman's claims may be taken metaphorically as displays of his hand in a game of bluff, to use the officer's own word, with the policeman, while not revealing everything, taking care to demonstrate that the hand is a strong one. These demonstrations are achieved in conventional linguistic ways and again are worked through in terms of the turn-by-turn operation of the interrogation as a speech exchange system. It is also worth noting in passing that the data in excerpt 1 indicates that interrogations by no means always consist of straightforward question-answer sequences, but can also comprise blocs of talk issued by one speaker.

Other features of the policeman's presentation of the reconstruction also work to achieve what Smith (1978:33–35) terms the "authorization" of the account, e.g., the policeman's statement that they have got Stuart "nailed to the wall," that the evidence has been assiduously collected, that the police aren't fixing the evidence against the suspect, that the police aren't conning or bluffing him; see also the policeman's statement that there is no reason to believe that the witnesses are lying, and that their statements also coincide with independently-collected evidence. Many of the policeman's statements serve to present his account of certain events as being disinterested, cohort-independent, as being transcendental objects, as it were, rather than, for instance, idiosyncratic guesswork or a self-serving production of a particular interested party. Note how even the witnesses are presented as not having falsely accused the suspect; nor can these witnesses be readily seen as part of the policeman's "team." To be sure, these people seem more likely to be part of the suspect's team, since he allegedly told them of what he was doing, and since the police had information even before these statements were made. The policeman's claims serve to forestall any counter-accusations by the suspect, based on the discrediting of the origins of the policeman's information. The conventional *ad hominem* device for undercutting a speaker's claims is no longer available at least without special "relevance-establishing" work by the accused.

These elements consequently help bolster the policeman's claims as being warrantably correct, as being "(known) fact," so to speak, rather than "mere" belief, supposition, conjecture. Similarly, the policeman's contrastive use of the characterization "(the truth" as opposed to "(a) con," "lying," "(a) bluff" works to upgrade and authorize the policeman's account. As Dorothy Smith points out (1978:35-7), such characterization procedures work in parallel with authorizations to elevate the account to the level of "facticity" or to bolster the account against straightforward challenges. They work by presenting the claims as independent of any particular single perceiver, or any interested standpoint. The claims are, in effect, presented as "hard and fast" characterizations, having the external and constraining properties which Emile Durkheim uses to characterize social facts and which the policeman presents as having Stuart "nailed to the wall." Externality and constraint may be seen as commonsense as well as analytic criteria for the construction and characterization of fact. Similarly, one might treat Parsons' (1952: 58-88) "pattern variables" as commonsensically-based criteria which, *inter alia,* can work to characterize particular claims about states of affairs as "factual." In our culture we might use the criteria of affective neutrality, specificity, universalism, etc., as authorization procedures to upgrade our account as "fact" in contradistinction to competing accounts. One might even treat the pattern variables as glosses of a set of commonsense language-embedded practical recipes for the achievement, monitoring, and assessing of (scientific) facticity.

In making these initial and still tentative comments on upgrading and authorizing particular versions or accounts I am not suggesting that people, in their everyday practical affairs, always have in mind, so to speak, a variety of specific competing versions of a past or present state of affairs. I am not implying that people are constantly oriented to a complex set of alternative candidate interpretations of "what happened." Instead, I am simply suggesting that the version which *is* produced may well contain built-in authorizations which serve to present it, at least *ab initio,* as "what really happened."

In other words, then, accounts or versions may not be just blandly presented; indeed, it is hard to imagine what a "bland presentation" would look like. Nor does it mean that authorized versions may not prove to be eventually superceded, discredited, transformed, etc., by other versions. However, this is typically an occasioned matter and even then the differing versions may well overlap or be fitted together in a variety of ways.[3]

However, the above comments do mean that since the authorization procedures built into the original version will contain elements which can forestall the straightforward, subsequent "flat" introduction of other possibly subversive versions, then a succeeding version will have to be designed so as to deal with the forestalling devices in the prior version. Other versions, then, can only be credibly established by virtue of some special work which addressed the features of the earlier account. Moreover, it should be reiterated that it is by no means certain that the original version will be treated as problematic; also any subsequent versions may differ only in matters of detail or even nuance, rather than revealing yawning discrepancies or disjunctures in co-conversationalists' respective representations of what happened. This is not to say that detail is inconsequential; for example, the policeman states that the victim had a hole in the side of his head, and asks Stuart Riley how it happened.

SR: By a hammer.
Policeman: A hammer?
SR: Yeah.

(Further talk reveals that Stuart took the hammer out with him. The policeman says that a hammer was found on the scene of the crime, but Stuart says he didn't use that hammer, but instead used a larger, "family" hammer.)

Another way of warranting a particular account as "having been the case" is by citing direct, first-hand experience. This statement by Stuart Riley shows how first-hand experience and agency can be used to warrantably correct an item suggested by the policeman. Such claims of direct first-person experience and agency are by definition found in confessions. Confessions are conventional conversational vehicles for the avowal of first-person experience and agency, and this, doubtless, is why the confession is seen as the sole responsibility of the suspect despite a considerable amount of substantive and organizational input by the interrogating officer(s). Certainly, such first-person "experience-licensed" claims are seen to be best avowed on one's own behalf and in that sense are—again *ab initio*—difficult to gainsay; in this sense the suspect has an element of control over the nature and direction of the interrogation and confession. One might say that a confession gains much of its illocutionary and perlocutionary force from the *experience-licensed* nature of the claims comprised in the confession, to use Bernard Harrison's term.

Again, however, such statements can be challenged by, for instance, the first-hand accounts of other witnesses or parties to the action or some phase of it. These accounts can also work on an explicit or implicit "I (or he/she) was there and you weren't" warrant. Other procedures, too, can be used by the policeman, e.g., his assessment as to whether the confession "fits" the "hard evidence" available from other sources and gathered on other bases.

Here, of course, we can usefully point out the relevance of Garfinkel's (1967:76-103) explication of the workings of the "documentary method of interpretation," whereby members assemble coherence in a set of particular documentary evidences by reference to an imputed underlying pattern; the particulars are taken together as "pointing to" a presupposed underlying pattern which in turn adds coherence to and elaborates the particulars in their relation to each other. There exists, here, a hermeneutic circle of reciprocal determination of meaning concerning "what happened," etc. Also, the documentary method provides for retrospective *re*-interpretation of appearances. Michael Williams' (1975) and Harvey Sacks' (1972:280-98) analyses of the imputation and relevance of incongruity in such evidence in occasioning a re-documentation of a given reported event, deed, or state of affairs constitute significant contributions to our understanding of sense-making practices used by the police and society members in general. The interpretive procedures constituting the documentary method may be seen as operative in and through speech exchange.

The family of commonsense interpretive procedures we call the "documentary method of interpretation" is of fundamental relevance with regard to the question of the alignment of the documentary evidences both as presented in the interrogation itself and as assembled prior to the interrogation. It seems that it is often a confession plus the statements surrounding the confession which provide for the imputation of coherence and consistency to what may be a diverse array of knowledge-claims and other documentary evidences gathered from a variety of sources and assembled through different handling procedures. One might argue that in the cases we have at hand, the documentary method of interpretation works as a fundamental locus for the operation of persuasive devices in the elicitation of confessions. In the police officer's reconstruction, (excerpt 1, lines 29-41), the fragments of evidence from the three murders—Stebbins, Morris and Dawson—can only be seen as "going together" in some sense by making the underlying presupposition that Stuart Riley, the suspect, was in each case the culprit.

Moreover, a central feature of the documentary method is, of course, that it is a public matter, that is, a held-in-common feature of every culturally competent society member's commonsense knowledge of sense making practices. Consequently, the officer (excerpt 1, lines 45–49) can enjoin Stuart to perform his own checking-out operation on the particulars of the reconstruction—an operation which involves using the documentary method to generate the same product, i.e., the imputation that Stuart is (and is known to be) the agent in the murders; in addition to this, Stuart, if he is indeed guilty, can also match the particulars of the reconstruction with further particulars derived from his own first-person experiences and agency. This matching procedure again involves his use of the documentary method and again the imputed underlying pattern is that of Stuart's guilt; the particulars Stuart, if he is guilty, knows on his own behalf serve to elaborate, and to provide a broader context for, the particulars contained in the policeman's reconstruction without substituting or revising the imputed underlying pattern. One aspect of the consequentiality of the documentary method, then, is that through its operation the suspect's "guilty knowledge" can do persuasive work.

The interlocutors' joint performing of the operations comprising the documentary method constitutes a procedural foundation for the achieved orderliness or coherence of the interrogation. The policeman, in indicating that Stuart has at his disposal a procedure for checking out his truth-claims (thus presenting these claims as nonrhetorical) can use the conjointly performed nature of these operations to further bolster the claims. The intersubjective availability and use of the same procedures and (in this case) the same product can establish for members a sense of the cohort-independence of the underlying imputations.

Confessions and Story Format

The alignment of information from the interrogation and from other sources, plus other kinds of "packaging," characteristically seem to be achieved through the format of an *invited story*, a narrative format which can typically work as a vehicle for a confession, and can also work as a means whereby such evidences can be aligned. Confessions frequently take more than one utterance to achieve, as both Stuart Riley and the police officer seem to attest, when the utterance Stuart produces at one point ". . . . I just did it, that's all" (see example ii, p. 274) is apparently taken as "insufficient" both by the suspect and policeman. Stories, too, involve more than one utterance and it will here be argued that they comprise basic vehicles for the articulation and imparting of an extensive array of items of information or knowledge, as we shall presently see. With respect to knowledge-claims and imputations, I wish to take the long way round by making comment on some features of stories that are present in the data.

Contrary also to what John Searle (1969) and some other ordinary language philosophers often seem to assume, a speech act such as a confession may take more than one utterance or one sentence or "statement" to perform. Members may not simply need to know that deed "x" was done but also how, why, where, when, and so on. These matters are germane to their (members') *assessment* of "the" speech act, i.e., whether the confession is sincere, convincing, whether it involves claimed extenuations, or even whether the utterance comprises a confession at all. The policeman's relevances (themselves matters of members' orientation) may in some respects be treated as formalized versions of these commonsense relevances, i.e., the police are formally enjoined to establish, if possible, motive and *modus operandi,* to match the confession with evidence collected from other sources, and the like. Stories contain a wide variety of devices for the achievement of these tasks, and indeed are frequently addressed to the "un-glossing" of a single-statement confession. Not least among the tasks achieved through the story format is the marking of the beginning (e.g., the story-invitation and the indication of "starting at the beginning" in the Strawson confession) and ending of the confession, (e.g., utterances which mark the initiation of the closing sequence). For instance

Officer:	Do you want to say anything before we end this conversation Lewis?	pre-closing
Strawson:	No I don't.	sequence
Officer:	This videotape conversation with Lewis Strawson now ends at, ah, two thirty one p.m. March 16th 1974.	(closes story and interrogation).

Such marking devices have great interactional utility. Since speech acts frequently take more than one sentence to effect, the beginning and ending of "the" speech act can of course not be taken as automatically coterminous with the beginning and ending of a sentence; instead, the beginning and ending of the act have to be interactionally adjudged, negotiated, achieved, and displayed. Thus the transacting of what one might have seen as a single speech act dissembles into the transaction of a considerable array of other actions which are organized relative to each other. At the very least, confessions are composite actions built up through the interactional accomplishment and coordinating of these other actions.

In both cases at hand, the story or account is invited by the policeman, and in the Strawson case a story format is prefigured.

Example i (Strawson)

P: Having these rights in mind, do you wish to talk to us now?
S: Well I signed the er card before, I might as well talk now.
P: All right, we're investigating the death at two-o-one Patterson.
S: Two ten.
P: Two ten Patterson, whose body was found (dismembered) in the tub at that address. Would you tell me in your own words what you know of this homicide?
S: Do you want me to start from the beginning?
P: Yes . . . . would you please –
S: [begins story/confession]

Example ii (Riley)

P: Well Stuart this is your opportunity to explain in your own manner, your own way, what happened.
S: I'm gonn' stop – seems everybody knows . . . . I just did it, that's all . . . . (continues).

also Example iii (Riley)

P: Stu, would you do ((out breath)) me . . . . the honor of telling me . . . . what happened in the Charley Dawson thing.
S: I just – man – I just say I'm gonna take him off and I took him off.
P: Well, how'd you get into the house, did he invite you in?
S: Yes . . . . (continues)

The preface of an invited (recipient-initiated) story exhibits systematic differences from the preface to a "volunteered" (teller-initiated) story. In volunteered stories, the prospective teller has to negotiate permission to tell the story to prospective recipients. Thus, the teller typically produces an utterance (a stereotypical example being "I saw a terrible accident on my way to work this morning") which presages an upcoming story, but then must hand the floor to the prospective recipient(s) to produce a next utterance out of which a decision granting or denying the teller rights to proceed may be glossed ("what happened?"); if such rights are granted, then the teller can proceed in the next turn to tell the story. As Sacks puts it, the prospective teller has to give the floor away in the hope of getting it back to tell the story. Here, we have three adjacently placed actions which provide for the teller being accorded rights to tell his/her story without "major" intercalation, by recipients, and without the teller having to constantly bid or negotiate for the floor during the course of the story. Some of the routinely encountered features of the turn-taking system in ordinary conversation are consequently suspended or modified for the duration of the story.

However, prefaces to invited stories are differently structured in that the inviter, the prospective recipient, produces the first utterance of the preface. This utterance characteristically involves the provision of materials to be incorporated by the teller into the story, though the degree of extension of this initial provision may vary considerably. The prospective teller typically indicates his/her acceptance or declination of the invitation in the immediately succeeding utterance, either by not agreeing to tell the tale or simply by beginning the tale itself, perhaps with a prefatory acceptance particle. Again we have a very tight social organization of conversational actions, and any intervening sequence is designed to address this adjacent serial organization; indeed, the sequence in the preface to the Strawson confession

S: Do you want me to start from the beginning?
P: Yes would you please?

is manifestly designed as an insertion sequence to address the organization and pair type of the adjacency-paired invited story preface.

It should, however, be noted at the outset that there are some significant similarities in the work done through the two types of story preface. Firstly, each preface works to signal that a story is upcoming or "on offer," and to achieve coordinated entry by all participants into a bloc of talk embodying a narrative format (though there may exist variations in such a format), a major part of which involves the casting of interlocutors into the capacities of teller and recipient(s) with the appropriate distribution of participation rights. Furthermore, each story preface provides recipients with a built-in motive for listening to the story—recipients can and must listen for the materials prefigured in the preface. Another dimension of this built-in motive for listening is that the recipient(s) can adjudge whether the story is yet to be completed; if the materials presented in the preface have not yet been incorporated into the story, then the recipient(s) may assume that the story is yet to be completed. Listening in conversations in general and stories in particular is an active matter which involves utilization of the resources provided in the preface. Moreover, recipients may use the story preface as a guideline as to how to respond after the story has been completed; the materials provided in the preface are frequently preserved in the post-story appreciation as one aspect of the demonstration of understanding of the story. These features, which have been explicated in detail by Sacks and his associates, are all addressed to the fact which we have already noted, namely that stories take more than one utterance to tell.

Invited stories, however, differ from volunteered stories in that the materials to be addressed in the telling of the invited story are provided by a prospective recipient, whereas in a volunteered story the teller him/her self provides the materials to be incorporated into the story. In volunteered stories, the teller has a considerable margin of control over the content of the story, whereas in invited stories the recipient has an increased margin of control than would be the case were he/she a recipient of a volunteered story. As might be expected, this element of recipient control has limits. For instance, the recipient's "intercalations" should be hearable as "transforms" of, or as falling under the *aegis* of, the materials presented in the story-invitation. Also, the "experience-licensed" nature of a considerable amount of the material in a confession gives the teller rights to incorporate materials on his/her own behalf.

In a sense, though, the teller of an invited story has to tell the story the recipient wants, and has asked, to hear. Indeed, in certain respects a recipient might be deemed by interlocutors as "knowing better" what is required in the story, when enough has been told, etc., particularly when recipients are incumbents of categories such as doctors, lawyers, social workers, teachers, police and the like, which are treatable to varying degrees as part and parcel of epistemic communities such that the medical, legal, etc., adequacy of the story might be considered by their interlocutors to be "better" adjudged by such recipients.

The increased amount of recipient control in invited stories may take on a variety of forms. For instance, the policeman may have considerable control over the segmentation of the story, particularly in respect of the alternation between the narrative thread and the scenic features such as the wheres and whens of the story and the identification of characters in the story. For instance, in starting the story, Strawson introduces the first narrative item.

S: I dropped off my girlfriend and started walkin' down:::
Brand towards Fisher.
P: What's yer girlfriend's name?
S: Elaine Stevens.
P: And where does Elaine live?
S: Forty six Stanley Street.
P: allright continue.
S: (.4) hhh(I) walked down Brand . . . .
[continues with narrative]

Here we can see the officer intercalating to elicit some background information, which, though tied in to the narrative, suspends the elemental "first this, then that" narrative relations.

Similarly, the officer has a significant margin of control over the issue of when "enough story" has been provided and, further, can initiate the closing of the story. Thus,

P: Do you want to say anything more before we end this conversation Lewis? — pre-closing sequence
S: No I don't.
P: This videotape conversation with Lewis
Strawson ends at, ah, two thirty one p.m.,
March sixteenth, nineteen seventy four.
[close of story and interrogation]

Interestingly enough, it appears to be characteristically the case in invited stories, that if the recipient initiates a closing sequence he/she may have to give the floor away (to the teller) in the hope of getting it back to close the story—a feature which does not seem to pertain to volunteered stories. It is my contention that since confessions are characteristically transacted by the use of stories as communicative vehicles a story-invitation comprises one persuasive device, or confession-elicitation device in such interrogations. Moreover, I contend that the story-invitation, effected by the officer, does further persuasive work in providing for what one might term the recipient control (the officer being the recipient) of the story/confession, whereby the officer can persuade—or, in some respect, "instruct"—the suspect to include certain items in the story. It is through a series of questions and other utterances which we might grossly term intercalations, that a story is built up, at least in the sense that a presented account is treated as having exhibited at least the following features: (i) a jointly oriented-to beginning (as Strawson himself attests), (ii) a jointly oriented-to closing, which in this case is characteristically initiated by the policeman's introduction of a pre-closing, and (iii) an internal narrative strcture where the teller arranges an order of events that apparently preserves the overall temporal order of events being narrated; this is what Sacks (1978:252) has called a "canonical form for narratives."[4]

It has already been observed that the policeman often takes turns—and not always particularly short turns—throughout the course of the story, requesting specific story-relevant (and therefore confession-relevant) material and the like. The officer may, for example, seek to elicit information which the teller might putatively have excluded from his confession. This is most interesting in view of one feature of stories as analyzed by Sacks, namely that speaker transition is suspended or heavily modified for the duration of the story; typically the teller holds the floor so far as rights to tell the story are concerned.[5] One might, therefore, have expected *a priori* to encounter certain incompatibilities between the interrogation and story formats.

Indeed it might, on the basis of present research, be anticipated that these putative incompatibilities would be rooted in the fact that interrogations, as a type of speech exchange system, manifestly include a considerable measure of pre-allocation of turns and turn types, e.g., questions and answers. In such pre-allocational systems there exists, though to varying degrees, a differential allocation of participation rights in the exchange of speech, where the next speaker is not selected by local allocational means or negotiations; rather, speaker selection is "pre-set," as it were, to alternate between given speakers or cohorts.

However, this and other data (Cuff: 1978) indicate that such incompatibility is likely to be minimized in invited stories in contra-distinction to volunteered stories. Intercalations by recipients do occur in volunteered stories but seem largely limited to utterances of the kind that Schegloff (1976) terms "continuers," namely very brief turns which, *inter alia,* display attention to an extended unit in progress, whether the recipient is signaling appreciation of the completion or approaching completion of the story, or whether the recipient is attempting to keep the story open. In invited stories, however, recipients can take relatively long turns providing these turns can be taken as eliciting "on-story" materials or as incorporating such materials into the story in a variety of ways. These turns, moreover, may alternate much more frequently with the teller's turns than is characteristically the case with volunteered stories.

In respect of these features, it may readily be observed that invited stories constitute felicitous devices for the maintenance of the pre-allocation of turns and turn types, not simply because invited stories permit of an alternation of teller and recipient so that the story materials are collaboratively introduced and built up, but also because this alternation permits of the increased turn size which would seem to be characteristic of pre-allocational systems (Sacks, Schegloff and Jefferson, 1978:46-7). Indeed, the issue of compatibility between pre-allocational systems—or at least those occupying a medial position on the continuum of types of speech exchange system varying from the local allocational to the highly, i.e., ceremonially, pre-allocational—may take on a stronger form. It might be suggested that many of the phenomena presently analyzed under the rubric of pre-allocation might usefully be deconstructed into more generic conversational devices, as is indicated by the case of invited stories—which, after all, are not exclusively found in pre-allocational systems. This suggestion seems quite compatible with Sacks, Schegloff and Jefferson's observation (1978:47) that ordinary conversation should be considered the basic form of speech exchange systems, with other systems comprising transformations of this basic form.

This approach would also, perhaps, give the analyst more leeway in dealing with the observation that the police officer's turns in the interrogation do not simply involve questions (though questions are very frequently found), but may involve compliments, instructions, suggestions, homilies, offers, assurances, agreements, and a variety of other items which may in various ways be tied into the narrative or some other thematic feature of the interrogation. Most of these items—and particularly those items which are "adjacency paired," (Sacks, Schegloff and Jefferson: 1978:28-31), such as questions—can work to keep the story or interrogation open; this is a feature of recipient control which will be discussed below. It will suffice for now to observe that such devices for keeping the story/interrogation open comprise particularly useful resources for the officer, whose concerns and interests would seem to require that the suspect keep talking. The most obvious example is that the officer's introduction of first pair parts of adjacency pairs maximizes the chances of the suspect producing at least one more utterance as an immediate next conversational action.

Persuasion, Power and the Interrogation Format

Some sociologists might be tempted to account for the element of control exerted by the officer in the interrogation in terms of objectively-existing power or authority relations pertaining between policeman and suspect. Such analyses may treat the course and content of the interrogations under inspection as the outcome of the working of an unseen hand, as it were, operating independently of, or, in analytic terms, prior to the observable features of the interrogation. These kinds of approach frequently involve many unhelpful rhetorical elements, not least of which is the often tacit according of privileged status to the characterizing concepts of power and/or authority. These approaches may well also lead the analyst into a veritable quicksand of tautology, where in specific terms the determinative power of some prior feature can only be demonstrated in its purported product. I feel that any approach involving even a trace element of such an analysis is likely to be unserviceable in providing resources that permit us to account for the fine detail and organization of the phenomenon under inspection, this detail and organization being attended to and established by co-participants themselves. On this level of detail, any analytic treatment of power or authority must be firmly located in the systematic examination of features integral to the discourse itself.

Power and authority in a relationship are, after all, oriented to by the relevant parties. Indeed, power and authority themselves are mundane concepts with conventional uses and are mobilized as part and parcel of members' sense-making practices. As is characteristically the case with members' accounting practices, orientations to power or authority are communicatively (and therefore interactionally) displayed, and it is through such displays that "another recognizable instance" of a typified power relation is achieved. Such displays may be highly specific matters but may also be diffusely present and pervade the interrogation; however, in the latter eventuality they can still be subjected to rigorous empirical analysis, and I hope here to indicate some directions which such an analysis could take.

One set of resources for the display and accomplishment of a power/authority relation in the interrogation is furnished by what we have alluded to above as the "pre-allocation of turns/turn types." Pre-allocational speech exchange systems can comprise quite efficacious techniques for the "doing" of power or authority in several ways. Through the working of pre-allocational systems, the differential distribution of rights regarding turns and turn types/activities is located in, and reflexively reproduces, a distribution of identities among the participants. It is the "social identity contrast," as McHoul (1978) puts it, which consequently comprises the locus for differential participation rights. In this respect, pre-allocational speech exchange systems may be said to show some of the properties of mutual determination and re-determination usually attributed to the working of a 'hermeneutic circle,' though an important rider in referring *tout court* to pre-allocation is to be found in section C of this paper; some features falling under the rubric of pre-allocation might be treated as more generic conversational devices.

A case in point can be found with regard to the distribution of social identities. In the interrogations under inspection, the interlocutors' orientation to the distribution of social identities seems to extend far beyond what is required for the working of the pre-allocation of turns and turn types. For instance, many of the suspect's utterances in the Strawson tape seem designed specifically to address the identification of the recipient as a police officer. More particularly, many of Strawson's utterances throughout the interrogation incorporate many features of "formality," and not just the general sense of formality generated through pre-allocational speech exchange systems, but a more specified kind of formality which seems manifestly addressed to the recipient *qua* police officer and, derivatively, to perceivedly display compliance. The following are two of the very many small examples of this, both from the Strawson interrogation:

a) 147: P: And then what did you do?
148: S: I proceeded to what you might say hack her apart.

b) S: . . . . I told (Teal) and gave him directions how to get down (0.8). He arrived and I asked him if he had a hacksaw. He said yes but I don't have a blade. I said I have the blade, just give me the handle and that was the extent of Ben Teal's connection with it.

Here such particles as "I proceeded" and "the extent of Ben Teal's connection with it" seem clear instances of the style used in reports made by the police. Conversation analysts have alluded to this pervasive phenomenon as "recipient design" and "membership analysis," where talk is tailored to address the specific identities of interlocutors (see Sacks, Schegloff and Jefferson 1978:43) and to address contexts which are cast in terms of such identities. One major resource in selecting such identities is that of membership categorization, to which we shall return below. Suffice it for now to observe that in an interrogation one way in which recipient design is accomplished by interlocutors is by addressing the known-in-common attributes that can be predicated on the categorizations "policeman" and "suspect," (though many subsidiary categorizations will be furnished during the course of the interrogation and can be similarly addressed). Such predicates may be informed, embodied and addressed through a held-in-common typification of the asymmetry of power or authority involved in this category-pair, as well as a typified conception of how the police, for instance, conduct and report their work. Indeed, when we examine the ways in which co-participants take this latter consideration into account, we can see that any attempt to characterize the substance and course of the interrogation purely in terms of the officer calling the tune in order to satisfy his esoteric (and perhaps even private or unknown to the suspect) concerns, e.g. his concern to assemble a legally sound case, would fall far short of the mark in any analysis which involved an attempt to examine members' orientations as data.

Consequently, one has to be fairly scrupulous when accounting for the interactional characteristics of the interrogation in terms of an asymmetry of power or authority—particularly if it is assumed that such an asymmetry is somehow built in and operative independent of the displayed orientations and practices of the participants. Some elements of what is sometimes taken to be the policeman's control (including his capacity to "pressure" or "persuade") over the interrogation by virtue of his objective position turn out in fact to be at the disposal of any recipient, and particularly a story-recipient—irrespective of whether the recipient invited the story. "Continuers" may be cited as an instance, as indeed may other tokens which may help keep the story open or close it down. Other elements of the policeman's control operate specifically through the device of an *invited* story, as has been indicated above. Still other elements of the policeman's control involve the systematic distribution of identities and their conventionally attributable predicates, (including conventionally imputable rights and obligations). All these elements are party-administered and interactionally managed (on a local basis), as Sacks, Schegloff and Jefferson (1978) put it, and are also found in interactional settings which cannot readily be characterized, either by members or analysts, in terms of power relations.

Indeed, a great many of these elements can be analyzed without trading on any notion of power and/or authority. To be sure, the reverse would seem nearer the case; characterizations of interaction cast in terms of power and authority gloss the very devices that permit of such characterizations. Power and authority are only observable through instances of the particular, contexted deployment of such devices and, on the whole, the concepts of power and authority relations characterize an outcome of the working of an extensive constellation of devices. If indeed power and authority can be seen as resources of a kind, they can only be so through being parasitic on this array of devices. Even then, we must acknowledge that there exist a variety of constraints on the policeman's control over the interrogation, as is suggested by my earlier observations on the experience-licensed nature of many of the elements in confessions and on the constraints on the nature of the officer's/recipient's intercalations in the invited story. While, then, one would in all probability not wish to demur from a gross characterization of the interrogation as either a power or authority relation, in a detailed interactional analysis such a characterization has to know its place.

Let us continue by looking at some other instances of what we might gloss as persuasive devices, largely—though not exclusively—mobilized by the policeman. Let us first note that in excerpt 2 from the transcript of the Stuart Riley interrogation, the perlocutionary force which I have termed persuasive power is re-doubled; not only is there a story-invitation—itself a persuasive device—but there are also two more features which comprise persuasive devices. The first of these is the officer's employment of a formulation of the gist of a foregoing stretch of the conversation where Stuart has been making various claims about himself and about what he would do under certain circumstances. Such formulations of gist and upshot typically feature prefatory particles such as "so," "well . . . .", "what you're saying is" and the like. John Heritage and I have analyzed formulations as conversational objects at length elsewhere (1979:123-62). Typically, the recipient of information furnished by another participant in the conversation may formulate the gist of that part of the conversation and the "information-giver" decides on (i.e., confirms or disconfirms) the proposed gist. Formulations and decisions therefore comprise an adjacency pair type. Here, we have an example of a gist formulation where the recipient, the police officer, says: "Well then you're telling me that you're a man of honor, right?" (excerpt 2, line 38) and Stuart Riley—the "information-giver"—confirms and indeed upgrades this gist: "yeah, I'm a man of honor" (excerpt 2, line 40).

Formulations are interlocutors' devices for describing (and for aligning their talk within) a conversation or some segment of it. They are generally available devices and are not only found in settings characterized by a perceived power imbalance. In this case we also have another kind of description working through the formulation, i.e., a description of a person ("man of honor")–a description introduced in the officer's formulation, applied to the suspect and preserved in the suspect's confirmation in his next utterance. The policeman can use the preference for confirmation of formulations as a resource for persuading Stuart to buy into the officer's description of him as a "man of honor."

Sacks (1974:221–4) terms such descriptions "membership categorizations" for the social identification of persons, and has outlined several conventional procedures for the systematic use of such categorizations in ordinary conversation. Again, we can see the generic nature of "knowledge how," of procedural knowledge, in the conducting of discourse. One of these procedures is that certain activities can conventionally be ascribed to particular categories. Sacks terms these activities "category-bound" activities. One activity which can, virtually by definition, be predicated upon the categorization "man of honor" is what we might term "doing the honorable thing," and it is this category-bound activity which can be read into the policeman's statement on lines 44–5 of excerpt 2. In this utterance we get the category-bound activity built into a story-invitation, whereby the persuasive "pressure" to produce a story/confession is not just generated by the preface; it is also generated by the presentation of the telling of the prospective story as being a manifestation of (the extent of) Stuart's honor, such that telling the story might be seen as "doing the honorable thing." While the description is built into the story-invitation, it is an analytically separable component which can be seen as redoubling the perlocutionary force of the utterance on lines 44–5 as (in this kind of environment) a confession-elicitation device.

A further feature of this sequence concerns the properties of the gist formulation as a conversational object. A central property of such formulations is that they preserve an orientation to the distribution of information. For instance, the formulation on line 40, excerpt 2, preserves the "man of honor" description as the gist of Stuart's description of himself. The policeman does not affiliate with or endorse the description. His formulation, however, might be taken by the suspect as presaging a possible prospective affiliation, particularly when tied with his utterance on lines 44 and 45, in that Stuart's provision of a story/confession might well occasion the policeman's affiliation with the man of honor description. In terms of the suspect's possible projection of the course of the conversation, any refusal to provide a story/confession might well mean that the policeman disaffiliates from the description ("so you're not a man of honor after all"). In the event, Stuart does not for the present provide a story. However, it is notable that he sees his declination to do so as being an accountable matter; and he does provide an account, namely that he wishes to speak with Mr. Gordon (his parole officer), a wish that has to be dealt with "here and now" by the officer.

Having indicated the practical *interactional* utility of stories as vehicles for the production and monitoring of information or knowledge, we can return to a more explicit consideration of the issue of knowledge-claims and ascriptions of substantive knowledge. In Strawson's story, the arrangement of events is carefully designed so as to preclude the ascription of (guilty) knowledge to other of the characters in the story; and, indeed, Strawson makes quite explicit attributions of lack of knowledge on the part of his associates, e.g., at one point he claims that the hacksaw blade used in the dismemberment was in the house, but that he obtained the hacksaw handle from one Ben Teal, that he told Teal that he (Strawson), needed to cut a section of pipe, and that Teal had "no idea as to what I was doing with it." See also Lewis Strawson's claim that Don Lane did not hear the girl's body fall ("it fell very lightly"). Such claims concerning situational elements may be glossed by members for their relevance to the imputation of knowledge. Now this kind of statement seems to work to exclude the character–in this case Ben Teal–from responsibility, or joint responsibility, for the action or for a *phase* of the action constituting the alleged offense. In this respect the suspect is using a variety of devices that operate through the story format in order to persuade the officer that a given state of affairs pertained at that time. Persuasive devices can therefore be seen to be reciprocally operative.

Knowledge and the Assessment of Conduct

In the last part of this paper, I wish to point to some fairly straightforward issues on the relationship between imputations of knowledge and imputations of guilt or responsibility for a given offense or ill effect, as these are represented in and through members' mastery of ordinary language.

"Knowledge" can be analytically treated as a concept with conventional uses, and, more specifically, as a member's concept comprising a dimension for the assessment–including moral assessment–of actions or deeds. We can, in part, assess a person's responsibility for an action in terms of that person's knowledge of the nature and consequences of the action. Moreover, knowledge is part of a "family" of dimensions for the assessment of social action or conduct. Other such dimensions are "intentionality," "(calculable) choice," and "control" (over outcomes, etc.). We can attribute guilt or responsibility for a given deed by imputing intentionality and choice to the agent, e.g., by claiming he/she "intended" to perform the deed and "freely chose" to do so.

These language-embedded dimensions can be taken as a family in that they "fit together" in the following senses. Each dimension can i) to a significant extent, be transformed in ordinary language into one or more of the other dimensions, or ii) be taken as presupposing or implying the operation of those other dimensions. For example, the claim that I *knew* what I was doing when I committed the deed I *did* commit might also be taken as entailing the claim that I *intended* to commit the deed, unless lack of choice (e.g., coercion) were cited in mitigation of that claim. Operating together, these dimensions can perhaps be treated as a commonsense, language-embedded template for assessing action. These three dimensions can be used as ordinary measuring rods for assessing guilt, blame, or responsibility of an agent for a given deed or purported ill effect.

With regard to the attribution of responsibility for a given deed, we might say that the maximization of the extent of an agent's knowledge, intentionality, or choice will also maximize or "aggravate" (as J. L. Austin puts it) the degree of guilt, blame, or responsibility for that deed. Claims which diminish the degree of an agent's knowledge, intentionality, or choice usually also diminish the degree of that agent's guilt, blame, or responsibility for the deed and its ill effects–in other words, mitigations or extenuations characteristically work through making inroads into the maximal applicability of those three dimensions (e.g., that the agent did not fully intend to perform the deed, did not fully know its consequences, or acted under duress). Excuses typically incorporate these dimensions.

The Strawson case gives us a good example of the ascription of lack of knowledge (on the part of Don Lane and Ben Teal) working to produce an assessment of the deeds of others which achieves mitigation on their behalf. Strawson attempts to implicate only himself rather more fully, and arranges the components of his story accordingly (though perhaps not always quite successfully, as the policeman's attempts–

not here transcribed–to find and use incongruities in the packaging of events, claims, etc. in the story suggest).

Finally, this matter of "knowledge" as a dimension for assessing action can be taken one step further, by examining a situation in which the ascription of knowledge comprises a feature in what one might for convenience call the "ratification" of "a" speech act–in this case a confession, namely the apprising of the suspect of his rights and the issuing of cautions at the outset of the interrogation (see excerpt 3).

For a start, let us treat the "Miranda" cautions and guarantees (i.e., guarantees of rights, facilities, etc.) in terms of the imparting and reception of specific items of knowledge–in this case, that the suspect has the right to remain silent, to have a lawyer present, and so on. Upon the displayed reception of such knowledge,[7] the interrogation can continue on the assumption that the suspect now possesses, "consults," and uses that knowledge as a background scheme throughout the rest of the conversation; or at least the subsequent conversation or any segment of it can be assessed *post hoc* by members in terms of the assumption that this knowledge has unrelievedly informed the utterances or statements of the participants, and particularly of the suspect. Put another way, knowledge is imparted at the outset of the interrogation and is subsequently imputed to the suspect; the assessment of the subject's subsequent utterances can be conducted on the presumption that the suspect possesses and utilizes this knowledge as a scheme of interpretation. This is particularly important in the assessment of the status of the suspect's confession.

A confession is in a composite sense "a" speech act, and therefore comprises social action, and it is only through an orientation to these dimensions for the assessment of action that we can treat the suspect's confession as being a confession at all, at least in the strict or full sense. In other words, the Miranda cautions and guarantees–themselves embodying a variety of speech acts–must be treated as resources that inform the suspect's confession; the suspect must be treatable as being aware of those cautions before his confession *counts* as a confession. The confession only counts as a confession if it is perceivedly voluntarily given, if the suspect produces the confession in full *knowledge* of his rights to remain silent and withhold the confession. Again dimensions such as knowledge and choice are seen to be reciprocally implicative in the assessment of conduct. The suspect is assumed (at least by the police, legal authorities, and the like), to be able to reason about the relevance of the cautions and guarantees to the ongoing discourse. The interrogation context is eminently a judgmental context for both the suspect and the officer–particularly since the officer too is legally presumed to know the Miranda provisions intendedly limiting his sphere of action.

In John Searle's (1969) terms we may treat the Miranda cautions and guarantees as providing the "felicity conditions" whereby a given type of speech act, in this case a confession, counts as having been adequately transacted and as being fully operative, so to speak. These felicity conditions involve in a most fundamental way the establishing of these dimensions for the assessment of actions, and particularly, perhaps, the dimension of knowledge. Typically, these felicity conditions are embedded in the interactional context within which the speech act is transacted. More specifically, judgments as to whether or not the felicity conditions for a given speech act are present or not are made in and through the specific interactional context, and typically involve an invocation and consultation of that context by participants or others making the judgments.

The issue of the social-interactional aspects of felicity conditions is assumed rather than explicated by Searle, since his interest is largely in the logical properties and relations of such conditions. With regard to the felicity conditions involving knowledge in relation to confessions, we can observe that if the suspect can be regarded as not having, or not competently using, the knowledge which should have been adequately furnished in the cautions, then the confession may quite simply not stand up as such and may be treated as null and void. Similarly, if a confession is perceivedly forced out of a suspect, it can be treated as null and void by reference to the dimension of choice or voluntarism; the suspect can be treated as having confessed under duress and is therefore not "responsible" for any putative "confession" that might have been elicited. So again, to make inroads into the knowledge, intentionality and choice model is to mitigate the force of the confession by mitigating the suspect's responsibility for it.

In this sense, then, the issuing of the Miranda cautions and guarantees may be seen to constitute at least as much of an interactional resource for the police officer as for the suspect. This is not really an either/or matter–the issuing of the cautions and guarantees performs double-duty, as it were, providing resources for the suspect which he/she can putatively use for his/her protection, and providing other resources for the policeman, which can be used to warrant the claim that the confession was indeed a confession in the fullest measure. This is especially crucial here, for the videotapes from which the transcripts have been drawn could be–and have been–used in evidence in court. This issue, of course, points to another layer of implicativeness, namely that the communicative devices (such as the knowledge-claims embedded in reconstructions) used by the policeman in order to persuade the suspect to confess may also work to persuade juries of the suspect's guilt. Similarly, the suspect's packaging of information so as to preclude the policeman's potential imputation of guilt to his associates can also work as a persuasive device for jury-members. To the researcher, this second layer simply reinforces the central significance of examining such persuasive devices.

This paper has attempted to point to some of the most general and grossly-apparent features of the data, and a close analysis of the fine-grained detail of the devices indicated above has still to be conducted. I hope, however, to have indicated some of the promise of such an analysis.

DATA APPENDIX

EXCERPT 1: Statement of Stuart Riley (2 excerpts)

1: Officer: I don'know you seem like a pretty smart fella t'me.
2 (3.4)
3: Officer: Are you smart enough tuh reali:ze thet the:: (2.0) police
4 he:re in the homicide bureau'v uh (·) build u(·)p uh::
5 (0.6) case against you: tih the point, (1.4) where we
6 feel yu- we gotcha::: (0.6) nailed t'the wal,
7: Riley: Couldn' say nothing about dat (boh),
8 (0.4)
9: Officer: Pard'n,
10: Riley: ˙t Ah couldn' say noth'n about dat.
11 (0.3)
12: Officer: Well,
13 (6.0)
14: Riley: We work very hard et ar ↓ job, (0.9) mghhm. (3.4) We've
15 taken statements::,
16 (1.0)
17: (Riley): °(hhm.)°
18 (1.8)
19: Officer: A:nd uh in these statements we have information, (3.0)
20 whur you ev to:ld, (0.9) people, (1.0) whatchu did. (3.5)
21 There's no reas'n:: (·) fer me tuh believe et this ti:me,

(1.4) thet the people who gave iss this information were
lying, (3.9) A:nd there's nothing in these statements
thet- would,hh (0.2) indicate tuh me, (·) thet they are
not the truth.
(2.2)
Officer: Based on ar ow:n? (0.3) independent, (0.5) investigation.
before the statements:. (2.2) we 'ad information. (2.4)
thetchu ed done this. (2.5) We 'ad a description::, (1.0)
of the fella who ran away fr'm: (0.5) Hank Stebbins'
place. (1.6) witha red leather ja:cket, (2.0) we know
thetchu:d ↓borrowed fr', a ↓friend. (2.0) ˙tlk We also
know about the ↓gun, (1.2) in the Morris (1.9) homicide.
(0.4) (Herb) Morris, (3.2) We know thet after:: (2.9) some
time durin' that da:y you fired a shot, over on Emburey
Street. (0.4) mghhm. (0.4) intuh the bookcase:, (0.2) in
t'th'kitchen, (2.4) ˙tk (0.2) We know thetchu gave the gun
tuh Jaine tuh put in'er purse et one time, (0.4) u-durin
that da:y, (4.2) We have recovered,h (3.5) a stereo:: (·)
unit, (1.2) an' a tape, (1.4) recorder, (0.4) tha'we know:,
(0.4) came fr'm the apartment, (0.3) of Charley Dawson
(2.0)
Officer: No:w,
(5.0) ((door squeaking))
Officer: I'm not trying to: (1.2) con you? (1.0) I'm only telling
you the truth. If you:, (1.3) fer one moment:, (2.0)
thought, (·) or noo: fr'm what I toldju (0.3) that I wz
trying tuh bluff you, (3.2) then you noo:, (·) ur: you
would know, theh we didn't have (·) anything ↓ahn you.
Riley: Right, °(Mh)°
(0.2)
Officer: But fr'm what I've to:ldju: (1.0) I wantchu tuh think
about it keep en open mi:nd,
Riley: °( ).°
(1.4)

EXCERPT 2

Riley: Cuz mah oncle 'ee a faggot en all the stuff he go through
(w'th) his wife you know, (0.9) She truthf'l yihknow all
a'stuff she go through she know w't 'ee is 'n evrythi:ng
(eu abu) she don't sa:y nothing °(y'know).° (0.3) She go

21 tuh church ev'ry day take care a'(th') kids'n evryt'ing,
22 °(y'nuh).° (0.4) 'N ah (sed) wo::w yihknow, (0.3) 'n den
23 she own th'sahd a'God yih know °((0.2)).° B't 'n ah
24 se:z you gotta be thez gotta be somethin the way she go
25 through yihknow.
26 (0.5)
27: Officer: We:ll dihyuh think thet uh::: half'v 'er effort'n going
28: Officer: tuh chu:rch is uh:::::: maybe t'pray fer 'im?
29 (1.4)
30: Riley: °Who.° m:Might be y'nuh (·) Ah think it i:s y'nuh.
31 (2.2)
32: Riley: But ah:'m not 'f ah don:'t (0.2) believe'n it ah'm nah
33 gon' (·) try tuh do sump'n (di:vh'nt.) (0.3) Yu- Ah try
34 tuh p- prac (·) preach tih you den you look aroun'n see
35 me doin sump'n else thet ah told you not t'do,
36: Officer: ˙t
37 (0.2)
38: Officer: W'l then yer: telling me now thetcher a man'v honor. right?
39 (0.3)
40: Riley: Yeh ah'm a man'v honor.
41 (0.8)
42: Officer: Awright?
43 (1.5)
44: Officer: Ah you honorable enough:? (0.7) et this ti:me tuh tell
45 me:, (0.8) what (·) motivatedju?
46 (0.7)
47: Riley: Ah: tol' y-you ah don' ha:ve'm gonna have t'think about
48 da:t. Dass wah ah wanna talk t'Mistuh ↑Gordon.
49: Officer: Awri:ght.
50 (1.2)
51: Officer: MGHHM:. Then I think thet uh:::: (1.3) this is wut you
52 sh'd do.

EXCERPT 3 (Strawson)

1: Officer: Well (1.2) before I: ask: you any more questions:, (.6)
2 I advise:(d) you of your constitutional rights: befor:e:
3 (.3) bt fer the benefit: ofer::::: (·) the: camera (·)
4 Im gunna as:(·) advise: you of your rights: again:.
5 (.5)
6: Officer: you have te remai:n: sirlent doyer understand: tha:t:

Strawson: °yes I do
(.3)
Officer: anythin:g: you say can or will be used agains:t: you in a
court of la:w::, doyer understand: that
Strawson: °yes I do:
Officer: you have the right te talk to a law:yer: an have him
present with you while you: are being ques:tioned: ?
(.4) do you understan:d tha:t,
Strawson: yes I do
(.3)
Officer: If: you cannot: afford to hire a lawyer:: one will be
(a)ppointed to represent you before: any questioning:
if you wish one (.6) doyou understand: that:
Strawson: yes I do
(.3)
Officer: having: these: rights: in min:d: (.2) doyuu wish: te
talk: to us: now:::.
(.5)
Strawson: Well:: I signed: the::(·) card before: I might as well
talk now:
(.9)
Officer: al::right (·) were: investigating the death (·) of a
gir::l (.7) at two o one Patterson
Strawson: two ten:
(1.2)
Officer: two ten (.2) Patterson: (.7) whoose body waz foun::d:
(1.0) dissem:bered: (.2) in the: tub at: that address.
(.6)
Officer: er: will you tell me? (.3) in your own words: (.2)
what you know:: about this homicide.
(.9)
Strawson: duyou want me to star:t from the beginning?
(.7)
Officer: yers would you please?
(1.2)
Strawson: I dropped off my girl:friend, (1.0) an:d: (1.2)
[continues with story].

ACKNOWLEDGMENTS

This analysis was presented in an earlier, less developed form at the British Psychological Society's London Conference (Criminological and Legal Psychology Section), December 1978, at University College, London.

The themes of this analysis were first delivered in their present form at the 1979 Language Sciences Summer Institute, International Christian University (Dept. of Linguistics) Tokyo, Japan: Director; Professor Fred C.C. Peng. I wish to thank participants in these sessions for their useful observations and Professor George Adoff of State University College at Buffalo for advice and practical assistance. I also wish to thank Gail Jefferson, John Lee, Peter Halfpenny and W.W. Sharrock of Manchester University, and also John C. Heritage of Warwick University, J.M. Atkinson of Wolfson College, Oxford, and C.C. Heath (University of Surrey) for many helpful comments at various points in the writing of this paper. My thanks are also due to the Chief of the Homicide Squad in the North American city where the recordings were made, and to each of the interlocutors in the interrogation for allowing the interrogation to be recorded.

NOTES

1. Although as trial evidence the videocassettes are public matters, I have still adhered to the social scientist's convention of changing proper names of persons and places and of changing date references.

2. This utterance is included in example ii, page 274.

3. For a detailed and critical consideration of analytic issues raised by the potential or actual existence for members of more than one version, in talk, see Cuff (1980).

4. It is notable that the two (in principle distinct) types of story organization, the *temporal* and the *sequential*, are in the main used in co-ordination; they dovetail, at least in large part, in a variety of ways in the confession-stories produced in the interrogations here under inspection. In other words, some point in the story counts on the appreciation of some sequentially-prior point and the relation of these points to each other purportedly preserves the temporal order of the events being reported. One might suggest that Strawson's utterance "shall I start at the beginning?" indicates such a dovetailing as does, in large part, his subsequent telling of the story. The policeman's intercalations, (if they may be so described; no implication of interruption is intended), may be seen as such by virtue of their occasioning a sequentially subsequent introduction of a temporally prior point or item. Insofar as this runs counter to the overall dovetailing

of temporal and sequential organization this may on occasion perceivedly disturb the smooth-flowing character of the story. An element of this backtracking may be found in the officer's "I mean, I thought maybe .... he might have heard the girl fall."

5. As indicated above, this is not to say that story-recipients say nothing, even if the story is teller (as opposed to recipient)-initiated. As Gail Jefferson points out (1978:245), a story is not a monolithic bloc of talk *per se* but is composed of a set of segments where the teller's talk can alternate with that of the recipient(s) in ways which articulate with the overall turn-taking system for conversation. This having been said, the teller may claim rights over the imparting of the story, and story prefaces typically incorporate an orientation to such rights. It is these rights to which my comments on recipient control are addressed. Owing to the considerable length of the transcript, the entire story cannot, unfortunately, be presented in this paper.

6. For some observations on the pre-allocation of turns, see Sacks, Schegloff and Jefferson (1978:45–7); see also McHoul (1978), who addresses his analysis to the issue of "formality," which is briefly treated in the present paper in section d.

7. Note that such a "reception" does not, for members or analysts, necessarily *display* understanding; instead it comprises a (possibly rhetorical) claim to understanding rather than providing the resources whereby understanding may be "checked out" by others. The *pro-forma* minimum requirements–which are, of course, routinely and unproblematically taken by the police and by other recipients as quite adequate in the circumstances for the indication of understanding–cannot be seen as assuring recipients that the suspect understands the cautions and the legal rights he/she has. On displays of understanding, see Sacks (1969:1–4).

REFERENCES

Austin, J.L. "A Plea for Excuses," pp. 175–204 in his *Philosophical Papers.* Oxford: The Clarendon Press, 1961.

Coulter, J., Beliefs and Practical Understanding, in G. Psathas (Ed.) *Everyday Language: Studies in Ethnomethodology,* New York: Irvington Publishers, 1979.

Cuff, E.C. and D.W. Francis, "Some Features of 'Invited Stories' about Marriage Breakdown," *International Journal of the Sociology of Language,* 1978, vol. 18.

——, "The Problem of Versions in Everyday Life," *Occasional Papers in Sociology,* Number 3, Department of Sociology, University of Manchester, Manchester M13 9PL, England, 1980.

Garfinkel, Harold, *Studies in Ethnomethodology.* Englewood Cliffs: Prentice-Hall, Inc., 1967.

Heritage, J.C. and Watson, D.R., "Formulations as Conversational Objects," in *Everyday Language: Studies in Ethnomethodology,* pp. 123–63. George Psathas (Ed.). New York: Irvington Publishers, 1979.

Jefferson, Gail, "Sequential Aspects of Storytelling in Conversation," in *Studies in the Organization of Conversational Interaction,* pp. 219–48, Jim Schenkein (Ed.). New York and London: Academic Press, 1978.

McHoul, Alexander W., "The Organization of Formal Turns at Talk in the Classroom, *Language in Society,* vol. 7, August 1978, pp. 183–213.

Parsons, T., *The Social System.* Glencoe, IL: The Free Press, 1952.

Sacks, Harvey, *Lecture 9, March 5,* Mimeo, Sociology Department, University of California at Irvine, 1969.

——, "Notes on Police Assessment of Moral Character," in *Studies in Social Interaction,* pp. 280–98, David Sudnow (Ed.). New York and London: The Free Press, 1972.

——, "On the Analysability of Stories by Children," in *Ethnomethodology,* pp. 216–32, Roy Turner (Ed.). London: Penguin Books, 1974.

——, "Some Technical Considerations of a Dirty Joke," in *Studies in the Organization of Conversational Interaction,* in Jim Schenkein (Ed.), *op. cit.,* pp. 249–269.

Sacks, Harvey, Emanual A. Schegloff and Gail Jefferson, "A Simplest Systematics for the Organization of Turn-Taking for Conversation," in Schenkein, J. (Ed.), 1978), pp. 7–55, a variant of the originally published version in *Language,* 50, 4 (1974), pp. 696–735.

Schegloff, E. A., "On Some Questions and Ambiguities in Conversation," in *Pragmatics Microfiche,* pp. D-8 to G-12, vol. 2, fiche 2. Cambridge, England: Cambridge University, Department of Linguistics, 1976. Reprinted in Atkinson, J. M. and J. Heritage (Eds.) *Structures of Social Action,* Cambridge: Cambridge University Press, 1984.

Schenkein, J., (Ed.), *Studies in the Organization of Conversational Interaction.* New York: Academic Press, 1978.

Searle, John, *Speech Acts.* Cambridge: Cambridge University Press, 1969.

Smith, Dorothy E., "K is Mentally Ill: The Anatomy of a Factual Account," *Sociology* 12:1, 1978 (January), pp. 23–53.

Williams, Michael L., "Seeing Through Appearances: Procedures for 'Discovering' Criminal Activity," Mimeo of paper presented to the Colloquium on Ethnomethodology and Conversational Analysis at the University of California at Santa Barbara. Mimeo produced in the Department of Sociology, University of Portland, Maine, U.S.A., 1975.

Appendix: Transcription Symbols

Compiled by George Psathas

With a few exceptions, the transcription symbols are those developed by Gail Jefferson and reported in several places. The major sources relied upon for this listing are: H. Sacks, E. Schegloff and G. Jefferson, A Simplest Systematics for the Organization of Turn-Taking in Conversation, *Language,* 50, 1974, 731-734 (also reprinted in J. Schenkein, (Ed.), *Studies in the Organization of Conversational Interaction,* Academic Press, New York, 1978); G. Psathas, (Ed.), *Everyday Language,* Irvington, New York, 1979; C. Goodwin, *Conversational Organization,* Academic Press, New York, 1981; and J. M. Atkinson and J. Heritage (Eds.) *Structures of Social Action: Studies in Conversation Analysis,* Cambridge University Press, Cambridge, 1984.

The system was developed to "record phenomena in the stream of speech relevant to the organization of conversation . . . it notes such sequential phenomena as the precise location of both silence and simultaneous speech, changes in duration . . . and phenomena relevant to units larger than the sentence such as differences in time between sentences or turns." (Goodwin, 1981). Although the system obviously does not capture all the distinctions that can be made in the analysis of speech, it aims to provide the reader with a description of those features of speech most relevant to the analysis of the organization of conversation.

Certain conventions used in the presentation of research reports are also included here.

I wish to thank Gail Jefferson for her helpful comments and suggestions.

I. Sequencing

1. Simultaneous utterances

Utterances starting up simultaneously are linked together with double left hand brackets.

Tom: [[I used to smoke a lot when I was young
Bob: [[I used to smoke Camels

2. Overlap

A. Beginning of overlap

When utterances overlap but do not start up simultaneously the point at which overlap begins is marked by a single left hand bracket.

Tom: I used to smoke [a lot
Bob: [he thinks he's real tough

An alternative notation for beginning of overlap is to use double oblique markers to indicate the point at which the overlap begins.

V: Th'guy says tuh me- .hh my son // dided.
M: Wuhjeh do:.

A multiple-overlapped utterance is followed, in serial order, by the talk which overlaps it. Thus, C's "Vi:c" occurs simultaneously with V's "left" and C's "Victuh" with V's "hallway."

V: I // left my garbage pail in iz // hallway
C: Vi:c,
C: Victuh,

B. End of overlap

The point where overlapping utterances stop overlapping is marked with a single right-hand bracket.

Tom: I used to smoke [a lot] more than this
Bob: [I see]

An alternative notation for end of overlap is an asterisk to indicate the point at which two overlapping or simultaneously started utterances end, if they end simultaneously, or the point at which one of them ends in the course of another or the point at which one utterance component ends vis a vis another.

M: [I mean no no n'no*
V: [P't it back up*

M: [Jim?? wasn' home* uh what.
V: [Y'know:w?*

3. Latching or contiguous utterances

Equal signs indicate latching, i.e., no interval between the end of a prior and start of a next part of talk.

A. Latching with change of speakers

Tom: I used to smoke a lot=
Bob: =He thinks he's real tough

B. Latching by more than one speaker

Two speakers begin simultaneously and with no interval between their start and the end of the last speaker's talk.

Tom: I used to smoke a lot=
Bob: =[[He thinks he's tough
Ann: [[So did I

C. Latching at end of overlapped speech

Two utterances end simultaneously and are latched onto by a next.

```
Tom:  I used to smoke [a lot ] =
Bob:                  [I see ]
Ann:  =so did I
```

D. Latching within same speaker's talk

V: well my son didit=I'm gladjer son didn't get hurt . . .

E. Latching as a transcript convenience

When a speaker's lengthy utterance is broken up arbitrarily for purposes of presentation, especially when overlap occurs, the equal sign is used to indicate continuity in the same speaker's utterance.

V: my wif // caught d'ki:d,=
R: yeh
V: =lightin a fiyuh in Perry's <u>ce</u>lluh

```
Tom:  I used to smoke [a lot more than this=
Bob:                  [you used to smoke
Tom:  =but I never inhaled the smoke
```

II. Timed intervals, within and between utterances

Silences, pauses and gaps, as intervals in the stream of talk, are timed in tenths of a second and noted where they occur.

1. Numbers in parentheses

The number indicates in seconds and tenths of seconds the length of an interval.

```
Lil:  When I was (0.6) oh nine or ten
                            (0.4)
Joe:  Are you talking to me
```

A. One alternative is to use dashes within parentheses.

Each dash is a tenth of a second; each full second is marked with a plus sign.

J: How's uh, (- - - - - - - - - + - -) Jimmy

B. A second alternative is the use of plus markers within parentheses.

Each plus mark is one tenth of a second: each full second may be marked by a space.

J: How's uh, (++++++++++ ++) Jimmy

2. Untimed micro-intervals

More or less than a tenth of a second is indicated by:

A. A dot within parentheses

J: . . . barges are struck (·) stuck that is . . .

3. Untimed intervals of longer length

If timing is not achieved, a pause, silence or gap may be noted as untimed.

John: Who all is over there
Kitty: Oh, Marcia and Judy stopped by,
((gap))
John: Who else.
Kitty: Oh, what's his name, ((pause)) Tom.
John: Oh.

III. Characteristics of speech production

Punctuation marks are used to describe characteristics of speech production. They are not to be interpreted as referring to grammatical units.

1. Sound stretch

A colon indicates that the prior sound is prolonged. Multiple colons indicate a more prolonged sound.

V: So dih gu:y sez

M: I ju::ss can't come

T: I'm so::: sorry re:::ally I am

2. Sound cut-off

A single dash indicates a cut-off of the prior word or sound, i.e., a noticeable and abrupt termination.

C: Th' U:sac– uh:, sprint car dr– dirt track championship

3. Intonation

A. A period indicates a stopping fall in tone.

F: So with every (·) economic failure. (0.5) they turn (0.5) more viciously. (0.5) on the local authorities.

B. A comma indicates a continuing intonation, e.g., the kind of falling-rising contour one finds after items in a list.

A: There was a bear, a cat, enna dog.

P: now if ya have thirteen points:, (1.0) counting: voi:ds?

C. Question mark indicates a rising intonation. (Question mark/comma indicates rising intonation weaker than that indicated by a question mark/period.

V: A do:g? enna cat is diffrent.

P: Yih ever take 'er out again?

P: t'morrow er anything?

D. Upward or downward pointing arrows mark rising or falling shifts in intonation immediately prior to the rise or fall.

T: I am however (0.2) very ↓fortunate (0.4) in having (0.6) a ↑marvelous deputy

E. Exclamation point indicates an animated tone.

C: An that! so what he sez

4. Emphasis

Emphasis is indicated by italics or underscoring. The larger the italics, the greater the relative stress.

Ann: It happens to be mine
Ben: It's not either yours it's MINE

V: I sez y'know WHY, becawss look

5. Pitch

The relationship between emphasis and prolongation (stretch) markers indicate pitch change (or non-change) in the course of a word.

A. Word stressed but with no change in pitch:

J: it's only venee:r though,

To indicate stress (and here stretching as well), the stress-mark is done on the first letter of the stressed syllable. Of course, if the stressing is greater, then the underscore is longer, e.g.:

J: it's only venee:r though,

B. Pitch drop:

J: it's only venee:r though,

To indicate pitch-drop, the underscore should be placed at the vowel immediately preceding the colon. Again, for more pronounced emphasis, the underscore is longer.

J: it's only venee:r though,

The idea is not to have the colon underscored and an immediately preceding vowel underscored.

C. Pitch rise:

J: it's only venee:r though,

To indicate pitch rise, the stress is marked upon the prolongation. If the rise occurs somewhere in the course of a prolongation, that can be shown as follows:

J: it's only venee::::r though

And one can show rising and falling:

J: it's only vene::::::r though

6. Volume–loudness or softness

A. Upper case letters are used to indicate increased volume.

V: In it dint fall OUT!

B. A degree sign is used to show a passage of talk which has a noticeably lower volume than the surrounding talk.

J: An' how are you feeling?
(0.4)° these days,°

IV. Aspiration–audible inhalation and exhalation

An h or series of h's is used to mark an outbreath unless a dot precedes the h's in which case an inbreath is indicated.

1. Outbreath

I'm not sure hh- who it belongs to

2. Inbreath

Marge: .hhh O̲ka:y, thank you Mister Hanys'n

3. Plosive aspiration as in laughter, breathlessness or crying is indicated by placing the h in parentheses.

Pam: An th(hh)s is for you hhh

Gene: So that shook up the old (h)house(h)hold up fer
a(h)whi(h)le heh

Joyce: ehh [hhhhhhh!
C: [oh(hh)h hah huh!

V. Transcriptionist doubt

Other than the timings of intervals and inserted aspirations, items enclosed within single parentheses are in doubt.

Ted: I ('spose I'm not)
(Ben): We all (t-)

Sometimes, multiple possibilities are indicated.

(spoke to Mark)
Ted: I ('spose I'm not)

(tough angle)
Ben: We all try to figure a (stuffing girl) for it

When single parentheses are empty, no hearing could be achieved for the talk or item in question.

Todd: My ( ) catching

( ): In my highest ( )

On occasion, nonsense syllables are provided in an attempt to capture something of the produced sounds.

R: (Y' cattuh moo)

VI. Verbal descriptions

Double parentheses are used to enclose a description of some phenomenon which the transcriptionist does not want to contend with. These may be vocalizations that are not easily spelled, details of the conversational scene, or various characterizations of the talk.

Tom: I used to ((cough)) smoke a lot
Bob: ((sniffle)) He thinks he's tough
Ann: ((snorts))

Jan: This is just delicious
((telephone rings))
Kim: I'll get it

Ron: ((in falsetto)) I can do it now

Max: ((whispered)) He'll never do it

VII. Presentation conventions

1. Arrows or dots in the left-hand margin of the transcript may be used to call the reader's attention to particular parts of the transcript. The author will inform the reader of the significance of the referent of the arrow (or dot) by discussing it in the text.

Don: If I had the money I'd get one for her
• Sam: And one for your mother too I'll bet

Don: I like that blue one very much
→ Sam: And I'll bet your wife would like it

2. Ellipses

A. Horizontal ellipses indicate that an utterance is partially reported, i.e., parts of the same speaker's utterance are omitted.

hhh (0.4) hhh <u>we</u> just want to get . . .

B. Vertical ellipses indicate that intervening turns at talk have been omitted.

Bob: Well I always say give it your all
.
.
.
Bob: I always say give it everything

3. Numbering of lines or utterance parts in a transcript is arbitrarily done for convenience of reference. Line numbers are not intended to be measures of timing or number of turns or utterances. Silences between talk may also receive line numbers.

11. Tim: Nice hand Chris:.
12. (0.4)
13. Jim: Th'ts a nice ha:nd.

NAME INDEX

NAME INDEX

SUBJECT INDEX

SUBJECT INDEX

ABOUT THE AUTHOR

GEORGE PSATHAS, Professor of Sociology at Boston University since 1968, has taught at the University of Colorado, Indiana University and Washington University, St. Louis. He has lectured on ethnomethodology and conversation analysis at universities and international conferences in Aberdeen, Ankara, Athens, Berlin, Calgary, Kyoto, London, Oxford, Paris, Plymouth, Sendai, Tokyo and Urasa in addition to many American centers. His most recent book is *Phenomenology and Sociology: Theory and Research,* 1989 and he has also edited *Everyday Language,* 1979, and *Phenomenological Sociology,* 1973. He is the founder and editor-in-chief of the international quarterly journal, *Human Studies.*

He resides in Newton, Mass. with his wife, Irma, formerly a professor of education at Dean Junior College and now teaching at Wheelock College. They summer in Wellfleet. Their three children, Christine, David and Anthony (with his wife Jeannine and son Alexander) also live on the East coast.